THE FUTURE OF STRATEGIC DETERRENCE

Strategic nuclear deterrence as it operated through the 1960s and into the 1970s is undergoing severe strain. Technological developments in the field of strategic weapons are undermining most of the conditions for stable mutual deterrence that have prevailed until now. At the same time – and partly because of these technological developments – strategic arms control is in difficulties. Changes in the political relationships between the nuclear powers and the relative failure of East/West detente have made it harder still to reach agreement restraining nuclear competition. Not only is strategic nuclear deterrence between the superpowers less predictable than it was but developments in the nuclear forces of other powers have had a strong impact on the central strategic balance. In the Third World too there is increasing concern not only about the perilous state of the Soviet-American nuclear relationship but also about the acquisition of nuclear weapons by Third World states and the profound effect this must have on stability.

This set of problems was examined at the 1979 annual conference of the International Institute for Strategic Studies in Villars, Switzerland. The papers presented and discussed at that conference have been edited and collected in this volume. They examine the future of strategic deterrence from many different perspectives – American, Soviet, Chinese, European and Third World. The challenge for the 1980s is to recognize the changing conditions of strategic nuclear deterrence and to manage the change so that the risks of conflict are reduced. These papers by prestigious and international figures are a substantial contribution to a debate which is likely to gather momentum in the next few years.

The editor
Christoph Bertram

The other contributors

Hedley Bull
McGeorge Bundy
Thierry de Montbrial
Yehezkel Dror
Lawrence Freedman
Curt Gasteyger
Benjamin S. Lambeth
Edward Luttwak
Laurence Martin
Richard Rosecrance
Michel Tatu
Gregory Treverton

The Future of Strategic Deterrence

Edited by

CHRISTOPH BERTRAM

Archon Books
Hamden, Connecticut

© The International Institute for Strategic Studies 1980, 1981

First published in the U.K. 1981 by
THE MACMILLAN PRESS LTD
and in the U.S.A. as an
ARCHON BOOK
an imprint of
The Shoe String Press, Inc.
995 Sherman Avenue,
Hamden, Connecticut 06514

Printed in Great Britain by
REDWOOD BURN LIMITED
Trowbridge and Esher

ISBN 0-208-01943-X

Library of Congress Cataloging in Publication Data

Main entry under title:

The future of strategic deterrence.

   Includes bibliographical references.
   Contents: Strategic deterrence thirty years later/
McGeorge Bundy – Future conditions of strategic
deterrence/Hedley Bull – Deterrence and vulnerability
in the pre-nuclear era/Richard Rosecrance – (etc.)
   1. Deterrence (Strategy) – Addresses, essays, lectures.
I. Bertram, Christoph, 1937–
U162.6.F87   1981   355'.0217   81-3598
ISBN 0-208-01943-X   AACR2

CONTENTS

Introduction

The reason for this collection of papers and for the Institute's 21st Annual Conference, held in 1979, for which they were prepared, is explained more easily in the negative than in the positive. We felt that the old concepts of deterrence, so ably and persuasively developed in the 1950s and early 1960s, were due for re-examination, that by the law of plausibility the changes in the world we are living in *must* have affected the tenets of strategic deterrence as they have everything else, and that it would be necessary to adapt the concepts to the realities in order to produce a basis for rational policies for the future.

There is no doubt, as both Curt Gasteyger and Laurence Martin remind us in their contributions, that change has been the rule over the past 30 years, in technology, as in the political environment, both international and domestic. The United States no longer holds a clear superiority in nuclear strength, conflicts are no longer manifested in the traditional arena of East–West relations, and new technologies have made nuclear weapons, theoretically at least, more usable. What is more obvious than that these and other changes should also affect nuclear deterrence – defined as the ability through the nuclear threat to make an opponent refrain from what he might otherwise want to do?

And yet the extent of change has been extremely difficult to measure. Somehow, there is a petrifying quality that surrounds nuclear weapons. Raymond Aron, almost two decades ago, called it the decelerating effect of nuclear weapons: changes in the *general* environment do not necessarily affect the specific environment of nuclear deterrence. Nobody can deny the changes. But, as McGeorge Bundy argues in his paper, the changes may not matter sufficiently to call for a major reassessment. Bundy's argument is straightforward: that *nuclear* weapons are in a category of their own, and that those with the

responsibility of releasing them will continue to realize and respect this. In the conclaves of the Oval Office or the Council Room of the Kremlin the games that strategists play lose much of their relevance. By nature politicians will be most careful to avoid steps that leave no way out, and for them – however old-fashioned this may seem to the architects of nuclear scenarios – limited nuclear war is not a controllable option. It is the uncertainty of control over events which is the fundamental reason why political leaders in Moscow and in Washington will be most reluctant to press the nuclear button.

It is this profound reluctance of the politicians to go down an uncertain and highly dangerous road, rather than any doctrinal value, which has made the concept of Mutual Assured Destruction (MAD) – the view that effective nuclear deterrence rests on the ability of either side to assure the destruction of the other, even after having been attacked with nuclear weapons – so persuasive. But it has the failings of all pragmatic approaches in that it is a strategy of the present and a strategy of risk. Politicians have been wrong before, pragmatism has failed before and miscalculations of the dynamics of crisis are the familiar stuff of history. Much of the current strategic debate therefore centres on the relevance of the concept for the present and future.

The Nature of the Problem
It is in the nature of the problem that the point where the slippery slope of change affects the credibility of deterrence cannot be pinned down with precision. Here lies the weakness in the argument that the famous 'window of opportunity' created by the theoretical vulnerability of America's ICBM forces to a Soviet pre-emptive strike can be turned into operational advantage by the Soviet Union, or of claims that the effectiveness of America's nuclear guarantee to

Western Europe has come to an end. They attribute *precise* consequences to *imprecise* events, and even the tendency of strategists to translate conceptual strategic problems all too eagerly into hardware issues can camouflage, but not effectively remove, this imprecision.

The imprecision in the nature and extent of change will persist. In spite of the new pluralism of the international system the bipolarity of deterrence remains essentially unchallenged; neither Chinese nuclear modernization nor nuclear proliferation will pose immediate problems – they may at this Institute's 31st Annual Conference but not at its 21st. Nor are these major changes affecting the core of deterrence – the ability of the Soviet Union and the United States to threaten each other credibly with nuclear devastation. Where the changes *are* visible, however, is at the periphery of deterrence: the relevance of nuclear forces for other than all-out conflicts and for threats other than those directed at the survival of either super-power. In fact, as this collection of papers shows, the doubts about the effectiveness of deterrence are essentially concerned with the effectiveness of this *extended deterrence*. Fortress America or Fortress Russia will remain secure, but security beyond the walls of these fortresses is more difficult to ensure with nuclear threats.

To make extended deterrence credible again a greater emphasis on nuclear counterforce would be required, both for continental and inter-continental delivery. But this would hardly demand profound changes in basic nuclear doctrine. What *seemed* an unbridgeable gap of views between McGeorge Bundy and his critics in fact is not: to argue, as Bundy does, that existing numerical differences in the strategic balance do not have a decisive impact, does not deny the need for strengthening the credibility of the deterrent by reducing vulnerability and offering nuclear options to the American President that are more than a threat of mutual suicide. And to favour the capability of nuclear weapons to destroy military targets, rather than cities, does not necessarily imply a war-*fighting* strategy but still rests on the need for deterring, rather than winning, a nuclear war. Insistence on doctrinal purity will not do justice to both technological and political change: deterrence has become more relative; the clarity of previous decades is gone.

How Much is Enough for Deterrence?

To point to the new relativity of deterrence may, in one respect, be no more than to pay tribute to common sense; after all, strategic doctrines have rarely been able fully to explain strategic reality. The American tendency to polarize relative differences over strategic policies has always seemed to many outside the United States a somewhat artificial exercise, particularly since strategic planners have tended to display in practice a much greater flexibility than official doctrines seemed to allow them in theory.

However, it is important to recognize the significance of doctrine, at least for a super-power that defines its security beyond its own territorial integrity. Doctrine may be expendable in the case of medium nuclear powers like Britain and France, where deterrence can be defined as a minimum or last resort capability; and doctrine is probably expendable in the Soviet Union where nuclear weapons are not set aside from, but are integrated into, the total spectrum of militarily usable force. The Paper by Benjamin Lambeth, in Part II, suggests some sympathy for this Soviet approach, but it is, I believe, a temptation that we must resist.

The reason for this lies at least as much in the nature of democratic society as in the need for strategic rationality. For all its faults MAD did have three important advantages which no strategic doctrine, if it is to be durable, should be without: it provided an answer to the old – but still relevant – question of how much is enough?; it provided a basis for democratic consensus; and it offered a coherent (if inadequate) framework for arms control. That we are all, today, wiser and yet more uncertain about the attainability of strategic stability à-la-MAD should not allow us to forget that there are more than strategic doctrinal differences distinguishing the West from the East. Democracies and democratic alliances cannot afford the strategic doctrines of dictatorships.

In spite of the growing *relativity* of nuclear deterrence, therefore, we cannot afford a nuclear doctrine that is open-ended – even if this were optimal for deterrence. Counterforce alone, in the sense that our own military requirements should simply be dictated by the targets and actions of the other side, is not enough. Open-ended doctrines in a democratic society will either lack political or financial support or both.

Therefore we must develop criteria for how much is enough, MAD or no MAD.

Laurence Martin hints at this in his Paper (in Part II) when he warns that the West should not try to deny the Soviet Union the ability to strike hostages in the West – even if this were technologically feasible: 'Do not try and get at the last Russian silo'! This warning is perhaps unnecessary simply because economic constraints will limit strategic technology and procurement. But to rely on this would mean not only leaving the definition of strategic policies to the Ministers of Finance; it also means that we have no criteria for developing a strategy of encouraging constraints on the other side.

It is no coincidence that, at a time of uncertainty about nuclear doctrine, there is also uncertainty about what it is we should try and achieve in arms control. But if we do not know what it is we want to restrain, and what it is we can afford to give up in return, will it make sense to enter into arms-control negotiations? The scepticism over the relevance of arms control to our nuclear problems has its root here: since we are not sure what it is we want to achieve through arms control, we are doubtful about the wisdom of getting involved in such a process. It is now more important to define the substantive criteria for restraint than the procedural devices through which arms control should be pursued. And it is an indication of the lack of criteria for the former that much of the present debate on arms control centres on the relative merits of choice among the latter.

The Function of SALT

If our objectives in arms control have become more modest, it is one direct consequence of the Soviet refusal to abide by Western criteria of stability. The very open-endedness of the Soviet military effort and the absence of visible doctrinal criteria of restraint in the Soviet system are simply not compatible with the approach that has dominated Western strategic arms-control thinking for the past decade.

There is a visible degree of frustration among those who were present at the conception of the effort to define criteria of strategic restraint, through negotiation, and there is a strong argument that the West should do unilaterally what it needs to do to shore up its security, irrespective of arms control. And yet we must ask ourselves to what extent we are falling into the familiar and persuasive trap of applying the lessons of the past (which we have only just realized) to the conditions of the future (which we do not fully know). Will the Soviet Union of the past two decades be that of the next two decades? Are we now designing a military response that might have been wise under the conditions of the 1970s but may be inadequate, or over-adequate, for the conditions of the 1980s? There are many who believe that the Soviet Union may pass the zenith of her military power by the mid-1980s. The balance of interest in the Strategic Arms Limitation Treaty negotiations (SALT) could shift between the United States and the Soviet Union in the next few years: over the past decade, the Soviet Union was trying to catch up, while the United States sought to maintain the *status quo*, not least through SALT; in the next decade, the roles may be reversed. How can we get these phases more in line with each other? And how can Western strategic decisions influence Soviet behaviour? This points to one important and continuing function of SALT: to serve as a framework for the avoidance of major miscalculations and misunderstandings, and to provide a boundary for strategic programmes and thus a degree of predictability in the strategic competition.

The Political Dimension

There is little in the next few years which threatens to change fundamentally the conditions of deterrence. But as deterrence becomes more relative, we will have to address longer-term trends. Nuclear proliferation will be a gradual process but, in the long run, it is probably irreversible. Professor Dror's Paper provides powerful arguments why this is so. The nuclear forces of Third-world countries will not matter in the central balance in the immediate future, but they will complicate it, particularly for the Soviet Union. ICBM vulnerability still affects only one part of the strategic triad, and it may be that new systems can mitigate that but the era of general strategic vulnerability is dawning. All this will strain the credibility of nuclear forces for other than contingencies of *vital* security importance, and we may have to think again, as the French theorists of the 1950s would have it, of multiple centres of deterrence. Similarly, the potential for non-nuclear deterrence in limited conflicts will have to be examined. So even if change continues to be gradual, change will occur.

Changes in strategic deterrence are not necessarily the primary pace-makers of political change. The degree to which the current Trans-atlantic uneasiness has spawned European nuclear concerns should not be underrated, just as frustration over the decline of American power and influence has generated concern over the *political* effects of asymmetries in the strategic balance that would otherwise be held tolerable. Laurence Martin reminds us in his Paper that the emphasis on counter-city strategies in the United States came at the end of a long period of isolationism. In contrast, the interest in counter-force may reflect a new mood of American assertiveness. Strategic balances are not very sensitive indicators of political relations; but political moods and concerns will tend to amplify shifts in strategic nuclear deterrence.

Strategic Deterrence Thirty Years Later: What has Changed?

MCGEORGE BUNDY

The first, and perhaps the most important, question about nuclear weapons is whether, or to what degree, they are truly different from others. There was not much doubt on this point in July 1945 at Alamogordo, and the reactions of statesmen and soldiers to the first private reports of that event show that one did not have to be present to be impressed. It was Churchill who called it 'the Second Coming in Wrath' and MacArthur who said, 'This will completely change all our ideas of warfare.' We have even earlier evidence, from those who worked on Tube Alloys in Britain and on the 'Manhattan' Project in the United States, that the special character of the prospective bomb was a crucial element in their extraordinary performance. Going even further back, we meet the powerful mixture of fear, hope and intense concern with which the small world of those who understood its meaning reacted to the discovery of fission by Hahn and Strassman in 1938.

So from the beginning men did think that nuclear weapons were different. But different in what ways? The question has persisted. In the first year after 1945 the weapons seemed different enough to persuade men as varied as Acheson, Lilienthal and Oppenheimer to make their remarkable effort to find a workable way of putting these things under an international authority. They seemed different enough to persuade too many Americans, more often civilian than military, that an inevitably temporary monopoly conferred some kind of world-wide supremacy. But most of all, this weapon seemed different – and here I think we hit something persistent – in that the thought that a hostile power might have it alone was intolerable. The technical promise that physicists were able to describe, through remarkable interpreters, was not in itself what fuelled the great American effort of 1941–5.

What did it was the thought of what might happen if Hitler got there before we did.

But are these weapons now more or less different than they were in the 1940s? Here we must take account of a double development. The explosive power so impressive in 1945 has now been both enlarged and blurred. When we think of strategic capabilities today, we must take account of warheads and delivery systems that go as far beyond Hiroshima as that event went beyond gunpowder. The welcome constraints of SALT II will still permit deployment of the order of 10,000 warheads on both sides, all designed to be deliverable in a single day and all more powerful – some by orders of magnitude – than the ones that first caused so much awe. At the same time there has been a vast proliferation of so-called tactical nuclear weapons; they have provoked almost continuous controversy among the experts, but there is no doubt that they are designed for use in the context of a battle that engages conventional military forces working for conventional kinds of military success. More recently, this problem of intermingling has assumed a new and complex form: there is now a possibility that highly accurate cruise missiles may be of considerable value to theatre forces in Europe with either conventional or nuclear armament.

But whatever the complexities surrounding tactical nuclear weapons, my own conviction is that the current and prospective strategic deployments do settle the question of whether these weapons are different. I think they are. Twenty years ago Bernard Brodie, surveying the prospect of a general strategic exchange between the forces then in existence, concluded:

Perhaps the most elementary, the most truistic, and yet the most important point one can

5

make is that the kind of sudden and overwhelming calamity that one is talking about in any reference to an all-out or total war would be an utterly different and immeasurably worse phenomenon than war as we have known it in the past.[1]

Brodie was not urging us to regard such a war as unthinkable; in the same pages he urged a sober recognition of the fact that it really could happen, and he was an early adherent of the lost cause – lost in the West at least – of civil defence as valuable insurance against the failure of deterrence. What he *was* urging was simply that we should understand the genuinely new nature of something not only instantaneously calamitous but wildly unpredictable, and very hard indeed to stop at any point short of 'grandiose, wanton destruction'. Evidence supporting his argument has multiplied since he wrote.

If only because specialists so often forget it, let me here emphasize one special characteristic of these weapons that, from the very beginning, has given reinforcement to Brodie's conclusion. Not only are these weapons enormously powerful, numerous and speedy in their arrival; they are also, by their very nature, weapons of mass destruction. In recent years there has been remarkable progress in the accuracy of delivery vehicles, and there has also been some small movement away from the weapons of enormous explosive power that seemed fashionable 20 years ago, but the overall destructiveness of full-scale strategic capabilities has steadily expanded, and no one has yet found a way to use these weapons on military targets without using them also on whatever else is in the neighbourhood. We sometimes forget that Hiroshima itself was construed as a highly military target, and that the bomb exploded within 100 metres of the aiming point.

Targeting Doctrines
From time to time, as in 1979, we have had learned debates on the nature of targeting, and recurrently we find the critics of such notions as mutual assured destruction telling us that these weapons should be targeted in a proper military fashion, not against populations and the civilian economy. In so far as these critics are claiming that *merely* to aim at cities is wrong, I agree with them, but in so far as they are suggesting that there can be large-scale use of these weapons

without unprecedented general destruction, I must express the gravest doubt about their good sense. We Americans know from the repeated declarations of our senior military leaders that our own strategic plans have always been focused mainly on military targets, but we also know from a recent unclassified report that a retaliatory strategic strike on just such targets would put some 60 warheads on Moscow. There may be room for argument about this 'military' target or that one, but niceties of targeting doctrine do not make the weapons themselves discriminating.

Yet it does not seem easy for experts to keep this point in mind. In the summer of 1979 a gifted younger analyst recommended that instead of populations, or even military targets, we should aim at the Soviet apparatus of political and police control, seeking to separate it from the peoples of the Soviet Union.[2] The assumption appears to be that a thermonuclear warhead can discriminate between *apparatchiks* and ordinary people. But 25 years ago Raymond Aron disposed of that notion, remarking that it 'will be indispensable, but singularly difficult, to convince the masses in the Soviet Union that the West bears no ill will except toward their tyrants, if atom bombs unite in death Stalinists and their opponents: women, children, and the secret police'.[3]

A final element in what makes these weapons different is that, so far at least, it is easier to deliver them than to defend against them. Delivery is not automatic, and the maintenance of credible delivery systems has been expensive for each of the two chief contenders. Yet so far the weapons of thermonuclear assault have outpaced efforts to defend against them, and the Anti-Ballistic Missile (ABM) Treaty made a virtue of what most experts thought a technological necessity.

The question does not die, however. Analysts of stature have maintained for years that defence against missiles can, in fact, become practicable if we work at it hard enough, and in the summer of 1979 their argument was revived, eloquently if not altogether convincingly, by Freeman Dyson.[4] I would like to believe Professor Dyson when he tells us that if we trusted engineers as much as we have trusted physicists, we could get ourselves a workable non-nuclear missile defence. To give up the ABM Treaty for that would be a good trade. The difficulty is that with *these* weapons it is not enough to defend fairly well. Just a 10 per cent survival of incoming warheads would be enormously too much for most of us, and I do not see how a defender could do even that well, all across the board, against an attack designed to saturate selected parts of the defence. What I do not see others may see better; at the very least it is important to keep asking whether and how we might expect a happy change in the offensive–defensive imbalance that has so far been a hallmark of strategic nuclear weapons. Such a change could probably never be clearly permanent, however, and the present prospects for it are not bright.

So for the present it seems a compelling conclusion that these weapons are different, and that the last 30 years have served to confirm and extend the difference.

Early Attitudes to Deterrence

The second great reality about nuclear weapons is that they burst upon a world in which the dominant political context was the existence of two, and only two, very great powers. As the initial German threat receded, and as the large (but quite special) question of ending the war in Japan was dealt with, what was left was the problem of the Soviet–American relationship. To be sure, British and French authorities did not accept any such formulation. The official British historian, Professor Gowing, remarks tersely of British attitudes in 1943 that 'the idea of the independent deterrent was already well entrenched'.[5] Yet even this special case tends to prove the point, for the British, from the beginning, had the Soviet Union uppermost in mind.

In the United States the primacy of the Soviet–American relationship was never in doubt. The debates of the first years, like those of every decade since, focused on what to do about it. This question was not made easier by the great difficulty the Americans had in understanding the attitudes of the Soviet Government, nor by the early development of what came to be called the Cold War – ironically, the phrase was introduced in 1947 by the same Bernard Baruch who had told the United Nations a year before that it was met 'to choose between the quick and the dead'.

The nuclear bipolarity so obvious in principle by 1945 did not become evident in fact until the 1950s. By the latter part of that decade it was amply clear to Western analysts that the competition in nuclear weapons was dominated by two, and only two, powers. No careful student or statesman could neglect the plans and prospects of other parties, but all such prospects were of a different order from those open to the United States and the USSR. In Moscow and Washington above all what was of central concern was what might be deployed and intended by the major rival. I think it has been that way ever since, and I should be surprised if many would disagree.

What is more remarkable is that by the late 1950s this nuclear bipolarity was widely understood as having become a strategic parity. In 1961 Raymond Aron wrote a brilliant analysis of the work of the leading American analysts of the immediately preceding years, and reached the conclusion that at the strategic level there was now parity between what he called the thermonuclear duopolists. He estimated that this parity dated from the moment in 1959 or 1960 when the Soviet Union began to possess a significant number of inter-continental missiles. It was a concept I shared at the time, and what is much more important, so did President Kennedy, for whom it was entirely clear that a general nuclear exchange, even at the levels of 1961, would be so great a disaster as to be an unexampled failure of statesmanship. Understanding this state of mind very well indeed, Aron later described the *ideé directrice* of his great work as that of 'the solidarity of the two Great Powers against the total war of which they would be the first victims'.[6]

Moreover, we must remember that the existence of this new strategic balance was also recognized at the time by relatively hard-boiled defence analysts. This was the season, for example, of Herman Kahn's brilliant but confusing *tour de force, On Thermonuclear War*. While Kahn's main emphasis was on the need to treat the possibility of such a war as real, he also believed that the evolving balance of thermonuclear forces had already created a situation in which the United States was unable 'seriously to threaten war' (p. 98). He wanted to change this situation, but he did not doubt its existence.

It is not too much to say that it was the prospect of general bipolar parity that dominated the development of the doctrine of strategic deterrence during the later 1950s and the early 1960s. The electric phrase had been Churchill's, back in 1955: by 'a process of sublime irony' the world was facing a situation 'where safety will be the sturdy child of terror, and survival the twin brother of annihilation'.[7]

The notion of strategic deterrence was the direct offspring of the two great realities we have so far described: that these weapons are different, and that at the higher levels of nuclear force the world has remained bipolar. The 'balance of terror' was the best we could get, men thought, and the object of analysis and action alike must be to ensure that the 'other side' would respect it. Strategic deterrence could be said to work if each of the two largest nuclear powers was reliably dissuaded both from any pre-emptive first attack on the other *and also* from any action that might lead to a general conflict between them.

In the largest sense, all sides in the West accepted the doctrine of deterrence. After the development of plainly survivable and deliverable Soviet thermonuclear weapons there was no one left, that I am aware of, who saw thermonuclear war as a desirable undertaking. Those who wanted more strength than either Eisenhower or Kennedy chose to supply wanted it, in the first instance, to make deterrence more effective.

US Doctrine of Deterrence
The United States' doctrine of deterrence led quickly to one absolutely fundamental requirement for her strategic forces: they must be such that they would credibly be able to inflict totally unacceptable retaliatory damage even after the strongest foreseeable first strike by the adversary. To meet this requirement the later Eisenhower and early Kennedy Administrations approved and then accelerated the deployment of what much later was named the Triad: the B-52s, the *Minutemen* and the missile-carrying submarines. Each of these forces was so deployed that a great deal of its strength could survive surprise attack. Even the aircraft, whose vulnerability in the late 1950s had been the proximate cause of Wohlstetter's trenchant but overstated warning that the balance of terror was delicate, were protected by the placing of a significant fraction on continuous alert.

The Triad was centrally a redundant, survivable, second-strike force, and it was so understood by President Kennedy and, later, by President Johnson. It was never seen by either of them as a force whose value came primarily from any numerical superiority over Soviet forces, or from any notion that a President would deliberately use it in a 'credible first strike'. Larger claims were made for it, to be sure. In early 1962 Secretary McNamara seemed to argue briefly for a large-scale counter-force capability, and throughout his time at the Pentagon, though decreasingly in later years, he stoutly asserted that the United States had and would retain superiority in strategic weapons. But he also believed and said that the value of such superiority would decline, and it was expected that each of the two sides could and would maintain a capacity for second-strike retaliation so great as to constitute stable mutual deterrence at the strategic level.

But let me fully recognize that while this was what was really believed by the Kennedy and Johnson Administrations, the heavy rhetorical emphasis on continuing American superiority was misleading. We did assert that we had strategic superiority, and we did assert that having it made a difference. What we did not say so loudly was that the principal use of this numerical superiority was in its value as reassurance to the American public and as a means of warding off demands for still larger forces.

In a similar fashion we may have spread confusion by using the measuring stick of 'assured destruction' to demonstrate that the deterrent power of our strategic forces was more than adequate. This measurement lent itself to the erroneous conclusion that the population itself would be the preferred target of any actual attack. I have already remarked that the Single Integrated Operational Plan (SIOP) throughout these years, as before and after, was designed by military men as a military operational plan, and 'assured destruction' measures were no more than an insensitive – and quantitatively conservative – shorthand for the hideous reality of nearly any full-scale retaliation. I think it can also be argued that no one really thought the Administrations were urging this kind of war – that was not how their chief contemporary critics read McNamara or his two Presidents. What was feared was rather that they would refuse to buy what was needed to keep – or, following Herman Kahn, to get – a usable superiority or even a credible first-strike force. That fear was justified.

Yet what deserves repeated emphasis in all this is that the one absolutely essential requirement for stable strategic deterrence was correctly understood and steadfastly set forth, both in speech and action, in the decade between 1958 and 1968: American strategic forces should be so designed that they could survive any attack and reply in such fashion that the adversary's advance knowledge of this capability would assuredly deter the attack in the first place. This was strategic deterrence. In terms of forces deployed, as well as in terms of what was held to be enough, it was, and was designed to be, much more than so-called 'minimum deterrence' and much less than a credible first-strike capability. And the scale on which the doctrine was applied in the deployments of that decade was defined less by the doctrine itself than by the parallelogram of political forces then at work: budgetary, bureaucratic, Presidential and Congressional.

Realities of Strategic Deterrence

Open recognition that usable superiority was neither necessary nor available did not come in the McNamara years. But as those years ended Carl Kaysen, who had given special attention to these matters in the Kennedy years, wrote a remarkable essay that stated the realities of strategic deterrence, under strategic parity, in a style that has not been improved on before or since. Kaysen underlined, as I have, the centrality of second-strike capabilities, and he explicitly noted that this capability, clearly and strongly achieved by both countries over the preceding decade, was not intrinsically sensitive to changes in numbers as such. The point had been made before; leaning in this direction himself, McNamara a year or two earlier had recalled that Bernard Brodie, as far back as 1946, even before thermonuclear weapons, had seen only 'relatively small significance' in even a three-to-one margin, once the bombs were measured in thousands. But Kaysen acknowledged it as a present reality:

[W]e cannot expect with any confidence to do more than achieve a secure second-strike capacity, no matter how hard we try. This capacity is not usefully measured by counting warheads or megatons or, above some level, expected casualties. Whether the result comes about with twice as many American as Soviet delivery vehicles – as has been the case in the past – or with roughly equal numbers, or even with an adverse ratio, does not change its basic nature.[8]

To its credit, the Nixon Administration abandoned the goal of strategic superiority, substituting 'sufficiency' and, later, 'parity'. And while he has recently repudiated his own most striking statement on the point, Henry Kissinger repeatedly argued, in his later years, that meaningful superiority was not available to either side.[9] There remained a significant doctrinal difference between McNamara and his successors, though it was never clearly spelled out by either side. The Republicans appeared to believe that a significant counter-force capability was desirable, and they regularly did battle with the straw man of a strategy of city-busting only. But the Nixon Administration showed no great sense of urgency about major new systems, and indeed it is reported that at one stage Henry Kissinger helped to block a proposal for mobile inter-continental ballistic missiles (ICBMs).[10] Once they had decided to trade out the ABM, the Republicans, again to their credit, made arms-control agreements their major goal, and they did a better job than some of them now choose to emphasize.

This is not a discussion of SALT, but it is well to remark that for all Administrations – and even more for most of the Senate – arms control is best understood as a modest reinforcement to strategic stability, even as an element of strategic deterrence. Starting too slowly, heavily hampered by the difficulties caused by mutual suspicion and deep differences in behaviour, usually behind the curve of development and deployment (as with multiple independently targetable re-entry vehicles, (MIRVs) though not with ABM) the SALT negotiations, throughout their ten-year life, have been aimed at reducing the risk of destabilizing change. Each side, of course, has feared the changes the other might make and has jealously guarded its own right to have whatever systems it wants most. Not all of what is wanted is clearly stabilizing, but the same criticism can be made of many proposals for drastic reduction. Both analytically and politically, strategic arms limitation is a part of, not a substitute for, the effort to keep the strategic balance steady.

Extended Deterrence

But what should the strategic deterrent deter? We cannot look to the language of political leaders for the answer. Characteristically, they have wanted to deter 'aggression', and they have been reluctant to define precisely which actions would trigger the deterrent. It is relatively easy to include under this umbrella the 50 American states, and we have South-East Asia and Africa to remind us that in distant regions dominated by their own internal forces there is no good role for strategic weapons. At the very most, the deterrent in such cases can have a modest effect in constraining the directness and visibility of Soviet activity. But what of Europe?

The American strategic protection of Western Europe is a classic case, so far, of doctrinal confusion and pragmatic success. 1949 was the year of the first Soviet test; six months earlier it was the year of the North Atlantic Treaty. The nuclear protection extended by Article V has endured, through thick and thin, for 30 years. There have been many alarms and great changes, none of them more remarkable than the original transition, in 1950–1, from a naked political assurance to a large-scale military deployment. But as its most recent student claims in his subtitle, there has been an 'enduring balance' in Europe all that time.[11] This balance reflects not only the deep political reality that both sides prefer what now exists to a large and unpredictable change by force, but also a balance of power in which the engagement of the American strategic deterrent is an essential element.

On the way in which this deterrent applies, or should apply, there has been recurrent debate. At one limit there are a few who have believed that there really is nothing to deter because the Soviet threat to Europe is not, and will not become, essentially military. Near the other limit some military men and a few civilian allies have argued that we must match (and even outmatch) the Soviet Union at all levels with nuclear forces in place in Europe. The arguments of the more assertive NATO Commanders are much the same, from Norstad to Haig. Periodically, prophets of varied persuasions have argued that the relation of strategic nuclear dependence is inherently unstable and that the new Europe will

want and need its own sufficient strength – I once thought that myself. A particularly intense and erroneous worry at one stage was that a revived West Germany could not indefinitely tolerate her own non-nuclear status in an alliance with three nuclear states. Experts have been found to doubt the comfort for Europe in each successive American doctrine, whether of massive retaliation, or flexible response, or the seamless NATO Triad. And Soviet threats of all sorts, political and military, conventional and nuclear, actual and hypothetical, have intermittently strained the balance. It endures.

This is not the place to sort out the doctrines of NATO or the issues of nuclear modernization. They are not trivial. Even though there is an inherent tension between military desires and peacetime budgets, in all NATO countries – even though NATO has served its purpose without ever coming close to its own force goals, and even though there is inescapable unpredictability in planning for any kind of third European War – there is some threshold of strength and plausibility beneath which NATO forces should not fall. So I support the general effort of the last two years.

But as to the future of the strategic deterrent over Europe, I find myself both conservative and optimistic. In its essence, it has never been a separate force. For many years NATO's most truly strategic weapons have been the assigned American submarines, and they in turn have always been only as reliable as the American guarantee. There is no way of changing this reality by new deployments of long-range weapons on land and no reason for the US to press that mode on her allies. Nor is the basic guarantee best measured by comparing the numbers of long-range American-controlled weapons in NATO alone against SS-20s and *Backfires*. Remembering that this strategic world is ineluctably bipolar, we must recognize that in any moment of serious stress neither Washington nor Moscow is at all likely to regard such American weapons as a separately usable or clearly limited kind of force. Any American-controlled weapons that can reach the Soviet Union will almost surely be all alike to them both.

It follows that the strategic protection of Europe is as strong or as weak as the American strategic guarantee, no matter what American weapons are deployed under NATO (I do not here exclude a useful contribution from the existence of British and French weapons, but that is not a major variable in the current debate, however one estimates it). And I believe the effectiveness of this American guarantee is likely to be just as great in the future as in the past. It has worked, after all, through 30 years, and, as we have seen, 20 of those years have been a time of underlying parity in mutual destructive power.

The enduring effectiveness of the American guarantee has not depended on strategic superiority. It has depended instead on two great facts: the visible deployment of major American military forces in Europe, and the very evident risk that any large-scale engagement between Soviet and American forces would rapidly and uncontrollably become general, nuclear and disastrous. The most serious assault on the strategic umbrella in those years was the campaign of Senator Mansfield for troop reductions and I take it as a very good sign that with his retirement from the Senate the reduction of our military engagement in Europe has disappeared as a political issue.

Now, of course, no one *knows* that a major engagement in Europe would escalate to the strategic nuclear level. But the essential point is the opposite; no one can possibly know it would not. Precisely because these weapons are different, and precisely because the existing balance in Europe is endurable to both sides, even a small risk of a large nuclear exchange is much too much. I am a believer in what Michael Howard has called 'Healey's Theorem' on the deterrent power of even an uncertain threat: 'if there is one chance in a hundred of nuclear weapons being used, the odds would be enough to deter an aggressor even if they were not enough to reassure an ally'.[12] And to reassure the ally I would point to the reality of my presence, the reality of my continuing attention to increased effort and the reality of the strategic stability. I would also point out that there is, in fact, great deterrent strength in detente itself. Who among us really believes that the Soviet Union is eager to stir us all back to the levels of arms expenditure we reached after Korea and *Sputnik*?

We must remember that at the upper levels of force the two greatest powers have been extraordinarily cautious with each other. This is not the result of estimates of each other's first-or second-strike counter-force capability, or a consequence of the possession or absence of escalation dominance; only occasionally have leaders in the two states known what such words mean. They do not dare get close to war with each other because of their fear of what would happen if it turned nuclear, as it always might. The Cuban case proves the rule. The two Governments scared themselves almost, but not quite, silly, and they did *not* get close to nuclear war. Both of them have been more cautious ever since.

Conclusion

My conclusion, then, is that marginal changes in strategic numbers are no threat to the American strategic guarantee in NATO. That guarantee rests not on numbers of warheads but on an engagement that poses a wholly unacceptable and innately unpredictable risk to the other side. Nor do I think the real effectiveness of this deterrent is highly sensitive to the ebb and flow of European confidence in any particular American Administration. Certainly two-way trust across the Atlantic is important, and certainly NATO has an unhappy history of recurrent misunderstanding. But the neutron bomb is not the shield of Europe. That shield is the American Triad, believably engaged by 300,000 Americans in place.

Thus the case of Europe, with all its complexity, leads us back to the balance of bipolar strategic deterrence. I think it is no coincidence that the American debate on SALT II has lately led in the same direction. Let me offer my own summary thoughts about the decisions that lie ahead in my own country.

The current focus on defence planning, caused by the warnings first of Senator Nunn and then of Mr Kissinger, is a backhanded compliment to the Administration's defence of SALT II, led by Harold Brown with an admirable combination of patience and intelligence. It also directs attention to the right subject. Our strategic deterrent is currently healthy, but one element of it is not as durably survivable as we would like. The USSR is not about to make a first strike at *Minuteman*. Soviet leaders know, even if some scenario writers do not, that the United States would be unlikely to accept passively the collateral devastation of eight states. But we have seen that redundant, survivable second-strike strength is of the essence of deterrence. It is right to tend to *Minuteman*.

It is also right to argue the matter out in a search for consensus. Because the deterrents on both sides are so ample, there is a large margin of safety, and it is reasonable to set out forces far enough above the danger level to ensure general public confidence. It is also right to put the question in the setting of the defence budget as a whole. If MX costs $30 billion, and perhaps will give us more than we need, would we not perhaps do better to buy something smaller and use the savings elsewhere? I do not answer the question. I assert only that the discussion will be good for us all, making it harder for critics to avoid the responsibility for sharing in the real process of real choice.

We must hope that in such a discussion we will succeed in keeping to the high road of this hard subject: that we need these weapons, in the measure that we do, for the determined purpose that they should never be used. We can remind ourselves, after all, that what may be the most striking single fact in the history we have been reviewing is that these weapons have not been used since Nagasaki. It must be our continuing determination to reinforce this record – in Thomas Schelling's phrase, this 'tradition of non-use'.

Finally, as we modernize we should remember, in all our choices, the judgments rightly rendered by two of our best students of these matters. The first is the view of Bernard Brodie that it is more important not to have this kind of war than to pursue some marginal advantage in fighting it.

Thucydides was right ... peace is better than war, not only in being more agreeable but also in being very much more predictable. A plan and policy which offers a good promise of deterring war is therefore by orders of magnitude better in every way than one which depreciates the objective of deterrence in order to improve somewhat the chances of winning.[13]

The second warning is from Raymond Aron: that the logic of strategic deterrence does not, of itself, promise us peace. The great states, he tells us, if they are rational, will not fight a war to the death with one another. He continues: 'But if philosophers have often called Man a rational being, they have rarely applied that adjective with the same assurance to the history of men'.[14]

The greatest single reinforcement of rationality is never for one moment to forget how different these weapons are.

NOTES

[1] Bernard Brodie, *Strategy in the Missile Age* (Princeton, NJ: Princeton University Press, 1959), p. 391.

[2] Colin S. Gray, 'A Case for a Theory of Victory', *International Security*, Vol. 4, No. 1 (Summer 1979), pp. 54–87.

[3] Raymond Aron, *The Century of Total War* (New York: Doubleday, 1954), ch. 8.

[4] *New Yorker*, 20 August 1979.

[5] Margaret Gowing, *Independence and Deterrence: Britain and Atomic Energy 1939–1945* (London: Macmillan 1964), p. 168.

[6] Raymond Aron, *Paix et Guerre entre les Nations*, 4th edn (Paris: Calmann-Lévy, 1966), p. 7 (my translation).

[7] I here follow Bernard Brodie and quote at second hand from his *War and Politics* (London: Cassell, 1974), p. 377, where Brodie also notes with reasonable pride his own earlier work on the concept of deterrence.

[8] Carl Kaysen, 'Keeping the Strategic Balance', *Foreign Affairs*, Vol. 46, No. 4 (July 1968), p. 672.

[9] His best effort was at Dallas on 22 March 1976, conveniently reprinted in *International Security*, Vol. 1, No. 1 (Summer 1976), pp. 182–191.

[10] The report is in John Newhouse, *Cold Dawn* (New York: Holt, Rinehart & Winston, 1973), p. 27.

[11] A. W. DePorte, *Europe between the Superpowers* (New Haven, Conn.: Yale University Press, 1979).

[12] Michael Howard, 'The Relevance of Traditional Strategy', *Foreign Affairs*, Vol. 51, No. 2 (January 1973), p. 262.

[13] Brodie, *op. cit.* in note 1, pp. 408–9.

[14] Aron, *op. cit.* in note 6, p. 12 (my translation).

Future Conditions of Strategic Deterrence

HEDLEY BULL

Deterrence has been the leading strategic idea of our times, at least in the Western world. Along with the idea of limited war, it has enabled us to persuade ourselves that force can still be used as an instrument of state policy, even while recognizing that the outbreak of an unlimited nuclear war would represent the breakdown of policy. Around the idea of mutual nuclear deterrence we have built our hopes of avoiding such a war.

It is worth reflecting for a moment on the extent to which, in the course of the last 30 years, the idea of deterrence has come to permeate our thinking. We began by accepting the simple proposition that a nuclear weapon state can make itself secure against attack from another state by the threat of nuclear retaliation. We learned to distinguish what Bernard Brodie called the 'anatomy of deterrence' and the components of which it is made up: our will and our capacity to retaliate, and the opponent's conviction that the destruction it will bring is assured and unacceptable. From this there followed the attempt to spell out, sometimes to quantify, the 'requirements of deterrence', to say how much destruction was necessary, how assured it had to be and what kinds and levels of force were sufficient to accomplish it. We came to speak of deterrence not only of nuclear but also of conventional and even 'subconventional' attack, and to recognize that the retaliation threatened could be graduated, ranging from massive nuclear retaliation at one extreme to limited conventional responses at the other. Thus the idea of deterrence came to infect realms of strategic planning far beyond the area of strategic nuclear weapons. We distinguished between deterrence of attack upon ourselves and upon allies and other third parties, and thus there arose concepts of 'extended deterrence', of nuclear umbrellas and of guarantees and their 'credibility'. It was pointed out that deterrence was only a special case of the political

exploitation of threats to inflict damage, that alongside deterrence there was what Schelling called 'compellence', and that both belonged to that wider domain of the application of threats of force in foreign policy that Edward Luttwak wants us to call 'suasion'.

Most important for our present purposes, we came to recognize that deterrence could be mutual and, by the late 1950s, that a relationship of mutual nuclear deterrence, or 'balance of terror', was growing up between the United States and the Soviet Union. This relationship of mutual nuclear deterrence was the fortuitous consequence of the efforts of each super-power to deter the other, and the deterrent capacity of each was in no way welcome to the other. But some observers in the West came to regard the 'balance of terror' not merely as a fact, but also as providing the basis of a system of peace and security, at least in the short term – a system notably inferior to theoretical schemes for total disarmament or world government, but having an advantage over these in that it actually existed. They also came to believe that the two sides could be brought to co-operate in maintaining a 'balance of terror' that was not wholly fortuitous but partly contrived. They sought to redirect arms control away from its accepted goal – the reduction and limitation of armaments – and towards the stabilization of nuclear deterrence, at least as the chief proximate goal.

These ideas, for better or worse, have had a very considerable influence on the course of events, and those of us who – in an intellectual or a practical way – have been collaborators in the system of deterrence bear a certain responsibility for them. As we contemplate the period from now until the end of the century it is appropriate that we should ask ourselves the following questions:

—To what extent, in thinking about peace and security in the future, should we continue to rely upon concepts of strategic deterrence, and especially upon the notion of a stable relationship of mutual nuclear deterrence? How valid are the old premises?

—To the extent that we *do* continue to rely upon these notions, how will our efforts be affected by the political and technological conditions likely to prevail between now and the year 2000? What are the future prospects for strategic nuclear deterrence?

—Should arms control continue to be directed towards the stability of mutual nuclear deterrence and, if so, what can arms control do to promote it?

The Validity of Old Premises

The first of these questions is the most important. There is a great danger in this kind of discussion that we may consider merely how to promote deterrence, and not also whether this is what we should be promoting.

On the evidence so far, the system of mutual deterrence is fulfilling its promise. There has been no nuclear war, nor war of any kind between the super-powers or between the European alliances built around them, nor indeed any war between fully industrialized powers. The limited conflicts in Europe, which Kissinger and others in the late 1950s believed to have been made more likely by the rise of mutual deterrence at the strategic nuclear level, have not materialized. Furthermore, by contrast with the anxieties manifest during the second Berlin and Cuban missile crises, there is a strong public feeling of security over the issue of nuclear war – so much so that the phrase 'balance of *terror*' is something of a misnomer when applied to the present time.

It is true that there is no way of proving that it is the nuclear stand-off that has led to these happy results. (Would either super-power, in any case, have sought to launch an attack? Was it, in fact, the prospect of assured destruction or other factors – memories of World War II, fear of domestic turmoil, fear of economic dislocation – that led the Soviet Union to conclude that any attack was not worthwhile?) But it is a reasonable supposition that strategic deterrence is not unconnected with them. It is true that a single, accidental nuclear explosion might quickly blow away public feelings of security and expose the fragility of the structure of mutual nuclear deterrence. But the structure would still be there,

more truly a 'balance of terror' than in periods of normalcy. It is true, too, that if peace prevails within the industrialized world, it does not prevail outside it: super-powers and their allies, as they range around the globe, practise a new version of the old doctrine of 'no peace beyond the line'. The indigenous conflicts among Third-world countries are not yet much disciplined by the growth of military nuclear capacity among them. But this fact can be used (and is used by advocates of nuclear proliferation) as an argument for the efficacy of mutual nuclear deterrence in promoting security rather than as an argument against it. Are not war and insecurity in the Third World the expression of the lack of relationships of mutual nuclear deterrence among contending powers within it, of the incompleteness of the 'unit veto system'?

Our starting-point, then, has to be the recognition that the doctrine of the pacific effects of mutual nuclear deterrence between the super-powers is, to say the least, not yet confounded. Nevertheless, it appears that those in the Western countries who plan strategic and arms-control policies are unduly reliant upon ideas of deterrence and mutual deterrence, and feel too comfortable about the bases of their own position. As we contemplate the future it is important that we ask not simply how strategic deterrence can be preserved against the dangers that menace it, but also how far peace and security can be provided in this way. Some of the limitations of the doctrine of peace through mutual nuclear deterrence are the following.

First, mutual nuclear deterrence provides at best an incomplete formula for dealing with even the immediate military dangers of the Soviet–American confrontation. For as long as it 'works', what the relationship of mutual nuclear deterrence accomplishes is the avoidance of the outbreak of war by a deliberate or calculated attack. As critics of 'deterrence only' policies pointed out almost from the beginning, this leaves unanswered the question of what happens if war nevertheless breaks out. The doctrines and weapons most suitable for maximizing deterrence are not necessarily those most suitable for the rational conduct of a war or for survival in one, and to the extent that the former requirement is in conflict with the latter, some balance between the two has to be struck. It also leaves unanswered the question of how we are to avoid the outbreak of war by accident or miscalculation. The frontiers between war by calculation and war by miscalculation are not easily defined, but thére is undoubtedly a distinction between seeing clearly that the course one has embarked upon will lead certainly to the destruction of one's country and failing to do so.

All this is familiar: the need to think beyond 'deterrence only' so as to plan rational conduct in the event that deterrence fails, and the need to cope with the danger of war by accident or miscalculation, especially by seeking to avoid or control crises, are well understood. The point is that the existence of a relationship of mutual nuclear deterrence, even one that is 'stable' in the sense that it has a built-in tendency to persist, does not in itself provide solutions to these problems (a point often obscured by loose use of the term 'stability', which can refer to the stability of the peace or of the 'arms race' as well as to that of mutual deterrence).

Second, deterrence is a technique, the art of finding the means to a given end, in this case that of causing a potentially hostile opponent to desist from resorting to an attack. Within the framework of deterrence policy what we discuss is the means by which we can best achieve this goal: with this or that mix of forces, targeting doctrine or device for demonstrating commitment or resolve. In deterring wars (as in fighting them) the tendency of the experts or professionals is to become absorbed in the choice of means and to lose sight of the choice of ends – the more so in this area because of the scope it provides for elegant analysis and quantification.

But we cannot afford to lose sight of the choice of proper ends, which are likely to be too complex and subtle to be accommodated in a conception as wooden as that of 'deterring the opponent'. Peace and security may require efforts not so much to respond to an enemy's hostility as to attempt to make the enemy less hostile – as George and Smoke argue in their admirable study, *Deterrence in American Foreign Policy*; such efforts may be served less well by threats of punishment than by the prospect of rewards for willingness to compromise, by diplomacy rather than deterrence – and this will require willingness to modify our own objectives as well as encouraging an enemy to modify his.[1] A preoccupation with deterrence, especially when it becomes a self-contained devotion to the

choice of technique, will direct us away from these wider dimensions of the problem.

Deterrence (and mutual deterrence) theory was formulated in the setting of the Cold War and reflects the assumptions that there are two actors, that these actors are roughly comparable and that they are very hostile to one another, yet have certain common conceptions of what constitutes 'rational action'. The theory does not tell us what modifications have to be made if one or more of these assumptions cannot be made – if, for example, there are three or more actors, if the actors are radically different kinds of power, if the hostility between them is much less (or much greater) than it was between America and the Soviet Union in the Cold War, or if there are not shared beliefs about 'rational' behaviour. George and Smoke have criticized the attempt to translate the theory of deterrence into the context of limited war and sub-limited war. There are similar problems about the transposition of it from the Cold War to the detente to the post-detente phases of Soviet–American relations, and about its applicability to other pairs of nuclear and potentially nuclear antagonists and to conflicts in which more than two actors are involved.

Some time ago I pointed out that underlying contemporary Western strategic analysis there is a conception of 'strategic man', a cousin of the 'economic man' whose existence is assumed in classical economic theory and that, like his cousin, 'strategic man' does not provide the key to human behaviour at all times and in all places.[2] If we are to apply deterrence theory to a host of international political situations other than that of the Soviet–American conflict at the time of the Cold War, we have either to develop a conception of a genuinely universal 'strategic man' or abandon the concept.

Third, the doctrine of peace through mutual deterrence assumes that those who have the capacity to initiate nuclear warfare will act 'rationally', at least in the sense that they will act in ways that are both consistent internally and with the principle of not deliberately willing the destruction of their own society.[3] This is the cardinal weakness of the doctrine, the reason why our hopes for peace cannot be allowed to rest permanently upon it. We can say that nuclear decision-makers have so far acted 'rationally' in this sense, a point that is stressed

15

in the paper by McGeorge Bundy in this volume. But history gives us no reason to expect that present nuclear decision-makers, the decision-makers from other states, and perhaps non-state groups that will join them, and the successors of all these throughout the ages can be relied upon to act as the theory requires them to.

Fourth, underlying all Western (and, in so far as it exists, Soviet) thinking about mutual nuclear deterrence there is a glaring inconsistency. This is the inconsistency between the view we hold that mutual nuclear deterrence is a source of security in the relationship between the United States and the Soviet Union, and our rejection of the view that it might also be a source of security in the relations of other antagonistic powers that are at present non-nuclear. As the nuclear 'have-nots' never weary of pointing out, the doctrine that nuclear proliferation is good for ourselves but bad for others rationalizes the existing distribution of power. Of course, many arguments can be adduced to show that nuclear weapons in the hands of possible newcomers to the nuclear club would be likely to be more dangerous than those that are at the disposal of the present custodians. Some of these arguments have a good deal of force, but there is no way in which the present nuclear powers can convince the rest of international society that the logic of mutual nuclear deterrence applies only to themselves. While it is true that much of the impetus towards nuclear proliferation derives from conflicts among nuclear 'have-nots' rather than from rivalries of the latter with the 'haves', our attitude to mutual nuclear deterrence has to be determined not simply by its place in Soviet–American or East–West relations, but by its meaning for the international political system as a whole. In the long run, the best course is to work against all nuclear proliferation, that which has already taken place as well as that which may occur in future, however difficult this may be. This requires us to take every opportunity to push nuclear weapons – and the doctrines and practices of nuclear deterrence associated with them – as far into the background of international political relationships as possible. The inconsistency to which I refer is a genuine one, and we should resolve it not by concluding that mutual nuclear deterrence can bring peace and security to all relationships of conflict in world politics, but by questioning the assumption that it has brought peace and security in the conflict between the super-powers.

Fifth, all policies of nuclear deterrence, unilateral or bilateral, are morally disreputable. The deliberate slaughtering of millions of innocent people, for whatever reason, is wicked. So is threatening to do so, if this means that we actually intend to carry out the threat (as, according to official Western and Soviet doctrines, we do).

There are mitigating circumstances. The end which our deterrence policies serve – the preservation of our security and independence – has a high moral value for us, as the preservation of Soviet security and independence has for citizens of the Soviet Union. The alternative policy (that of relaxing nuclear deterrence to the point of jeopardizing our security) is also morally disreputable. There are moral difficulties, moreover, in the position of those individuals who elect to withdraw into a world of private moral rectitude and disavow responsibility. In this area there are no courses of action open to us that are free of moral difficulty, although this does not mean that any course of action is as morally good or bad as any other, or that the moral arguments for different policies all cancel one another out and can therefore be disregarded.[4]

If we are to persist in policies of nuclear deterrence, it is important to recognize that they do involve us in wickedness, and we must remain clear-sighted about what we are doing, whatever the efforts of the experts and the bureaucrats to obscure our vision. This awareness of the true moral character of our policies may not cause us to abandon them, but it will prevent us from being fully reconciled to them and will alert us to seize whatever opportunities may arise for improvements at the margin.

The Prospects for Strategic Deterrence
A review of the old premises, then, suggests that we ought to seek ways of making ourselves less dependent upon the concept and practice of strategic nuclear deterrence. We can agree with McGeorge Bundy, quoting Bernard Brodie, that deterrence should not be depreciated in order to improve the chances of 'winning'.[5] But it is important not to make a fetish of deterrence. We must break out of the intellectual straitjacket imposed by the professionals' attempt to make deterrence a technique and recognize that deterrence is not a sufficient goal of policy in

itself. In the long run it does not provide a sound basis for peace and security.

However, the opportunities that seem likely to arise between now and the end of the century for making ourselves less dependent on strategic deterrence do not appear great. There is today in the Western world a widespread, and by no means unjustified, expectation of what David Gompert has called 'strategic deterioration'.[6] On the one hand, we are not going to be able to do without strategic deterrence and, on the other, the political and technological conditions for maintaining it seem likely to be less favourable in the next two or three decades than in the last.

The central balance

Are we likely to witness a decline in the stability of the Soviet–American relationship of mutual nuclear deterrence as a consequence of the acquisition by one side or both of a disarming capacity or an effective population defence? Are there signs that the growing vulnerability of American land-based strategic missile forces, about which we hear so much, will be seriously destabilizing? And what about the greater threat to the Soviet Union's deterrent presented by vulnerability of her (proportionately greater) land-based forces? Will the alleged 'relative vulnerability' of strategic bomber and submarine-based forces, and the possible conjunction with these developments of some kind of breakthrough in defence against missile attack, make a substantial difference?

Twenty years is a long time, but all this is difficult to believe. At present the invulnerability of strategic forces other than the land-based missile forces is not in doubt. If it were, countermeasures would be taken that would be likely to restore their invulnerability or provide substitutes, as is happening now in the case of the land-based forces. More fundamentally, mutual nuclear deterrence does not necessarily require the invulnerability of land-based forces: at all events, even if it does as a matter of sound policy, it does not as a matter of logic. Richard Garwin has recently argued that even a *Minuteman* force that is entirely vulnerable has some deterrent value.[7] The point could be generalized. A potential attacker is deterred when his leaders are in a certain state of mind. Their state of mind, even when advised that the opposing retaliatory forces can be eliminated with near certainty, is still

likely to include feelings of uncertainty about weapons that have not been tried in battle. It may also include uncertainty about the gains that can be expected from going ahead with the attack, even if they could rely on the weapons to do the job: the deliberate unleashing of war with a great power is a momentous action, setting in motion a chain of events the ultimate outcome of which cannot be foreseen. This does not mean that, in a desperate situation, such a decision will not be taken: war by miscalculation is an ever-present possibility, and the decisions that do set off such chains of events are sometimes taken without much thought being given to consequences other than the most immediate ones. Nevertheless, the essential conditions of mutual deterrence are subjective or psychological, and these conditions may in principle be satisfied even in the absence of totally invulnerable retaliatory forces.

Still less does mutual nuclear deterrence necessarily require what is called Mutual Assured Destruction, a concept which implies not only that retaliatory forces must be able to survive attack, but also that they must be able to penetrate to targets to bring about a given level of damage or dislocation. Neither disarming forces nor (as Don Brennan has long argued) population defences are in principle incompatible with mutual nuclear deterrence. The Wohlstetter thesis of the 'delicate balance of terror' set out the technological requirements for maximizing deterrence but omitted the psychological and political dimension, which when inserted, helps to explain why, as Robert Jervis has said, 'deterrence seems easier than the theory implies'.[8] This is not to deny that steps should now be taken to restore the invulnerability of land-based missile forces or to find substitutes for them: no one, I think, would argue that the vulnerability of retaliatory forces is actually good for mutual deterrence. But the stability of mutual nuclear deterrence is less sensitive to degrees of force vulnerability than is pre-supposed in much of the recent argument.

The stability of the Soviet–American relationship of mutual nuclear deterrence is not called into question by recent developments. What is subject to debate is the state of the overall strategic balance between the United States and the Soviet Union. The achievement by the Soviet Union of rough strategic 'parity', the impression of superiority in some dimensions and the evident improvement of the Soviet Union's capacity for 'crisis bargaining', taken in conjunction with the growth of the Soviet Union's conventional forces and of her capacity for global intervention, have led to an understandable feeling in the West that the balance is shifting against it. We should notice, however, that the feeling that the balance is shifting towards the opponent is also evident in the Soviet Union, where the recent moves in the United States, Western Europe and Japan to draw closer to China raise the spectre of a Soviet Union isolated and encircled by a grand alliance of all the other great industrial powers. We should also consider that the fears on each side may be in some measure mutually reinforcing, and that a situation in which each side believes that the balance is shifting against it may be one in which the danger of miscalculation is considerable.

Peace will depend, as much or more than it does on mutual deterrence, on the ability of the super-powers to avoid or control crises for, although these are liable to occur whatever the state of the strategic balance, they are more likely to occur when the balance appears to be shifting. Until recently the super-powers appeared to be strengthening their capacity to avoid or control crises by agreeing on the rules of the game and, more generally, through developing structures of arms control and comprehensive detente. It is clear that the momentum behind these efforts has now slackened – and, indeed, that the existing structures of super-power understanding are in danger of crumbling.

Strategic Deterrence and General Deterrence
Strategic deterrence (that is deterrence of strategic nuclear attacks by threat of strategic nuclear retaliation) is only a particular case of general deterrence, which includes deterrence of other kinds of attack and deterrence by other kinds of response. An important issue is whether strategic nuclear weapons should and will be used only to deter the use of other nuclear weapons or whether they should also be used to deter other kinds of threat.

The prime concern of all the present nuclear powers is the deterrence of nuclear attack, but they have pointedly refused to cut the links between nuclear deterrence and general deterrence. The NATO powers are committed to the first use of nuclear weapons against conventional attack, and the Soviet Union maintains a similar policy *vis-à-vis* China. In cases where what is at stake is a possible conventional attack on the home territory of a nuclear state rather than on that of its allies, it is difficult to imagine that the government of the state concerned could make any distinction between nuclear deterrence and general deterrence – or be believed if it did.

Yet there is a strong *prima facie* argument for sharpening the distinction between nuclear deterrence and general deterrence and for cutting the link between the two wherever possible. A regime in which nuclear weapons are viewed as having the function only of deterring the use of other nuclear weapons might be thought to be a considerable advance upon the regime which exists at present.[9] Policies that help to cut the link (declarations of no first use of nuclear weapons are an example) might be thought to help push nuclear weapons into the background of world politics, to facilitate control of these weapons by nuclear powers and to remove an incentive to proliferation. Some elements of a regime of this sort already exist: the explicit nuclear threats made by both the United States and the Soviet Union against certain non-nuclear states in the 1950s, for example, have not been repeated since that time.

At present, however, the prospects for further separating nuclear from general deterrence are not favourable. In the case of the Western powers, the persistence of Soviet conventional superiority, the growing importance of West Germany in the context of the European Community and of NATO and the demand for a European-based response to the Soviet missile threat against Western Europe all militate against it. It is notable that in the Western world discussion of the long-standing question of how to balance pre-ponderant Soviet conventional forces in Europe centres upon the choice between various means of introducing a nuclear threat (the threat to initiate tactical nuclear warfare, threats from European-controlled nuclear forces, or the threat of a United States counter-force strike) and pays little attention to the attempt to match conventional force with conventional force. Richard Garwin's proposal to remove tactical nuclear weapons and Forward Based Systems (FBS) from Western Europe and to rely upon conventionally armed cruise missiles and

European access to a portion of the American strategic force (his proposal is not directed towards a NATO no first use position but is intended to help reduce the role of nuclear weapons) does not seem to take sufficient account of the psychological need felt in Western Europe for some locally based nuclear weapons.[10]

Strategic Deterrence and Extended Deterrence

In the past the super-powers have been prepared to extend nuclear deterrence to provide protection to other states, not only against nuclear but also in some cases against non-nuclear threats. Such protection has been extended to allies but also, at least on an informal or implicit basis, to other powers (for example, by both super-powers and by a Britain rediscovering her Himalayan frontiers in the early 1960s), and there have also been joint guarantees (of a not very serious kind) offered both separately and jointly to non-nuclear weapon states as inducements to adhere to the Non-Proliferation Treaty (NPT).

Such extended deterrence has already long been in decline as a consequence of the contraction of the two alliance systems and the disenchantment of Third-world states with practices suggestive of super-power condominium or hierarchy. Will the 'extended deterrence' provided by the super-powers continue to contract? Will new nuclear powers enter into the business of 'extending' deterrence – China, perhaps, to Cambodia? Britain and France to the rest of Western Europe? A nuclear Japan to Korea or Australia? Or will 'extended deterrence' eventually disappear completely, as every part of the world comes to be consolidated within one or another nuclear power, none of which looks beyond itself for deterrent support?

It seems unlikely that more will be heard of 'joint guarantees' extended by the super-powers. ('Joint guarantees', here implies 'positive' guarantees, or undertakings to come to the assistance of non-nuclear states; 'negative' guarantees, or undertakings not to attack them with nuclear weapons, still have a role, but these are not a form of deterrence.) Nor do we have any reason to expect a reversal of the decline of American 'extended deterrence'. The credibility of threats to use nuclear weapons on behalf of third parties depends less on 'commitments' ritually affirmed, or on demonstrations of willingness to fulfil them, than it does on the interest the deterrer is judged to have in carrying out the threats. When American interest in doing so is evidently very strong, as it is in relation to Western Europe, 'extended deterrence' may still have a long life, even though here also there are signs that the protected are growing dissatisfied with present arrangements. In Asia and the Pacific, perhaps, the strength of American interest is less clear. The achievement by the Soviet Union of nuclear parity, the progress of nuclear proliferation and the continuing fragmentation of the alliance systems all make it less likely that there will be a strong American interest in extending nuclear guarantees to other powers.

Will the super-powers be willing to 'extend deterrence' so as to stabilize regional balances in which nuclear weapons have become a factor, or will their impulse be to disengage and insulate themselves from the attendant dangers? In the event that Israel, Iran, South Korea, South Africa or Pakistan were to demonstrate possession of nuclear weapons and seek to exploit them in local conflicts, the super-powers might experience both impulses – on the one hand, to seek to control events by 'extending deterrence' to locally threatened parties; on the other hand, also to seek to avoid the dangers of involvement by cutting existing commitments to local parties and seeking safety through disengagement.

In the event that nuclear weapons fell into the hands of a so-called 'crazy state' or came to be possessed by a non-state group that seemed likely to use them, a Hobbesian instinct for survival might surface in the super-powers that might lead them to set aside all niceties and to intervene directly and at once to disarm the state or group concerned. Such a crisis, posing a direct threat to the survival of the super-powers, might also reveal in them a common interest in preserving a minimum of security in world affairs which up to that point had been lost to sight.

Strategic Deterrence and Proliferation

Further nuclear proliferation is widely anticipated between now and the end of the century, partly because of the spread of the capacity to acquire nuclear weapons and partly because the motives to do so in some cases appear strong. These include prestige in the case of Brazil, the 'Islamic bomb' and the desire for security in the case of expendable clients of the West such as

Israel, South Africa, South Korea, or Taiwan. We cannot know at what pace this proliferation will occur, nor even be sure that it will occur at all. Moreover, the idea that further proliferation is inevitable is potentially self-fulfilling and therefore irresponsible. But how will strategic deterrence and proliferation affect each other?

There are two competing doctrines about the relation between the strategic deterrence policies of the super-powers and nuclear proliferation. According to the first or 'high posture' doctrine, the super-powers can best discourage proliferation by maintaining a wide margin in military nuclear capacity between themselves and other competitors. This will enable them to convince would-be entrants to the nuclear club that it is beyond their reach and will also allow them to 'extend' strategic deterrence to third parties (West Germany and Japan are the classic examples) who might otherwise be forced to acquire nuclear weapons of their own. Underlying this doctrine is the belief that the hierarchical structure of power in the world today, at least in the realm of military nuclear affairs, can be maintained indefinitely. According to the second or 'low posture' view, the super-powers are more likely to stem the tide of proliferation if they seek to play down the role of nuclear weapons in their own policies and thus help to undermine the argument that nuclear weapons are a necessary status symbol or source of security. This points to the severing of links between nuclear and 'general' deterrence, to the termination of 'extended deterrence' and, ultimately, to the abandonment of nuclear deterrence itself and to nuclear disarmament. It is, of course, the logic of Article VI of the Non-Proliferation Treaty, and it implies acceptance of a less heirarchical distribution of power.

Looking to the future, it is clear that powerful forces are working against the 'high posture' doctrine. The United States and the Soviet Union will not maintain their ascendancy in military technology indefinitely; even now they enjoy it not because of any inherent technological superiority over the powers of Western Europe and East Asia, but because the latter have chosen not to devote their resources to this end. Nuclear guarantees to potential nuclear powers, even though the most crucial of them are still in good standing, have shown a steady decline, as we have seen. A large part of the world is in revolt against the hierarchical assumptions behind this doctrine: the discussion of the possible 'widening' of SALT III to include European participation and the declining authority of the NPT regime are symptoms of its decline.

Nor does the future look bright for the 'low posture' doctrine. The massive super-power rearmament that has been dramatized and partly generated by SALT does not augur well for the presentation of the SALT process as the run-up to nuclear disarmament. The super-powers do not appear to be contemplating the adoption of no first use positions or other steps to qualify their reliance on nuclear deterrence. The prospect for the 1980s and 1990s is that the stability of the 'balance of terror' will depend chiefly on unilateral measure taken by both sides, and that force levels will remain high. The argument, moreover, that relatively high force levels enhance the stability of the mutual deterrence relationship is a powerful one.[11] Nuclear proliferation is in any case being generated by conflicts among the non-nuclear (but potential nuclear) powers themselves. There is little reason to expect that the passing of super-power hierarchy will usher in a new and more tranquil era of world politics in which the time will be ripe for a futher downgrading of the role of nuclear weapons, for among the powers that are united against hierarchy there is no agreement as to what new distribution of power should replace it.

The forces which encourage proliferation, as they make themselves felt in the rest of international society, will in turn react upon the strategic relationship of the super-powers. For a long time the conventional wisdom has been that China, Britain, France – and, indeed, any new nuclear weapon states – will be so unlikely to acquire in the foreseeable future the sort of strategic capacity possessed by the super-powers that in practice (at least for the purposes of SALT) they may be discounted. But already the discussion of SALT is complicated by the idea of a separate 'Eurostrategic' balance which, even though it is now regarded as somewhat subversive, is likely to grow rather than diminish in importance, especially if American and Western European policies continue to diverge on issues such as detente, the Middle East and the conduct of economic affairs. China is a factor in the conventional balance in Europe, if not yet in the

United States–Soviet strategic nuclear relationship. The 'nuclearization' of international conflict in other parts of the world, should it proceed, will compel the United States and the Soviet Union to deflect some of their attention away from one another and will weaken the sense they now have that, if they can 'cap' their own volcano, they will be in a position to manage the nuclear danger throughout the world as a whole. If nuclear weapons and nuclear confrontations become widespread in the world, and are such that they are beyond the influence of the super-powers, the 'central' balance will not seem so central.

As proliferation takes place, it will highlight increasingly the inadequacies of our present deterrence theory. This assumes a two-power confrontation, whereas in future there will be greater need to consider deterrence in the context of several or many nuclear powers. It assumes that between the powers deterring one another there is a level of hostility above which deterrence would be impossible and beneath which it would be unnecessary. In the world of many nuclear powers that is approaching, there will be greater need to consider what meaning deterrence might have in relationships which exhibit a greater or a lesser degree of hostility than the received theory assumes. The theory assumes, moreover, that both sides in a relationship of mutual deterrence share a conception of rational action. It is easy to conceive of situations of nuclear confrontation in the future in which states, divided not only politically and ideologically but also culturally, do not share a conception of rational action to the extent to which the super-powers have done in the past. Professor Dror's argument about the difficulty of applying 'deterrence rationality' in a Third-world context bears on this point.[12] We need to recognize that our present theory of deterrence is a 'special theory', and that there is a need to proceed to a 'general theory' that will be based not on the ideas of rational action that are unique to Western industrialized society, but on those that are the common property of the many different kinds of society that exist in the world today.

Arms Control and Strategic Deterrence

Surveying the position of arms control today, it is possible to choose only between several kinds of pessimism. First, there is the pessimism of those who feel that, whatever the merits of strategic arms control in principle, it is in practice ruled out for the present by what they see as the Soviet Union's bid for military ascendancy. Arms control for them has become simply an obstacle to the restoration of the strategic balance by unilateral means, which should now be given priority. Second, there is the pessimism of the technical experts, reflected in recent publications of the IISS: their thesis is that SALT held promise once because of accidental historical circumstances, but that technological change is now sweeping SALT aside: distinctions between strategic and tactical missions, and between nuclear and non-nuclear delivery vehicles, can no longer be made and the problems of verification by national technical means are becoming insuperable.[13] Third, most bitter of all, there is the disillusion of the enthusiasts, the 'arms-control community', whose chosen vehicle, the SALT process, has contributed neither to disarmament, nor to the stability of the strategic balance, nor even to the preservation of detente. For myself, I am more optimistic, but only because at a deeper level I am more pessimistic: my expectations were never very high.

Formal arms control is not likely to have any marked effect on the stability of the strategic balance. This is our experience so far, and I do not know of any reason why this should be expected to change. The stability of the strategic balance – as distinct from the stability of the peace – is in any case assured for the foreseeable future, without the help of arms control. In any case, arms control, in my view, has become too closely identified with the attempt to stabilize the Soviet–American balance. The logic of mutual nuclear deterrence does not provide a secure foundation for peace. In our thinking about the other great subject-matter of arms control, nuclear proliferation, we reject that logic, and rightly so.

What, then, are the options for arms control in relation to the strategic balance?

First, we could continue as now, pursuing numerical ceilings of launchers and re-entry vehicles on the basis of parity, and hope to reduce them. The original justification for this approach was that, with parity as a benchmark, it would be possible to proceed to figures that would stabilize deterrence and lead to reductions. This will not happen. We should drop this approach, but will be lucky if we are allowed to.

Second, we could acknowledge that the stability of the strategic balance is a matter for Defence Ministries and concentrate instead on diplomatic relations between the two super-powers, in the spirit of Salvador de Madariaga's conclusion that 'the problem of disarmament is the problem of international relations'. Certainly a restoration of Soviet–American comity, well away from the now poisonous atmosphere of the arms debate, is vitally important for peace. But not only does this leave us without an arms-control policy, it also overlooks the fact that the arms balance is at the heart of the political relationship between the super-powers and this issue has to be addressed.

Third, some favour the attempt to negotiate a distinction between 'stabilizing' and 'destabilizing' weapons or forces, the contemporary version of the idea of 'qualitative disarmament' discussed at the 1932 Disarmament Conference. The difficulty with this is that ABMs, MIRVs and super-accurate missiles are not inherently stabilizing or destabilizing; their effect depends on their purpose and context. Moreover, this suggested course of action assumes that governments on both sides do not want to destabilize, which is not the case. A more sophisticated version of this plan is Christoph Bertram's proposal for an agreement to ban certain missions (silo-killing, anti-submarine warfare and anti-satellite missions) and the translation of this principle into kinds and numbers of weapons. This is a constructive idea, but there are difficulties. Since agreements about 'missions' still have to be translated at some point into agreements about kinds and numbers of weapons, the problems of arriving at the latter are not avoided. It requires that the super-powers reach agreement about 'philosophy', but the strategic doctrines of each side are so much the product of

internal pressures and comprise that it is difficult to see how they could be determined in international negotiations.

Fourth, some have suggested focusing upon the preservation of the strategic dialogue rather than on the negotiation of any particular kind of SALT agreement, perhaps by expanding the role of the Standing Consultative Commission. The development of a Soviet–American strategic dialogue, and of permanent machinery to give effect to it, has been one of the gains of the arms-control enterprise. The decline of the SALT negotiations, or of particular approaches to them, should not be allowed to affect them. But this is hardly in itself a sufficient objective for arms control.

Finally, there is a need to relate strategic arms negotiations to proliferation, and the collapsing momentum of the former to the gathering momentum of the latter. The super-powers will suffer a decline in the legitimacy of their custody of nuclear weapons and in their trusteeship for the world as a whole that in the past they have been able to make credible, at least to some of the people some of the time. Perhaps an institution might be created in which expert representatives of nuclear weapon states and others would be brought together. Here the former might be asked to provide information, to answer questions and to give assurances to the latter about their custody of nuclear weapons. The NATO Nuclear Planning Group – while, of course, quite different in its nature and function – may provide some hints here. In a world in which the attempt to stabilize the relationship of mutual nuclear deterrence at lower levels by means of arms control appears to have broken down, and in which the old rhetorical goal of a general and comprehensive reduction and limitation of arms is as remote as ever, there is a need to reassert somehow the idea of the responsibility of the super-powers to international society as a whole.

NOTES

[1] A. George and R. Smoke, *Deterrence in American Foreign Policy: Theory and Practice* (New York: Columbia University Press, 1974). I have also been helped by Robert Jervis's analysis in 'Deterrence Theory Revisited', *World Politics*, Vol. 31, No. 2 (January 1979), pp. 289–324.
[2] Hedley Bull, *The Control of the Arms Race* (London: Weidenfeld and Nicolson, 1961), p. 48.

[3] Jervis, *op. cit.*, argues that rationality is neither necessary nor sufficient for deterrence and might even undermine it. But he does not say what rationality is. I do not think there is any such thing as 'objective' rationality which can only be defined in relation to given goals.
[4] To this extent I agree with R. B. Midgley's strictures on the 'morality of antinomies and paradoxes' in contempor-

ary writing about international relations. See his *The Natural Law Tradition and the Theory of International Relations* (London: Elek, 1975) and my 'Natural Law and International Relations', *British Journal of International Studies*, Vol. 5, No. 2 (July 1979), pp. 171–181.

[5] See note 13, p. 12.

[6] See David C. Gompert *et al.*, *Nuclear Weapons and World Politics*, 1980s Project, Council on Foreign Relations (New York: McGraw Hill, 1977).

[7] See Richard Garwin, *Testimony to the Committee on Armed Services, U.S. House of Representatives, February 7, 1979* (Washington DC: USGPO, 1979). Garwin argues here that even a vulnerable *Minuteman* force, if it is part of a wider complex of retaliatory forces of which some are vulnerable, has deterrent value.

[8] Jervis, *op. cit.*, p. 303.

[9] On this point, see Richard Garwin's contribution to Gompert *et al.*, *op. cit.*, pp. 83–147.

[10] *Ibid.*

[11] See Michael Mandelbaum's discussion of 'The First Nuclear Regime', in Gompert *et al.*, *op. cit.*, pp. 15–80.

[12] See Yehezkel Dror, 'Nuclear Weapons in Third World Conflict', in *The Future of Strategic Deterrence, Part II*, Adelphi Paper No. 161 (London: IISS, 1980).

[13] See *The Future of Arms Control, I: Beyond SALT II*, Adelphi Paper No. 141; *The Future of Arms Control, II: Arms Control and Technological Change: Elements of a New Approach*, Adelphi Paper No. 146; *The Future of Arms Control, III: Confidence-Building Measures*, Adelphi Paper No. 149 (London: IISS, 1978, 1978, 1979 respectively).

Deterrence and Vulnerability in the Pre-Nuclear Era

RICHARD ROSECRANCE

The issue of war and peace is a matter of alternative risks. There is first the *risk of striking*, and most of the literature on deterrence and on vulnerability to enemy attack deals with this. Second, there is the *risk of not striking* and, as a result, of suffering a decline in political position or military or economic capacity. This risk has been much less thoroughly discussed. A theory of war prevention must balance these two risks. A power may run serious risks in deciding to strike if the risks of not striking appear to be even more serious. Thus it is not sufficient to be ready to mete out steady-state damage to deter a foe. Much depends as well on his perception of longer-term prospects and the degree to which he believes he will suffer *if he does not strike*. Inevitably, this means that the prevention of war is not a static problem. When the risks of not striking are low, the deterrents to a strike need not be particularly formidable. On the other hand, when the risks of not striking are very high, even substantial deterrents may not prevent a war. One of the uncertain assumptions of nuclear deterrent strategy after World War II was the premise that statically capable forces would cope with what, after all, is a dynamic historical process.[1]

In what follows it will be argued that war has sometimes occurred when the risks of striking (or the risks of failure) were above 50 per cent, and that war has sometimes *not* occurred when the probability of failure was much less than 50 per cent. These seemingly paradoxical cases are reconciled by consideration of the risks of not striking in the instances cited – the run-up to the two World Wars. The lessons to be derived from these case studies are applied to the future of deterrence in the conclusion.

Earlier German Calculations

German military calculations between 1871 and 1890 differed fundamentally from those after 1905. France had been isolated and defeated by Prussia in 1870–71. Despite French preparations after the Peace of Frankfurt, the new, enlarged Germany did not seriously doubt her ability to defeat France, should the latter begin a war of revenge. At the military level a German 'preventive war' was considered in 1875 and again in 1887. But a new factor in the situation was the possibility of a Russian threat to Austria in the East. To meet this eventuality, Germany had to be ready to wage war on two fronts. In an Austro–Russian conflict the elder von Moltke was initially ready to strike France at once. In terms reminiscent of 1914, German forces would then turn east to deal with Russia. As France added defensive fortifications along the Meuse and the Moselle, however, an earlier victory seemed possible in the East. Accordingly, after December 1878 von Moltke planned to stand on the defensive in the West and attack in the East. After victories over the slow-moving Russians, Berlin could then defeat the French by an aggressive defence, leading, they might reasonably have hoped, to exhaustion and a diplomatic settlement.

The two-front war always had to be held uppermost in the mind of German leaders. But Bismarck's diplomacy largely obviated the threat. After 1887 France was isolated, while Russia was pinned down by England, as well as by Austria, Italy, Turkey and Romania. The two beleaguered states could not join forces because of Bismarck's Reinsurance Treaty with Russia. Accordingly, Germany could have moved to settle France's revanchist claims. But what purpose would be achieved by attacking France? Germany could take no more French territory. As von Moltke saw, even after a victory over France it 'would have to be left to diplomacy to try to gain us relief from that side, even though only on the basis of the *status quo*'.[2] Even more important, there was no need to wage war against either France or Russia. The Germans enjoyed diplomatic supremacy in Europe, and both Russia and Austria were on notice that Berlin would not support their offensive ambitions in the Balkans. The German position was not deteriorating: it was improving. Considered in deterrent terms, therefore, we have a case in which an opponent (France) was vulnerable to attack, yet the Germans did not attack. The low risks of striking were more than counterbalanced by the even lower risks of not striking.

The situation in 1914 was different in both respects. The Triple Entente had come to challenge Germany's central position. Austria had become weak, Italy was now a cipher in the Triple Alliance and the link with Romania had been severed. As a single power, Germany's economic preponderance over France had increased and her population of 68 million dwarfed France's meagre 40 million. But between 1890 and 1911 British and French imperialism made continual gains in the Far East, Africa and elsewhere. Germany had to satisfy herself with three African territories and a few insignificant islands in the Pacific. As the Slavs became restive in the southern parts of the Austro–Hungarian Empire, it seemed possible that the Empire would collapse in internal turmoil. Only a resolute policy of facing down Slavic challengers (particularly Serbia) seemed likely to preserve the balance in Hapsburg domains.

The military position, however, was now more precarious. The original Schlieffen Plan had assumed a military vacuum in the east, which would be quickly exploited by a German offensive in the west. The stronger Russia became and the more quickly she could mobilize, however, the more difficult it would be to attain the requisite superiority over France. While it is not clear that the Schlieffen Plan ever promised victory on two fronts,[3] the balance before 1912 was much more favourable to Germany than that in 1914. The British contribution to French defence was reinforced after Agadir. Naval co-operation and British use of French logistics meant that British armies became potential participants in the defence of France. In the meantime the Russian challenge was mounting. Before 1912 Germany had some basis for thinking that Russia would stay out of an Austro–Serbian war. But after the crisis of late 1912 this was unlikely. In addition, Russia had recovered from her defeats of 1904–5 and had, by 1913, resumed her position as a first-rate military power.[4] As the younger von Moltke correctly sensed, the momentum of rearmament would favour Germany's enemies between 1912 and 1914.[5] This was because the great Russian rearmament and railway construction would begin to have a strategic effect (an effect that would be greater still in 1916 and 1917), while France was adopting a three-year service for her conscripts. Germany had initiated her own plan to add 117,000 men but, as Ritter remarks, at the outbreak of war 'the great German army act of 1913 had not been able to effect any essential change in the relative strength of the two power blocs – not even in the ratio of Germany *vis-à-vis* France.'[6] In fact, Germany erred by emphasizing her navy. The extra expenditure on a battle fleet might have been better spent on ground forces that were then feeling the financial pinch. The overall military balance moved against Germany between 1912 and 1914, and the performance of Tirpitz's navy was not greatly improved by the extra funds that it received.

Why, then, war in 1914? For two reasons: first, the longer term promised an even stronger balance against Germany.[7] The completion of the Russian rail network by 1916, and the vast rearmament and modernization plan which would add 40 per cent to Russian peacetime strength a year later, meant that Germany could not afford to wait for an issue. Second, the diplomatic reasons for hesitation were shrinking into the background. In 1912 Bethmann had rebuffed Austria and had observed that the conflict might be resolved under more favourable circumstances later because of a reorientation in British policy.[8] By 1914 this was less clear – or at least, the decline of Austria had become so marked that action seemed necessary if Vienna were to be propped up as a great power.

There is uncertainty about whether victory was still possible as late as 1914. Von Moltke's mood swung from euphoria to depression.

Several weeks before the outbreak he confided to Conrad, the Austrian Chief of Staff: 'we are not superior to the French.'[9] The ratio of forces was little different from that of 1912, when the peacetime armies stood respectively thus: Russia, 1,300,000; France, nearly 600,000; Germany, 624,000; Austria–Hungary, 450,000.[10] Von Moltke acknowledged that Germany's mobilized opponents would have a superiority of 12 army corps.[11] On the other hand, he noted on 1 June 1914: 'We are ready, and the sooner it comes, the better for us.'[12] Earlier he had told Lerchenfeld, 'the moment is militarily favourable to a degree which cannot occur again in a foreseeable future.'[13] Bethmann was initially optimistic, but this was because he believed the British would stay out. But von Moltke never founded his plans on such hopes. Conrad was even more realistic. He told a colleague shortly before the ultimatum was given to Serbia: 'In 1908–9 it would have been a lay-down for us, in 1912–13 a game with the odds in our favour; now, it is a simple gamble.'[14]

These considerations elude a simple summary. At minimum, however, they suggest that Germany went to war in 1914 not because she had attained military superiority, but because of fears that her opponents would, in a few years, reach a position of dominance. As Corelli Barnet wrote: 'the German plan of campaign was not at all an aggression plotted by a general staff conscious of great power, but a desperate sally by men haunted by numerical weakness.'[15] The risks of striking (or of failure) may even have been above 50 per cent, but the risks of not striking were much greater still. Austria–Hungary was weakening, and the Triple Entente was concerting its forces. Germany no longer enjoyed her pivotal position, as under Bismarck. Indeed, the basis of decisions appeared to be long- and short-term political prospects as much as military ones. Bethmann had temporized in 1912, restraining Vienna when he thought diplomatic forces were turning his way. Just as certainly, he acknowledged war and the 'blank cheque' when the long term looked bleak.

1887 and 1914 are thus very different, but it is not the question of greater or lesser 'vulnerability' (the risks of striking) which makes them different. The risks of not striking were negligible as Bismarck's diplomacy approached its zenith. They had become very great in July 1914.

British Plans in 1939–40

From 1938 onwards Britain had to reconcile conflicting requirements in her attempt to deter Hitler. First, she was concerned to maintain the balance of power on the continent of Europe. This meant, ultimately, supporting Eastern countries against whom Hitler was directing his very considerable energies. In the second place, however, neither Britain nor France (nor the two combined) had sufficient power to prevent Germany from dominating Eastern Europe. With no direct access to Poland or Czechoslovakia for defensive purposes, Britain and France had to be ready to wage offensive war against Hitler in the West if they were to protect Prague or Warsaw. While they had a bare equality with German forces and thus should have been able to prevent defeat in the West, they did not enjoy the five or seven to one preponderance that would have been required to succeed in an offensive.[16]

Hitler's *Drang nach Osten* posed ultimate strategic difficulties for the British Chiefs o, Staff. They reasoned that, with American helpf Britain would win a long war against Germany, for Germany did not possess the necessary raw materials and oil for a protracted conflict. Economic warfare, a war of attrition and a sea blockade would ultimately deprive Germany of the fruits of victory. Hence, at least initially, the Chiefs of Staff supported Chamberlain's appeasement policy and were convinced that Germany would not risk war with the major powers. Her military might did not promise victory over the Western powers in the short term, and her economic and strategic resources were inadequate for the long term. But when, in March 1939, it seemed that Bucharest might be imperilled, the Chiefs of Staff observed: 'If Germany obtains access to the economic resources of Romania, she will have gone a long way towards rendering herself immune from the effects of economic warfare.'[17] Acquisition of the Ploesti oil fields might make it possible for Germany to survive a blockade. This threat, as much as Hitler's rape of Bohemia–Moravia on 15 March, called for a new British policy. The dilemma was now presented in a new form. Britain had to stop Germany's eastward march. She could do so, however, only by threatening an offensive war in the West, for which both she and France were unprepared. How, then, might

Hitler be stopped? One possibility was an agreement with the Soviet Union. If concluded in time, a pact with Moscow would certainly make Hitler pause. Soviet troops could participate in the defence of Poland, and they would shift the numerical balance in the East which had allowed the German dictator to pick off smaller opponents one by one. The Chiefs of Staff pressed the Government to reach such an agreement. But the political leaders, led by Chamberlain, preferred a direct agreement with Warsaw and Bucharest, and what emerged was the British Guarantee of 31 March 1939.[18] From then on it appears that the Soviet Union made no serious attempt to reach agreement with Western nations. With the British guarantee 'banked', Moscow saw no reason to pay anything to elicit a British commitment, especially as this could involve fighting on Soviet territory. It was thus intrinsic to the situation that Moscow would agree (temporarily) with Hitler, to gain time and territory, and that was what happened on 23 August 1939.

Thus the British deterrent dilemma was compounded. A credible guarantee to Poland meant, in the final analysis, the readiness to launch a Franco–British attack on Germany's West Wall. Since Britain could not do this alone and France was unwilling to do it, the guarantee involved merely a defensive declaration of war. The guarantee did not, therefore, deter Hitler; it merely provoked him. Still more important, it contained unresolved contradictions. What if Hitler occupied Poland but failed to attack France? How could Britain bring war to Germany if the firm presumption of all British thinking was that Germany would take the offensive? What would Britain have done if Germany had simply ignored her?[19]

An effective guarantee would have involved risks and actions which Britain and France were not willing to undertake. How, then, could they have given the guarantee? Here one must inquire into political and international forces which were steadily turning against the Western democracies. Some felt that if Britain did not guarantee Poland, the latter would make her peace with Hitler. Many believed that Britain had to take a stand to stop German gains, even if this entailed the risk of war. Opinion within the Prime Minister's own party was calling for action. The Chiefs of Staff continued to be con-

cerned about the long-term balance of raw materials tipping in favour of Germany. The major reason for the guarantee, then, was to be found not in the risks of striking (or committing), but in the risks of not striking (or not committing). In a technical military sense Britain should have been 'deterred' from offering the guarantee. She was 'vulnerable' to German action in the East and could not prevent it. But the calculation of the alternative risks nonetheless justified the action. Britain could not deter Germany with the guarantee, but neither could she afford the political, economic and international losses which she foresaw if she did not give it.

In the euphoria that followed the outbreak of war British leaders were even willing to involve themselves in hostilities with the Soviet Union as a result of the latter's attack on Finland. They avoided what probably would have been the most fateful blunder in British military history only because the Finns surrendered on 6 March 1940, before the Anglo–French expeditionary force could set sail. Once the risks of not striking (or not committing) had become uppermost in British calculations, the risks of striking were at a discount.[20]

Germany in 1939

In certain respects Hitler's deterrent plans were more carefully drawn than those of his opponents. The British guarantee of 31 March did not block his plans for an invasion of Poland; indeed, they stimulated them. The Führer's orders for *Fall Weiss* came on 3 April, with the initial target date of 1 September 1939. Two conditions had to be met before invasion could take place. First, Hitler had to make sure that Britain and France would not launch an offensive in the West while his back was turned in Poland. Second, the Soviet Union had to be prevented from aiding Warsaw. The question of whether France could have attacked across the Siegfried Line while Germany was thus preoccupied (that is, between 9 and 15 September) has given rise to much speculation. Perhaps she could have breached the line and broken into the interior of Germany. But she did not know it. Her own intelligence indicated that there were 43 well prepared German divisions in the West Wall.[21] In any event, French doctrine was against offensive war, and the most General Gamelin would consider was a reconnaissance in force, and that only later.

General Halder was confident that France would not be able to attack,[22] and his confidence was shared by others. Thus one pre-requisite was met; the other, Soviet agreement to the dismemberment of Poland, was achieved by 23 August.

Accordingly, Hitler could believe that Britain and France would now stand aside. They could not save Poland by their own efforts, and they had failed to enlist the only power (the Soviet Union) that could actually help them. Thus the Russo–German Non-Agression Pact would be a 'bombshell' to London. Hitler declared that Anglo–French military intervention was 'out of the question'.[23]

But he was wrong. Hitler's first inkling that Britain would stand firm came on 23 August, when both Ambassador Henderson and Chamberlain (in a private letter) made it clear that England would fulfil her obligations to Poland. On 25 August Britain formalized her commitment in a treaty with Poland signed in London. On the same day Mussolini told Hitler that he could not enter the war unless supplied with many vital raw materials; his abstention was now clear. Hitler then postponed the order for the invasion of Poland, hoping for a British reconsideration. But it never came. When Germany offered a propagandistic recital of her claims and demands on 29 August it was meant to justify war, not to prevent it.[24]

After 26 August Hitler failed to heed the risks of striking. He was prepared to act even though Britain and France would probably go to war with Germany. To be sure, in the short run that would not mean much, for Hitler dismissed their threat to attack in the West, and they could not help Poland directly. On the other hand, he had no military plan for eliminating them. He might have brought about the worst of all worlds by simply ignoring their declaration of war, but it was a foregone psychological conclusion in Hitler's thinking that he would eventually attack them. Hitler told his generals on 22 August:

A permanent state of tension is intolerable. The power of the initiative cannot be allowed to pass to others. The present moment is more favourable than in two or three years' time. An attempt on my life or Mussolini's could change the situation to our disadvantage. One cannot forever face one another with rifles cocked. . . . We are faced with the harsh alternatives of striking or of certain annihilation sooner or later.[25]

This meant that a British–French challenge could not go unmet or Hitler would lose the initiative in world politics. When Czechoslovakia had stiffened her resistance in the spring of 1938 Hitler had decided to rebuff her – politically if possible, militarily if necessary. Similarly, after the British and French declarations of war it was inevitable that Hitler would strike them. In this way, of course, Hitler validated the original British assumptions of 31 March and made it unnecessary for the Allies to plan offensive operations. That he could do so, however, was testimony to the degree to which the risks of not striking had come to determine his planning, to the neglect of the risks that striking clearly involved.

Hitler was aware that the British rearmament programme would peak later than his own. The British Army was tiny; naval improvements would not be felt until 1941 or 1942; only the Air Force had grown significantly. The longer war was delayed, the worse the equation would be for Germany. But Germany's position in 1939 was still quite different from that of 1914, and it contrasts with Britain's plight on the eve of World War II. Both Germany in 1914 and Britain in 1939 could fasten upon the real and relative decline in their positions. Britain's role in Europe and the world had suffered greatly since 1934. Germany could believe that the diplomatic and military balance was increasingly turning against her in 1914. In both cases statesmen could conclude that the risks of not striking (or not committing) were high. Hitler, however, had no such problems. The Nazi leader's star was in the ascendant within Germany and in Europe. Economically, he was bringing Eastern Europe under his thrall. The longer-term military balance mattered only if war was inevitable. But with German diplomacy at its height, this should not have been the case. Objectively, there should have been no need for precipitate actions, especially when these entailed military risks that were distinctly avoidable. That the risks of not striking seemed high to Hitler in August 1939 was testimony to his sense of personal mortality and impatience, not to any concrete reversal of German fortunes.

Conclusions and Implications

This analysis has focused attention on the risks of not striking as equal in the deterrent conspectus to the more commonly stressed risks of striking. In three historical cases the former, more than the latter, seem to have been decisive. It would be rash in the nuclear age, however, to draw direct conclusions from a pre-nuclear era. The thermonuclear weapon is so destructive, and the numbers of weapons remaining on both sides even after a first strike (or even after a first strike *and* a counterforce response) so awesome, that the threat to use these instruments may alone prevent war. But if there is any lesson to be learned from these cases, it is that the quantitative balance in numbers of weapons is not likely to be the crucial (to say nothing of the determining) factor in the decision to wage war. Germany did not use her military superiority on various occasions, nor did Britain's inferiority prevent the latter nation from mounting a frontal challenge. Of greater importance is the long-term political and diplomatic situation and the allied question of internal stability. Germany's action in 1914 was precipitated as much by Austrian internal weakness as by the not entirely imaginary German fears of a rearming Triple Entente.

Today most commentators believe that the Soviet Union has been very cautious in resorting to force in the post-war period, although recent events in Afghanistan tend to alter this perception. But it is always conceivable that if she were pressed into a corner, she could again respond militarily. Until Afghanistan, the two occasions on which Soviet troops have crossed frontiers in anger were in such a context: when Communist régimes were on the verge of collapse in Hungary in 1956, and Czechoslovakia in 1968. Some are prepared to assert that the Soviet invasion of Afghanistan was also the result of a feeling of being cornered. This suggests that one should worry less about large Soviet forces and more about the situation that might emerge if the Soviet Union came to believe that the tide of events in world politics was turning against her. This situation might be approached if the so-called 'window' of strategic opportunity were not only decisively closed to the USSR, but opened glaringly after 1986 to the United States, in a context in which there was also considerable turmoil in Eastern Europe. The latter is the more likely, as Eastern countries, pressed by resource shortages, are forced ever more into an interdependent world economy.[26] Western attempts to take advantage of this ferment could have a dynamic effect on the then new Soviet leadership. To look ahead, it is impossible to imagine another World War II, but it is not entirely unthinkable that some of the features of 1914 could be replayed. Many have contended that we must now close the strategic and tactical gaps that have emerged as a result of Soviet force increases. In doing so, however, we should be aware that a sudden reversal of Soviet military fortunes, conjoined with unrest in Eastern Europe, could lead Moscow to take drastic and unsettling actions to recoup its position.

NOTES

[1] Typical second-strike formulae are of this kind, emphasizing the destruction of a fixed percentage of enemy industry and population.

[2] Quoted in Gerhard Ritter, *The Sword and Scepter*, Vol. 1 (Coral Gables, Fla.: University of Miami Press, 1969), p. 230.

[3] See Gerhard Ritter, *The Schlieffen Plan* (London: Oswald Wolff, 1958), p. 7.

[4] Imanuel Geiss, *German Foreign Policy 1871–1914* (London: Routledge & Kegan Paul, 1976), pp. 148–9.

[5] In December 1912 Moltke complained: 'The navy would not be ready even then (1914) and the army would get into an increasingly unfavourable position, for the enemies were arming more strongly than we were, as we were very short of money.' Quoted in Geiss, *op. cit.*, p. 143. See also F. Fischer, *The War of Illusion* (New York: W. W. Norton, 1975), p. 162.

[6] Ritter, *The Sword and Scepter*, Vol. 2, p. 226.

[7] As Bethmann recalled later: 'Yes, my God, in a certain sense it was a preventive war. But when war was hanging above us, when it had to come in two years, even more dangerously and inescapably, and when the Generals said, now it is still possible without defeat, but not in two years' time. Yes, the Generals!' Quoted in Imanuel Geiss, 'The Outbreak of the First World War and German War Aims', *Journal of Contemporary History*, Vol. 1, No. 3 (July 1966), p. 82.

[8] F. Fischer, *World Power or Decline* (London: Weidenfeld & Nicolson, 1974), p. 24.

[9] Quoted in Norman Stone, 'Moltke-Conrad: Relations between the Austro-Hungarian and German General Staffs', *Historical Journal*, Vol. 9, No. 2 (1966), p. 214.

[10] L. C. F. Turner, *Origins of the First World War* (New York: W. W. Norton, 1970), p. 29.

[11] Corelli Barnett, *The Swordbearers* (London: Eyre & Spottiswoode, 1963), p. 31.

[12] F. Fischer, *Germany's Aims in the First World War* (New York: W. W. Norton, 1967), p. 50.

[13] Quoted in Luigi Albertini, *The Origins of the War of 1914*, Vol. 3 (London: Oxford University Press, 1957), p. 7. See also Fischer, *op. cit.* in note 12, p. 60.

[14] Quoted in Stone, *loc. cit.*, p. 228.

[15] Barnett, *op. cit.*, p. 31.

[16] A. J. P. Taylor, *The Origins of the Second World War*, 2nd edn, (Greenwich, Conn.: Fawcett Publications, 1961), p. 114. See also B. H. Liddell Hart, *History of the Second World War* (New York: Putnam, 1971), pp. 70–73. This conclusion is buttressed by the experience of the closing phases of World War II when the allies needed a five-to-one superiority to defeat Germany.

[17] CAB 53/10 Chiefs of Staff 283 MTG, 18 March 1939.

[18] Simon Newman remarks: 'the decisive objections to Russia's inclusion were political ... open inclusion of Russia would undermine potential support'; *March 1939: The British Guarantee to Poland* (Oxford: Clarendon Press, 1976), p. 140.

[19] A fuller statement of this argument occurs in Alan Alexandroff and Richard Rosecrance, 'Deterrence in 1939', *World Politics*, Vol. XXIX, No. 3, (April 1977). pp. 407–13.

[20] See CAB 80/8 COS (40) 252, *Military Implications of Hostilities with Russia in 1940*. This paper emphasized the feasibility of air attack on the oil supplies of the Caucasus and concluded: 'We are advised that the interruption of these supplies would in time paralyse the Russian military machine and disorganize Russian national life.'

[21] When, in fact, there were only eight front-line and 25 less ready divisions. These divisions did not have tanks and possessed supplies for only three days of fighting. Jon Kimche, *The Unfought Battle* (London: Weidenfeld & Nicolson, 1968), pp. 89–95.

[22] This was, at least partly, because he did not realize how early they would in fact mobilize.

[23] Speech by the Führer to the Commanders in Chief, 22 August 1939. *Documents on German Foreign Policy, 1914–1945*, Series D, Vol. 7, *The Last Days of Peace, August 9–September 3, 1939* (Washington, DC: Department of State, 1956), pp. 202, 204.

[24] General Halder confided to his diary on 31 August: 'Intervention of West said to be unavoidable: in spite of this Führer has decided to attack.' Later he confused Hitler's apparent serenity with confidence that Britain and France would stand aside. Norman Rich, *Hitler's War Aims* (New York: W. W. Norton, 1973), p. 130.

[25] Speech by the Führer to the Commanders in Chief, 22 August 1939, *Documents on German Foreign Policy*, p. 202, fn. 24.

[26] New CIA forecasts see the Soviet Union importing 700,000 barrels of oil a day by 1982. This would force East European nations into world markets. *New York Times*, 30 July 1979, p. D1.

The Problems of Extending Deterrence

EDWARD LUTTWAK

Extended Deterrence in American Politics

It has been reported that on the eve of his assumption of office President Carter asked the Joint Chiefs of Staff to supply him with an estimate of the minimum number of strategic nuclear weapons that would suffice for deterrence; the Chiefs were specifically invited to consider the possibility that 200 ICBMs might be enough.

Even without knowing the exact form of words employed by the President, it is a fair speculation that the 'deterrence' he had in mind could only have been simple, strike-back-only deterrence – that is, deterrence for the self-protection of the United States *strictu sensu*. It will be recalled that during that same period President Carter was insistent on expressing his devotion to the North Atlantic Alliance; in fact, he was then actively sponsoring an all-for-NATO defence policy whose immediate implications were the (abortive) decisions on the withdrawal of American troops from Korea and the redeployment of major naval units from the Pacific to the Atlantic. There was much emphasis on the need to strengthen NATO's (conventional) military strength.

Subsequent events show that it would be wrong to attribute sinister motives to the conjunction of presidential enthusiasms; no conscious intent to decouple European security from strategic nuclear deterrence is to be imputed. One is not dealing with holy selfishness, nor indeed with strategic logic of any kind. It is rather a case of unstrategical pragmatism, apt to pass virtually unobserved in a political culture itself profoundly unstrategical. For the President NATO is one subject and strategic nuclear policy quite another; why confuse matters by connecting the two? When strategic nuclear questions are considered it is the techniques and tactics of the mechanical interactions of the two

forces, and above all the possibilities of arms control, that dominate attention in a framework naturally bilateral. Equally, when NATO and its travails are considered the business-like thing to do is to focus on the administrative detail of 'rationalization'.

President Carter has been allowed to remain perfectly consistent in his inconsistency: he does not appear to have declared himself even once on extended deterrence, under whatever name. Certainly, he has not emulated his predecessors, who used to reiterate with some frequency the nexus between the security of the Alliance and the *ultimissima ratio* of strategic nuclear punishment.

The context, so far, of the SALT II debates in the United States Senate shows that President Carter's inadvertence on the question of extended deterrence cannot be counted as one of his eccentricities. A great deal has been heard of the Allies during the July 1979 hearings before the Senate Committees on Foreign Relations and the Armed Services but, with the single exception of Henry Kissinger, no witness and no Senator has expressed any reasoned position on the role of American strategic nuclear weapons in the deterrence of Soviet military action against NATO Europe. Certainly, there was no depiction of the part that strategic weapons might play in inhibiting Soviet attacks against European-based nuclear weapons – this being, of course, the most obvious intra-conflict function of extended deterrence.

Instead, there has been a great deal of discussion of Allied 'perceptions' of the strategic balance and of the impact of ratification – or its denial – upon those perceptions. As used in the debates, the word 'perceptions' is invoked to explain why things that do *not* make a difference in 'reality' are nevertheless important. Thus Secretary Brown, in explaining why he felt it

31

necessary to react to the Soviet acquisition of a partial counter-force capability (against the American *Minuteman* force), first denied that such a capability made a 'real' difference, and he then went on to argue the need to match it for the sake of the beneficial effect on third-party 'perceptions'.

What makes everything so complicated is the highly specialized meaning of 'reality', itself defined in terms of the theory of Mutual Assured Destruction. According to that theory, which remains devastatingly influential even when ostensibly repudiated, *no* meaningful advantages can be derived from the acquisition of strategic nuclear capabilities in excess of the mathematically prescribed requirements of assured destruction and below the (very much higher) requirements of a fully disarming counter-force capability. True believers still firmly deny the need for any reaction to the projected emergence of sundry Soviet superiorities in the ICBM sector. Secretary Brown and his colleagues also explicitly reject the contention that the Soviet Union could extract any 'real' advantage from the acquisition of a *partial* counter-force capability (against the American *Minuteman* force). Specifically, they have ridiculed various crisis/blackmail scenarios put forward by Paul Nitze and others. But they part company from the true believers by nevertheless advocating the need for the MX programme, explicitly to achieve perceptual effects which they hold to be necessary to maintain 'essential equivalence'.

It was only in this psycho-political realm that the connection between the central balance and the Alliance was recognized during the July 1979 debates. The Allies were accorded the role of important spectators whose opinions of the central balance would be very important, but there was no suggestion that the central balance might actually affect their security directly by conditioning Soviet conduct – no suggestion, that is, that the spectacle might actually have a concrete effect on its audience.

Thus the question of extended deterrence has not so far figured in the debates on the SALT Treaty. 'Perceptions' always excepted, minimalists and maximalists agreed to treat the central balance as a closed bilateral system. The pro-Treaty minimalists have denied that discrete shifts in the strategic balance in favour of the Soviet Union would have any significance what-

ever, since the United States would still retain an Assured Destruction capability; the anti-Treaty maximalists argued that these adverse shifts were highly significant, since they revealed that the Soviet Union was attempting to attain a fully disarming counter-force capability. What seemed to be at issue was the reliability of self-protecting deterrence (as well as perceptions of the same) and not the scope of deterrence.

For the minimalist the omission of extended deterrence from the argument is a matter of strict logic: the theory of Mutual Assured Destruction inherently defines a purely bilateral world in which the values of allies, and even the protection of United States forces overseas, is only possible to the extent that these things are fully assimilated into the body of national territorial interests (so that attacks upon them would warrant an automatic retaliatory response). For the maximalists, it would be equally logical to define *desiderata* in terms of the requirements of extended deterrence, but in fact they have failed to do this. With rare exceptions, they define the significance of increments in Soviet strategic nuclear capabilities strictly within the closed bilateral framework, saying little or nothing about third parties.

Since it is only at the level of strategical thought that the connections between things are revealed, it is not surprising that extended deterrence should have been the ignored issue of the SALT II debates, even though it could have served very well as an evaluative criterion of genuine significance.

The Theory

It is against this sobering background of political inadvertence that the theory of extended deterrence should be reviewed.

The mechanism whereby inter-continental nuclear deterrence is extended to offer protection to Allies and American forces overseas (and thus beyond the minima set by national boundaries) is, of course, the mechanism of escalation. It addresses the total *potential* scope of weakness at conflict levels below the inter-continental nuclear – that is, the sum total of values whose protection cannot be adequately provided by either defence or deterrence at each of those lower levels. It is obvious enough that protection obtained from extended deterrence must always be a second-best solution, for there is always some inherent reluctance to escalate and this automatically offers a corresponding opportunity for coercive diplomacy by the other side. What counts, of course, is the degree of this reluctance, which naturally varies sharply from time to time and more gradually over time with changes in the balance of inter-continental nuclear vulnerabilities. More precisely, the *actual* scope of extended deterrence is defined by the interaction of two quite different balances: the balance of relative inter-continental nuclear vulnerabilities on the one hand, and the 'balance of perceived interests' on the other. It is the interaction of these two balances, as viewed from both sides, that determines the credibility of escalation in any one particular case and thus determines the scope of extended deterrence.

The connection between the degree of absolute vulnerability of the would-be protector and the scope of extended deterrence *ceteris paribus* is obvious enough: the more vulnerable the would-be protector, the less convincing is his promise to mete out punishment, given that retaliation is expected. But that is only half the story, since the risk of extending deterrence also depends on the expectations of the other side: the more vulnerable the antagonist to be deterred, the less likely he is to invite punishment in pursuit of a given objective. For each side there is the further consideration that, in facing a conflict which is apt to continue, the amount of damage that can be inflicted on the other side is a significant value in itself – on the assumption that the damage expected at this stage is still very far from the entirely catastrophic. It is for these reasons that the balance of *relative* vulnerabilities is the operational criterion on the risk side of the equation.

The factors that govern the balance of relative vulnerabilities are physical in nature and easy enough to define, if often very hard to measure. These factors are: the capabilities of each side's forces (offensive and defensive); the quality of the civil defence and industrial recovery organization and the scope and robustness of passive defences. Certainly, it is not the simple balance of inter-continental nuclear forces that defines the risk side of the equation.

By contrast, the factors that govern the 'balance of perceived interests' are political and diplomatic, atmospheric and therefore evanescent. The intensity of each side's interest in a given value can change drastically over time (for example, the American interest in maintaining West Berlin's independence from Soviet control increased very sharply between 1945 and 1961), and, of course, there is always much room for error in each side's assessment of the intensity of the other's interest in a given extra-territorial value. Thus the balance of perceived interests, of sentiments and their reciprocal assessment on each side, is a complex and uncertain thing, sentiments being, of course, variable over time, while assessments may lead, lag or be plainly in error.

Indeed, error is unavoidable. The intensity of a given interest may increase sharply and precisely in response to a challenge – thus retroactively turning what was a correct assessment into an underestimate. Conversely, the unmet challenge stimulates retroactive justification through the downgrading of the interest. The process that determines the relative value of a given thing to its would-be protector is, of course, political in the broadest sense, with the dynamics of internal politics often being activated by external challenges. Thus the evolution of the Berlin value, which was finally equated with a national-territorial interest (President Kennedy's 'I am a Berliner'), owed much to the internal political reaction to external challenges, French as well as Soviet. Equally, non-territorial and non-substantive values can be devalued by oblivion – that is to say, by tranquillity.

In addition to the declaratory dimensions of commitment-making or disengagement, there is the cumulative effect of diplomatic action and reaction. Urgent and hard responses to attempted encroachments or implied challenges will strengthen the true intensity of the interest protected, as well as affecting assessments of the same. Hesitant and yielding responses will, by contrast, affect the balance of perceived interests adversely, increasing the risks of extended deterrence much as a deterioration in the balance of vulnerabilities might. Diplomats may be forgiven if they attach greater value to the benefits of flexibility, while, for the most part, strategists are more mindful of the added risk of misperceptions that a flexible stance entails.

Extended Deterrence Today
The Case of Europe
As far as Central Europe is concerned, extended deterrence now comes into play in two very

33

different circumstances: in negating the effects that the Soviet ability to attack European cities with nuclear weapons would otherwise evoke, and in deterring a Soviet disarming offensive against European-based theatre nuclear weapons. Given that European-based nuclear weapons do not threaten Soviet cities as convincingly as Soviet medium-range ballistic missiles (MRBMS) and intermediate-range ballistic missiles (IRBMS) and bombers threaten European cities, the latter must be hostages unless protected by the extended deterrence of American inter-continental nuclear weapons. It must be assumed that the British and French independent deterrent forces only protect British and French cities, if they protect anything at all. The rationality assumptions of deterrence itself define the problem as a matter of denying opportunities for coercive diplomacy rather than one of actual protection. Does American extended deterrence still meet the need? Will it continue to do so given an American–Soviet balance of vulnerabilities that increasingly favours the latter? The answer must be yes, although for reasons not altogether reassuring.

In this case it is the balance of perceived interests that dominates the matrix. On the one hand, there is the enormity of the deed and the lack of Soviet gain in actually executing it; on the other, there are the sentiments that would be evoked. More realistically, the latent threat to the cities is dominated by the availability to the Soviet Union of other (and infinitely more plausible) instruments of military pressure, at much lower levels of conflict intensity. American extended deterrence thus meets only a very feeble requirement in this case: to negate a blackmail option, which must rank very low in the Soviet repertoire. Thus even the advent of an increasingly dubious parity should not abridge the effective scope of extended deterrence in this case. This should apply equally during conflict: only a Soviet Union in the process of being defeated in combat at lower levels of intensity might plausibly threaten European cities to force a cessation of hostilities. In the above case it is implicitly accepted that the Soviet threat to European cities would suffice to inhibit a NATO attempt to impose a cessation of hostilities (at lower levels of intensity) by threatening to attack Soviet cities (for example, with the *Poseidon/Trident* warheads allocated to Supreme Allied Command, Europe). It is not, of course, the recent sharp increase in the relative vulnerability of the United States that would determine the result, but rather the long-standing, absolute vulnerability of the European cities, including those that the British and French nuclear forces might protect by deterrence in other circumstances.

In this case, therefore, we find extended deterrence to be as fully applicable, as credible and as stable as it has ever been; but this happy situation reflects weakness rather than strength – specifically the wide range of other opportunities for Soviet coercive diplomacy in peacetime and the utter implausibility of a victorious NATO offensive (or for that matter counter-offensive) in wartime.

The Case of Japan
In the case of extending deterrence to negate Soviet nuclear threats to the population of Japan, matters are not quite the same. Here too the sheer enormity of the deed must greatly inhibit Soviet action, quite independently of any fear of direct retaliation. But, of course, there is still a difference between the prospects of the victim and those of the aggressor, and here too the difference must be equalized by extended deterrence to deny a corresponding potential for coercive diplomacy. A significant difference between the two cases is the fact that the Soviet Union does not have, *vis-à-vis* Japan, a comparable repertoire of high-intensity threats (while having an even broader repertoire at the low-intensity end of the spectrum). Specifically, the Soviet Union's ability to carry out a successful amphibious invasion of Japan is altogether more dubious than her ability to advance against NATO forces in a non-nuclear conflict. This would increase to a corresponding extent the saliency of nuclear threats in a crisis of sufficient severity.

It follows that the requirements which American extended deterrence must meet are somewhat more demanding in this case. Since the Soviet Union is acquiring such abundant inter-continental nuclear forces, the fact that American extended deterrence must cope with a threat now emanating from Soviet weapons of lesser range does not alter the character of the problem. Nothing much would be gained by deploying American weapons designed to be directly comparable with the SS-20 and *Backfire*. What *would* make a great deal of difference would be an American counter-force advantage, for this would provide a plausible and straightforward instrument of deterrence in this case: silo-killing ICBM warheads would be much more plausible as instruments of extended deterrence in this particular case than less accurate dedicated weapons of lesser range. (In nature, range and accuracy go together, but given the deployment choices actually available, the two would not be congruent in this case).

Deterrence by Counter-Force

The wider question of the role of counter-force capabilities in extended deterrence is best discussed in the more specialized context of the Soviet threat against European-based theatre nuclear weapons.

The Soviet ability to attack those weapons has greatly increased of late, and it is still increasing. The difference between the new SS-20 and the old SS-4s and SS-5s is not merely greatly increased accuracy but also greatly diminished vulnerability. Because of their vulnerability, SS-4s and SS-5s could scarcely be used in a selective, discrete fashion: all would be immediate candidates for destruction if any were used. SS-20s, by contrast, are mobile and easily concealed, so that selective attacks by them are a true option. Even though its present warheads are relatively large, the SS-20 has a potential for high accuracies that would allow the useful deployment of low-yield warheads suitable for pre-emptive precision attacks upon Quick Reaction Alert (QRA) air bases, *Pershing* pre-dispersal depots and any future ground launched cruise missile (GLCM) basing points (the currently envisaged USAF deployment scheme does little to minimize the threat).

Given the role that these theatre nuclear weapons play in the structure of NATO security, even a fully equivalent countervailing threat (against Soviet MRBMs, IRBMs and G- and H-class submarines and nuclear-armed aircraft) would not dispose of the problem. In the NATO structure conventional forces serve to deter incursions and to defend against conventional attacks; battlefield nuclear weapons serve to deter a full-scale conventional offensive and to defend against one that appears to be within measurable distance of success, as well as to deter the prior use of Soviet battlefield nuclear weapons. Theatre nuclear weapons in turn serve to deter Soviet attacks against NATO battlefield nuclear weapons, as well as to defend against a successful Soviet offensive that features the use of nuclear weapons of any kind.

Unless they are fully confident of NATO's self-deterrence, Soviet war planners must undertake to peel away these layers of protection one by one: superiority in non-nuclear offensive potential is their base capability, and some sort of equivalence in battlefield nuclear weapons is sufficient for the Soviet Union, given the former advantage. But as long as American extended deterrence covers European cities, the deterrent effect of European-based theatre nuclear weapons cannot be negated by Soviet threats of retaliation against European cities. Nor can the Soviet Union achieve her goal by threatening reciprocal use, for Soviet theatre nuclear attacks upon NATO forces in the process of being defeated would have by no means the same significance as NATO theatre nuclear weapon attacks upon victorious Soviet forces. It follows that the logical Soviet goal must be to acquire a disarming counter-force capability against European-based theatre nuclear weapons.

In theory, this particular threat could be negated by a combination of active and passive defences in addition to dispersal and mobility, the major means of protection for these weapons. In practice, however, the *unalerted* theatre nuclear-weapon force is highly vulnerable. Of particular concern is the fact that the refinement of Soviet military capabilities provides the possibility of a *non-nuclear* disarming offensive, in addition to the already manifest trend towards a precise nuclear offensive offering the prospect of low collateral damage.

The latter threat already generates a requirement for extended deterrence quite distinct from the much less demanding requirement associated with the threat of nuclear attacks upon European cities. Very specifically, it is a selective counter-force option that is called for. In this case the straightforward balance of American and Soviet offensive forces is of central significance to the scope of extended deterrence. The emerging Soviet advantage in ICBM counter-force capabilities is undoubtedly depriving the United States of the most effective instrument of deterrence *vis-à-vis* the threat of a disarming counter-force attack upon the European-based theatre nuclear forces. The reciprocal threat of selective strikes against Soviet ICBMS loses plausibility when the Soviet Union can count on achieving a net improvement in the residual balance by a (non-escalatory) response of identical form. Given an American advantage in ICBM counter-force capabilities, the deterrence of low-casualty Soviet attacks against European-based theatre nuclear weapons could be accomplished by the threat of low-casualty American attacks against Soviet ICBMS or theatre nuclear assets. Given the deterioration in the ICBM balance, the scope of extended deterrence has effectively been abridged.

Nor would the deployment of the 2,000-warhead MX force which is now envisaged suffice to restore the situation. This would undoubtedly re-establish the ICBM component of the 'triad' for the purposes of self-protecting deterrence, but it could not restore the American ascendancy in the ICBM sector of the competition, given the planned characteristics of warheads and guidance. Nor can compensation be found in other categories of weapons. In the case of air-launched cruise missiles, the selective use of the force is improbable on operational grounds alone; it is also apt to be counter-productive, given the vulnerability of the bomber bases, including dispersal bases, to which the B-52 is confined. As for submarine-launched ballistic missiles (SLBMS), neither the *Poseidon* nor the *Trident* have the requisite counter-force characteristics, while the inherent counter-force potential of the large-diameter tubes in the *Ohio*-class submarines remains as yet unexploited.

What applies to the extended deterrence of Soviet attacks upon theatre nuclear weapons based in Europe is true, *a fortiori*, of the extended deterrence of such threats as a Soviet invasion of northern Norway or a seizure of Berlin or attacks upon lesser allies overseas. In all such cases the threat of selective counter-force attacks would in the past have provided the most plausible deterrent, one that would capitalize on the very great political and psychological difference between threats to uphold and threats to change the *status quo*. In both cases, there is not now a conventional defence nor a battlefield nuclear deterrent of sufficient plausibility. In both cases only the hope that the Soviet Union might anticipate wider consequences that she would judge to be broadly unfavourable stands between these exposed positions and Soviet power.

As the overall military balance continues to change adversely, it is important to remember that the outpost can receive deterrent protection from the prospect of a wider conflict only to the extent that the *initiation* of that wider conflict is more frightening to the potential aggressor than to the victim. In the case of northern Norway there is, in theory, much scope for dealing with the problem *in situ* by endowing the outpost itself with formidable defences and a battlefield nuclear deterrent also.

In the case of Berlin (as, for that matter, in the case of an American aircraft-carrier moving within range of Soviet attack submarines) the protection of the lesser thing must derive from the strength of the security system as a whole. Given weakness in the whole, the outpost is correspondingly less well protected from afar. How plausible is it to a potential aggressor that the centre would indeed choose to widen a conflict if the expected outcome were no better for the whole than for the outpost on its own? (And, of course, infinitely more catastrophic).

Here, then, a partial answer may be given to the prescribed questions: if extended deterrence remains as reliable and credible as before in the presence of a deteriorating military balance, it is the stability of the system that is being compromised. In the past military decline would exact its price *pro rata* in a corresponding loss of control over territory. In modern conditions boundary lines do not adjust as easily to absorb change, for there is no frequent conflict in detail at the margins of civilized states. The delusion that adverse changes in the military balance will have *no* consequences is easily inspired by such conditions. But military decline is as costly as it ever was. Instead of a visible retreat, the result is progressive fragility in the system of deterrence, and this is a process which may long continue to be hidden from view, especially in conditions of political tranquillity, which are themselves contrived for the sake of their strategic consequences.

All remains the same on the surface, while the substance of deterrent protection is increasingly eroded. Eventually, the plausibility of the threats on which deterrence is based may collapse overnight. The exposed positions that are protected only by perceptual lags will then have to be conceded by a prudent victim when the hollow deterrent is challenged. Even then, the results of military decline could still be denied, but only to the extent that the victim can persuasively promise to react to the challenge in a manner reckless and by then self-destructive. Such a policy, whether adopted in protection of Berlin or designed to nullify Soviet counter-force advantages by a 'launch on warning' firing doctrine, certainly offers a most economical response to the broad and serious military effort of the Soviet Union – but then the stability of the entire system would be sacrificed for the most marginal of our peaceful comforts.

China's Nuclear Forces and the Stability of Soviet–American Deterrence

GREGORY TREVERTON

The first obvious fact about China's nuclear force is how little is known about it in the West. The second is the asymmetry of its apparent impact on the nuclear balance. There is little to suggest that China's missiles target any country but the Soviet Union, but to some extent ambiguity about her nuclear forces must be calculated Chinese strategy. For the Soviet Union in particular, such uncertainty must play on her deep-rooted anxiety about China.

Uncertainty makes this (or any) assessment of China's nuclear role speculative. With American and Soviet nuclear arsenals exceeding 10,000 warheads in the 1980s, why should 100, or even a few hundred, relatively crude Chinese weapons matter? On the one hand, it is tempting to say that except for Soviet paranoia, which is more political than military, there is no reason why anyone should care much about Chinese nuclear forces. On the other hand, however, Chinese forces do seem to constitute a minimum deterrent of a sort *vis-à-vis* the Soviet Union.

The Chinese case is so special that it is hard to see other nations emulating her forces or apparent rationale for them. (And it is worth remembering that by the end of the 1980s only three nations are likely to have any claim to the status of 'medium' nuclear power – the same three as today.) Chinese forces are likely to remain in the 1980s what they are today – a special concern to the Soviet Union and a complication in nuclear relations between the super-powers. It would take radical changes in her own forces and in the situation of Asia for China to provide an example of nuclear possibilities for other nations.

China's Nuclear Force

The Chinese nuclear programme began in the late 1950s, with the co-operation of the Soviet Union. China exploded her first atomic bomb in October 1964, at the Lop Nor test site. Over the next six years China progressed from fission weapons to thermonuclear ones; the testing programme suggests a smooth transition, and China made it in the very short time of three years, less time than the United States, the Soviet Union, Britain or France. The pattern of testing in the 1970s suggests an effort to get more yield from lighter weapons.[1]

At no stage has China built nuclear weapons in large numbers. Rather, what is known about her nuclear programmes suggests a careful effort to master the technology step by step and to have the capability to build nuclear weapons in considerable numbers if those were required. Nor is there any sign of a 'crash' programme to build the means of delivering nuclear weapons. As the table on page 39 indicates, China appears to have been developing an ICBM since at least 1973, and has only recently deployed the first one or two 'limited-range' ICBMs.

China has not yet built any solid-fuel missiles. Since 1970 she has had a *Golf*-class submarine with two missile-launching tubes but no missiles for it. That may be due to technical problems, but it is more likely to reflect a lack of priority. According to Central Intelligence Agency estimates, China's military expenditure remained constant between 1972 and 1977, though industrial productivity grew by more than half. Whatever the reason – conscious choice or antagonism between 'civilian' and 'military' after Lin Piao's abortive coup in 1971 – there is little evidence that nuclear programmes fared significantly better than any other military expenditure.[2]

At present China's nuclear force consists of one or two 'limited-range' ICBMs, with a range

China's Nuclear Capability: 1970 to 1980

	1970–1	1971–2	1972–3	1973–4	1974–5	1975–6	1976–7	1977–8	1978–9	1979–80
Submarine	1 G-class submarine with missile-launching tubes but no missiles	↑	↑	↑	↑	↑	↑	↑	↑	↑
Fission/ fusion weapons	approx. 120	approx. 120	approx. 150	approx. 200	200–300	200–300	200–300	several hundred	↑	↑
MRBM	none deployed	approx. 20 deployed (range: up to 1,609 km)	approx. 20–30	about 50 deployed	about 50 deployed	about 50 deployed (range: 1,127 km)	30–50 may be phased out	30–40 CSS-1 1–3 MT deployed	30–40 CSS-1	40–50 CSS
IRBM	–	–	developed 15–20 (range: 2,414–4,023 km)	produced 15–20 (range: 5,633 km)	20–30	20–30 (range: 2,414–2,816 km)	20–30 now operational	30–40 CSS-2 1–3 MT?	30–40 CSS-2	50–70 CSS-2
ICBM	–	–	–	being developed	(being developed) produced but not deployed	ready for deployment (range: 5,633 km); ICBM with 12,875 km range being deployed; not operational	ICBM with 5,633 km range now operational; ICBM with 12,875 km range still in development	ICBM with 5,633-km range may now be deployed; 12,875 km ICBM still in development	limited ICBM (range: 6,437 km)	2 CSS-3 (limited range of 6,437 km)
Tu-16	some	at least 30 (range: 2,575 km)	100	100	100 (radius of action: 3,219 km)	60	65	80	80	80–90
Tu-4	some	↑	↑	↑	↑	some	↑	↑	↑	↑
Il-28	150	150	200	200	200	300	300	400	300	300
Tu-2	–	–	100	100	100	100	100	100	100	100
F-9	–	–	200	300	some	some	↑	↑	↑	↑

Source: The Military Balance (London: IISS, various years).

39

of 6,437 kilometres, 50–70 intermediate-range ballistic missiles, with a range of 2,414–2,816 kilometres, and 40–50 medium-range ballistic missiles, with a range of about 1,125 kilometres. The yields of the missile warheads are presumed to be in the range of 1–3 megatonnes; all the missiles are driven by storable liquid fuel. In addition to missiles, China has a number of aircraft capable of delivering nuclear weapons, but most of those planes are obsolete, based on Soviet prototypes of the late 1950s and early 1960s. There are some 90 Tu-16s, with a radius of some 3,220 kilometres, plus some Tu-4 and F-9 bombers and about 100 Tu-2 and 300 Il-28 aircraft.

Chinese aircraft hardly pose a substantial nuclear threat to the Soviet Union. Few of them could be relied on to penetrate Soviet air defences. Fragments of evidence suggest that China, aware of that problem, does not put much faith in a nuclear role for her aircraft. For instance, Chinese inventories of nuclear weapons seem not to include many gravity bombs, and the emphasis in nuclear testing on improving weight-to-yield ratios suggests a shift away from air-delivered weapons.

Nuclear Weapons and Chinese Security

China's nuclear force therefore amounts to her missile force. That force can threaten the Soviet Union but not the United States (even its limited-range ICBM could reach no American territory save Alaska). Chinese launch sites – near the Korean border, south and west of Peking and south and west of Outer Mongolia – suggest a focus, perhaps exclusive, on the Soviet Union.[3] Is that force a deterrent? What does it deter? What role does it play in the Soviet–American nuclear balance?

Nuclear weapons, at the other end of the technological spectrum from a People's War, reflect the same emphasis on self-reliance and on defence. China has stated over and over again that she will never use nuclear weapons first.[4] Those statements serve to reassure Asian neighbours, for whom even China's limited nuclear force could be an instrument of coercive diplomacy. But they also reinforce the emphasis on the Soviet Union as the only possible target of a second use of Chinese nuclear weapons. Certainly, the lack of a push to produce an ICBM fits with the shift away from a view of the Soviet Union and the United States as more or less equal enemies to a view of the latter as not particularly threatening. From that perspective, it makes little sense for China to deploy a full-range ICBM, which would be of use primarily against the United States.

None of this, however, explains why China has not developed larger or more sophisticated nuclear forces. Three sets of explanations, in some combination, are possible.

First, China may not believe there is much to be deterred. She may rate the possibility of any major Soviet attack to be low, and a pre-emptive nuclear strike extremely low. Certainly, Chinese rhetoric has given less and less credence to the Soviet threat, and the border has been relatively quiet since 1969. The story persists that only American signals to the Soviet Union in 1969 prevented a pre-emptive attack on China's nuclear capacity, but China may feel that the period of acute danger has passed.[5] Chinese statements emphasize the Soviet threat against Europe. How much of that is real and how much is rhetoric is hard to know.

Second, China may believe she has enough to deter. This explanation would focus more on the adequacy of Chinese forces than on the paucity of the threat. It would derive both from a Chinese belief that her nuclear forces would be deterring in themselves and from their place in broader Chinese defences. Chinese statements frequently assert that nuclear weapons are not the decisive element of war.[6] Those statements must reflect a real perception and a desire to create a self-fulfilling prophecy. The risks of nuclear attack are less if the would-be attacker believes his opponent does not regard even a massive nuclear attack as the end of the battle. Mao's exhortation to 'dig tunnels deep, store grain everywhere and never seek hegemony' dovetails with such a view. A nation that is prepared to survive an attack is less likely to receive one. Chinese statements assert that any attacker would have to follow massive nuclear strikes with the occupation of Chinese territory.

Third, China may simply be prepared to wait out a period of vulnerability, in the expectation that technological advance will make new generations of nuclear weapons cheaper. Again, of course, a perception that Chinese vulnerability was neither too great nor too important would make the waiting period less uncomfortable.

While there is little about the pattern of Chinese nuclear development to suggest that technical problems have been overriding, they have no doubt existed – for instance, in the development of solid fuel. It is more likely that the cost of producing nuclear weapons in large numbers, as opposed to continuing research and development, has seemed too high.[7]

Implications for the Soviet Union
It goes without saying that the Soviet Union is pre-occupied with China. Yet exactly what it is about China that pre-occupies Moscow is harder to specify. The record of the gradual Soviet military build-up in the 1960s hints more at a desire to put political pressure on China than at preparations to deal with a military threat. The 12 Soviet divisions in the Far East in 1960 became 17 by 1965 and 21 by 1969. However, China responded not with acquiescence but with border probes of her own in 1969.

After 1969 the perception of a Chinese military as well as political threat is more and more evident in Soviet actions. By 1972 the Soviet Union had a quarter of her armed forces (44 or 45 divisions, including three in Mongolia) in the Far East, with over 3,000 tanks and as many as 1,400 combat aircraft. In the late 1960s about a quarter of the Soviet I/MRBM force – mostly SS-4s with 1-megatonne warheads – was moved to positions in the Far East facing China. More recently a quarter of the SS-20s appear to have been deployed in the Far East, with perhaps the bulk of the rest in a 'swing zone' from where they threaten China and Europe. There are also shorter-range SS-12 missiles. In all, some 2,500 nuclear tactical warheads are thought to be under the Soviet Far East Command.[8] Chinese considerations no doubt loomed large in the Soviet Union's decision to build the SS-20. In particular, her long-range missile force (5,000–6,500 kilometres) permits the Soviet Union to target most of China from a safe distance; her development of the 3-MIRV warheads and improved accuracy may have been fuelled by the desire to try to target Chinese military targets, including Chinese missiles.

China's nuclear forces are hardly a credible first-strike arsenal. And China has repeatedly disavowed any such purpose for them. Whether they constitute a credible second-strike deterrent depends on the view of the power to be deterred – the Soviet Union. Soviet uncertainty about where Chinese missiles are and, to a lesser extent, how many exist, is as great as that of the United States – probably greater. Moscow reportedly spends something like half its total satellite reconnaissance effort on China. China plays on Soviet uncertainty by occasionally revealing missiles to satellite passes or by publishing photographs of them.

How much of a deterrent China's force would be in Soviet calculations depends, first, on how much of it would survive a first Soviet strike. Obviously that question cannot be answered with any precision. What *can* be said is that China is apparently trying hard to reduce the vulnerability of her forces. Her missiles are deployed in much smaller clusters than those of American and Soviet systems. Many are deployed in caves; others are camouflaged. Most of the missiles can be moved and they are occasionally deployed far away from their operating bases.

Certainly, Moscow must reckon that no matter what first-strike it launched against China, *some* Chinese missiles launched in a retaliatory strike would reach Soviet targets. With all Soviet anti-ballistic missile (ABM) defences around Moscow, Chinese missiles would be able to penetrate to a number of other major Soviet cities. If as many as 100 missiles survived and were able to be launched, China could destroy about half the industrial capacity in 17 major Soviet cities, killing about 15 million people, if the Chinese missiles each carried only a 50-kilotonne warhead.[9] (These figures probably understate potential damage because of technical factors in their calculation and because many of the Chinese missiles probably carry much larger warheads.)

With her nuclear forces and her general attitude towards nuclear attack, China tells the Soviet Union, in effect: 'We will not be deterred by the prospect of massive destruction of industry and cities.' With her dispersed population, China could absorb enormous losses in a nuclear attack. And she has said she is prepared to do this: Chou En-lai once remarked that China could lose 100 million people if need be. China reportedly began building a network of underground tunnels and shelters, primarily in large cities, after 1969. They were designed to disperse urban populations and to store food in case of

41

an attack. Of course, the extent and effect of these civil defence preparations are impossible to estimate with any accuracy, but they stand as an earnest of China's commitment to deter nuclear attack by preparing for it. (The corollary to 'We will not be deterred by massive destruction' is 'You have to come after our nuclear forces, and you cannot strike them' – minimum deterrence with a vengeance.)

Still, in military terms it is hard to see what the Soviet Union has to fear from China. Clearly, she could deal with any conventional military threat posed by China, and it is hard to imagine that China would contemplate the use of nuclear weapons other than in retaliation. In neither a first nor a second strike could Chinese weapons threaten the USSR's own nuclear weapons.

Why should Moscow worry about China's nuclear weapons? The possible reasons merge with more general Soviet military and political concerns about China.

First, nuclear weapons would present the Soviet Union with a particularly frightening version of the 'two-front' problem. Chinese nuclear weapons cannot threaten Soviet weapons, but neither could Moscow pre-empt all Chinese nuclear weapons. Hence any slow-moving crisis (or major war in Europe) would confront the Soviet Union with the continuing possibility of a war with China and an accompanying nuclear threat. Moscow would have to retain a reserve of nuclear warheads for use against China.

Second, the Soviet Union may, in fact, feel deterred, at least from any pre-emptive strike. That feeling may merge with a more general sense that while China poses little military threat, Soviet military preponderance has little utility. Moscow's ability to exact military punishment for political purpose is limited. Nuclear weapons are too risky to be used, in part because China's nuclear forces deter, but also because the political costs to the Soviet Union of a first use of nuclear weapons in Asia would be exorbitant. Similar considerations may apply in regard to major conventional air strikes against Chinese military and industrial targets, while military incursions, even major, into Chinese territory would only play into Chinese hands. Probes along the border are possible but may seem pointless. (Calculations such as these may have frustrated Moscow in framing military options against China in support of her Vietnamese ally

during the Chinese incursion. However, it may be that China withdrew before Moscow felt compelled to act.)

Third, Moscow may find the present acceptable but may fear the future. China could probably have a nuclear force to be reckoned with by the mid-1980s if she chose. She could deploy significant numbers of ICBMs by then, if the effort were given appropriate priority. Moreover, the shapes of warheads on existing ICBMs suggest an interest in accuracy, an interest that may be corroborated by the Chinese satellite programme. China has launched at least eight satellites since 1970, the last few apparently reconnaissance satellites for military purposes. China could not pose a limited threat to Soviet nuclear weapons in the 1980s, but she could threaten many more Soviet industrial and military targets. If she built solid-fuel missiles, China could deploy one or two missile-firing submarines, which would further complicate Soviet targeting.

Nuclear weapons may serve as concrete symbols of Soviet anxieties. Regionally, they suggest a rising power to the East, not only a competing Communist state but one giving the lie to the Soviet claim to be the country of the future. Internationally, the more strength the Soviet Union builds against China, the more she drives China towards alignment with the West in general and the United States in particular – surely an enduring Soviet nightmare. Cooperation with the West in nuclear matters would touch Soviet nerve endings and so make Moscow attentive to Western transfers of a wide range of computing and electronic equipment.

Western Interests

Recent American – and Western – policy towards China smacks too much of the adage 'my enemy's enemy is my friend'. Does that extend to the nuclear realm? Does any of this matter to the West, or is the West merely the happy beneficiary of China's lopsided effect on the strategic balance? Certainly, China will complicate efforts to deal with one major source of instability in the strategic situation of the 1980s – concern over the credibility of the American nuclear guarantee to Western Europe (and, conceivably, Japan).

Much of the Soviet I/MRBM effort is directed at China – probably much more than is usually concluded in Western analyses. It is likely that Chinese considerations matter more than European ones in determining the configuration of the SS-20 and pacing its deployments. Yet since the SS-20, not to mention *Backfire*, could be moved from the eastern Soviet Union to the west, the United States and her NATO allies are bound to consider them as potential threats to the West, to be dealt with accordingly by NATO forces and arms-control efforts.

The question of who is racing whom will complicate efforts to negotiate over so-called 'grey area' systems in Europe, like the SS-20. Should all SS-20s count as a threat to Europe? Or should the Soviet Union be permitted an allowance to deal with the Chinese threat that she – but not the United States – faces? A similar set of considerations would prevail if future SALT negotiations focused on deep reductions in aggregate launchers (or warheads) for the two sides. Because of the Chinese threat the Soviet Union would be likely to demand an allowance, or to insist that the number be not too low. That would be a problem even if China's force grew no larger or more sophisticated. It would be harder still if China's nuclear arsenal improved.

From the West's perspective, the other major source of instability in the strategic balance of the 1980s, intertwined with anxieties over the credibility of American guarantees, is the vulnerability of American land-based ICBMs. China will matter little to the substance of that issue, but she is intriguing commentary on how it is viewed. If the Soviet Union cannot be confident of pre-empting 100 Chinese missiles, surely she cannot be sure of taking out the entire American *Minuteman* force. And if Moscow is effectively deterred, at least from certain kinds of action, by the knowledge that a few Chinese warheads might strike Soviet cities, Soviet–American deterrence may be much more stable than is sometimes implied.

The fact that 100 warheads may constitute a sufficient deterrent for China but a few thousand may not for the United States says something about the different meanings deterrence has for the two countries. For China deterrence is minimum in all senses: China has foresworn any first use of nuclear weapons – and thus any nuclear coercion – and has no allies to cover with deterrence. Nuclear weapons may play only

a small role in a broader Chinese deterrent, but the target of the deterrent is specific: the Soviet Union. In all these ways China also differs from would-be nuclear proliferators of the 1980s. Most of them will have small, unstructured nuclear forces with no real rationale. For them nuclear weapons will be part military instrument, part symbol of prestige, part source of political leverage and part insurance against a neighbour's acquiring nuclear weapons first.

Still, the lesson that a small nuclear force can deter even a super-power cannot be lost on China's neighbours. Arguably, once China built nuclear weapons to deter the Soviet Union, India felt she had to consider them with respect to China. Similar logic would be applicable to Taiwan if she felt completely abandoned and unable to defend herself, or to South Korea (or North Korea), or even to Japan, if doubts about the American guarantee became severe and relations with China or the Soviet Union, or both, became sharply hostile.

It seems more likely that Chinese nuclear forces will merely complicate super-power nuclear relations in the 1980s. For instance, China could serve to increase Soviet interest in ABM systems. The Soviet situation is reminiscent of the American debate over ABMs in the late 1960s, for a relatively 'thin' – and cheap – system might suffice to give the Soviet Union considerable protection from China. China has thus been, with Britain and France, a primary beneficiary of the ABM Treaty of 1972. The Soviet Union could be tempted to develop, under the ABM Treaty regime, a network of SA-5 missiles capable of knocking down Chinese missiles or, conceivably, to seek an end to the ABM Treaty. Any Soviet effort is bound to fan concern in the West that the Soviet Union is developing an ABM system surreptitiously for use against the West as well, or that she is acquiring a capacity to do so quickly if the ABM Treaty were to be abrogated in the future.

While the Soviet Union appears to have ruled out a pre-emptive strike against Chinese forces for the moment, it is not obvious that this would be the case in a time of crisis. With some anti-Chinese ABM system in place, Moscow might be tempted to make such a strike even against a much larger future Chinese force. That would confront the United States with some unpleasant choices.

The requirements of crisis management may appear to demand some collusion between Moscow and Washington in putting boundaries around the Chinese force. Suppose, for instance, that China built several missile-carrying submarines. She might then have an incentive to deploy these in areas known to contain American (or British, or French) submarines. In any Sino–Soviet crisis the Soviet Union would thus be confronted with considerable uncertainty about the precise nationality of the missile coming at her. China might then achieve some 'coupling' of her fate with that of the United States. The scenario is far-fetched, but Soviet worries about it need not be.

In any event, it is probable that China will remain a special case at the margins of nuclear relations between the super-powers – a source of anxiety for the Soviet Union and of complication to super-power arms-control efforts but of limited use as a model for other would-be nuclear nations. China has been moving steadily away from reliance on People's War, in fact if not in rhetoric, and recent military contacts with Western nations underline her interest in developing a more modern military force. Nuclear weapons will be part of that modernization, but there is little to suggest that they will be given special priority. The existing Chinese arsenal contributes something to deterrence; a greatly improved force is likely to continue to seem too expensive to justify its cost, and more likely both to provoke Soviet reactions and to unsettle Asian neighbours than to contribute to China's security.

NOTES

[1] For a chart on Chinese testing, see S. K. Ghosh, 'Nuclear Weapons Programme – China', *Strategic Analysis*, (November 1977), p. 23.

[2] See Jonathan D. Pollack, 'The Implications of Sino–American Normalization', *International Security*, Vol. 3, No. 4, (Spring 1979), p. 40.

[3] Jonathan D. Pollack, 'China as a Nuclear Power', in William H. Overholt (ed.), *Asia's Nuclear Future* (Boulder, Colorado: Westview Press, 1977), p. 55.

[4] A 1964 Government statement is representative: 'The Chinese Government hereby solemnly declares that China will never at any time and under any circumstances be the first to use nuclear weapons.'

[5] The most explicit account of that episode is by President Nixon's Chief of Staff, H. R. Haldeman, in *The Ends of Power* (New York: Times Books, 1978).

[6] For instance, a 1961 internal military document: 'Though the power of atomic weapons is great, they can only attack the other party's centers in strategic air raids . . . Afterwards they can only be used primarily . . . as firing vanguard before an attack. To resolve the battle . . . and to achieve victory, it will still rely upon the ground force, the army, and conventional weapons'. Cited in Pollack, *op. cit.*, p. 51.

[7] The chronology is again suggestive. Chinese missiles and bombers began production in the spring and summer of 1971, just as Western observers began to detect a 'steel versus electronics' debate in China between those who gave priority to basic development and those inclined to invest more in advanced technology, perhaps including defence. See Jonathan D. Pollack, 'The Logic of Chinese Military Strategy', *The Bulletin of Atomic Scientists*, Vol. 35, No. 1, (January 1979), pp. 27–8.

[8] These numbers are from *The Military Balance, 1979–1980* (London: IISS, 1979).

[9] These estimates are, of course, crude. They are based on targeting and population data in Geoffrey Kemp, *Nuclear Weapons for Medium Powers*, Parts I and II, Adelphi Papers Nos 106 and 107, (London: IISS, 1974), especially Part I, p. 18, and Appendix.

The Rationale for Medium-Sized Deterrence Forces

LAWRENCE FREEDMAN

It would be misleading to suggest that there is, or is about to be, a serious search within Britain and France for new rationales for their nuclear forces. The old rationales saw the Governments of these countries through stormy debates in the 1960s, survived the 1970s and will probably suffice in the 1980s.

Further expenditure will be presented as maintaining existing capabilities, not as some radical new departure in national policy. Because the British *Polaris* force will suffer group obsolescence during the 1990s, a decision has been taken to replace it with a force of *Trident* missiles. Because the Labour leadership (if not its rank and file) tended to a similar view in Government, we can expect such opposition to the *Polaris* replacement as it mounts to be provoked by its cost or timing or its imperviousness to control rather than by scorn for the strategic rationales. The decision emphasizes continuity rather than novelty.[1] The prospectus for the French *force de frappe* suggests incremental improvement within an established framework (with possible innovation in modes of delivery). All major segments of the political community appear reconciled to this. Recent arguments in France have been over whether too little rather than too much is being done – hence the authorization of a sixth SSBN.

Rationales phrased in strategic terms are often rationalizations for objectives related more to NATO's internal political balance than the military balance between East and West; for example, as an advantage over Germany, to compensate for her economic and conventional military strength. Britain is encouraged to cling to nuclear status as a means of preserving the vestiges of her former international position, intimacy with the United States (where nuclear co-operation,

along with intelligence, provides the residue of the 'special relationship'), permanent representation on the UN Security Council and regular invitations to Summit Meetings. Few arguments for retention of Britain's nuclear force touch such sensitive nerve endings as the prospect of leaving France as the only strategic nuclear power in Europe, a prospect that rarely induces a 'So what?' The French enjoy claiming to be the world's 'third nuclear power' (which the British could, though rarely do, dispute), as if this added to the greater glory of France.

For both powers tangible political benefits have proved elusive. Nuclear power has not earned France leadership of the European Community, nor compensated for Britain's wretched economic performance. Britain has been able to take a seat when the mighty have met to discuss all nuclear issues, but without being able to influence greatly the course of ensuing negotiations. Britain dare not participate in SALT III: there is insufficient flexibility in her force structure to provide for any bargaining position. France has recognized that arms-control negotiations are more likely to result in pressure for unacceptable concessions than in opportunities for influence and has therefore kept clear of negotiations, typically presenting this as a reflection of superior international wisdom.

Furthermore, these forces have ceased to be controversial in NATO circles. A repeat performance of the acrimonious debates of the 1960s does not appear likely. Once the United States Administration had failed in its attempt to persuade the French not to go ahead, there was little point in continuing the argument. Official NATO recognition came to British and French forces when the Ottawa Declaration of 1974 described them as 'capable of playing a deterrent role',[2] hardly a ringing endorsement. The United States now refrains from criticism of her Allies' nuclear forces, but has little positive to say. When mentioned in Annual Defense Statements, they are usually considered as part of the theatre nuclear balance.[3]

Arguments over the introduction of new capabilities are generally more ferocious than those over continuation. The European forces are now familiar (if not prominent) features of the strategic landscape. Familiarity has bred indifference rather than contempt. However, Alliance appreciation of these forces has risen recently with the felt need for virtually any counters to the Soviet build-up and growing sensitivity to the detail of the theatre nuclear balance.

Diminishing Rationales

The contention here is that the European forces' low profile and the feebleness of the debate that surrounds them result from their becoming subject to the twin laws of diminishing rationales and diminishing critiques. They have not become as important, in either a positive or a negative sense, as their respective proponents and opponents once expected them to be.

Britain

As the early pace-setter and wartime accomplice of the United States in atom bomb development, Britain felt that she had right of access to the secrets of the atom. Her January 1947 decision to press on alone was not controversial, confined as it was to an extremely exclusive circle. No special rationale was deemed necessary. It was a capability developed for a Government with world-wide interests and responsibilities. What was unthinkable was that Britain should be without the most modern weapons available. The programme was fixed 'in relation to the availability of raw materials and scientific and engineering effort; it had never been properly related to strategic and tactical needs and probabilities'. In July 1947 the first crude calculations of military needs indicated the improbability of producing an autonomous force of a size that could be decisive in a war with the USSR.[4]

In an East–West confrontation Britain expected to complement the United States in providing a Western deterrent that would ensure a sufficiency of weapons for all significant Soviet targets (it was still assumed that atomic bombs would remain a scarce commodity for some time). Britain, sensing her own vulnerability to nuclear attack, desired always to deter attacks on herself as much as Soviet aggression on the Continent. In the early 1950s the plan was to concentrate on Soviet targets of particular relevance to Britain and perhaps of low priority to the United States. Nevertheless, the essential frame of reference was that of a war in which the country acted with allies and not alone. Strategic thinking concentrated on the appropriate use of nuclear weapons by the Alliance as a whole and not on any uniquely British role.

In 1952, when the Chiefs of Staff concluded that NATO should rely more on the Great Deterrent of nuclear weapons and less on stronger conventional force levels, they had in mind Strategic Air Command and Royal Air Force Bomber Command. When Duncan Sandys announced in 1957 that British forces were henceforth to be organized around nuclear weapons, allowing for cuts in conventional forces, he was following an approach that the United States had already adopted and NATO had endorsed. When the leading British strategists of the day – Blackett, Buzzard and Liddell Hart – criticized 'massive retaliation', it was as contributors to an Alliance debate. Even when the Campaign for Nuclear Disarmament began to make calls to 'ban the bomb', it hoped for exemplary action by Britain that others could follow. It did not argue that growth in American capabilities rendered the British force unnecessary; the critique was directed at *all* nuclear forces. In short, throughout the 1950s there was barely any suggestion that a distinctive strategic rationale was required for British nuclear forces. The 1958 amendments to the McMahon Act in the United States, facilitating nuclear co-operation with Britain, plus the rhetoric of the 'special relationship', discouraged strenuous effort to devise a force that was truly 'independent', let alone a distinctive rationale to support it.

The position changed in the 1960s as the Kennedy Administration promoted a NATO doctrine. Gestures could be made towards strengthening NATO's conventional option, but Britain was quite unable to follow Robert McNamara's flights of strategic fancy with counter-force targeting and rules of engagement scrupulously avoiding cities. While not wedded to attacks solely against populations, Britain made little pretence that military-relevant targets could be destroyed without vast loss of life, or that weapons of sufficient quantity or quality could be developed to impress the enemy by a threat other than that of mass destruction. The sophisticated infrastructure necessary for controlled and contrived strikes was unattainable. British nuclear plans could only be for a short and brutal war.

Furthermore, British strategists, including those with wartime experience in Operations Research, considered the elaborate scenarios constructed in the American research institutes unreal and devoid of historical and political insight.[5] Of the new concepts, only the first strike/second strike distinction appeared at all useful. Otherwise, somewhat condescendingly, Britain put down the new strategy, devised at Rand and applied by McNamara, as evidence of an American susceptibility to waves of fashion.

Any sense of superior wisdom was soon dented. The American strategic reappraisal was accompanied by derision of small nuclear forces. This might have been merely irritating, were it not for Britain's dependence upon the United States. It had been decided to purchase the American *Skybolt*, an air-to-surface missile (ASM) that unfortunately failed to fit in with McNamara's plans. The hurried Accord of December 1962, to supply *Polaris* submarine-launched ballistic missiles (SLBMS) instead, sustained the British deterrent but limited it even more to counter-city attacks and exposed the problem of a convincing rationale.

The growing size of the US force, covering all suitable Warsaw Pact targets, plus ascendent theories of controlled escalation, left the British force looking puny and unsophisticated, adding little to NATO's nuclear capabilities. Continued reliance on the United States undermined its representation as a symbol of national independence. Nor was it acceptable to question the American nuclear guarantee to Europe, still considered to be of the utmost importance. Optimism about European security without America might further tempt the United States to withdraw from NATO commitments. Only political rationales, never far from the surface, were left, emphasizing opportunities for the exercise of benign influence when all nuclear issues, from disarmament to NATO planning, were discussed.[6]

As part of the Nassau Understanding, Britain assigned her *Polaris* fleet to NATO, while reserving the final decision on whether 'supreme national interests' were 'at stake' in any crisis. The official line since then has been that *Polaris* represents a contribution to NATO and not an alternative. Only secondary importance is attached to its value as insurance should the Alliance collapse and Britain find herself alone. However, unofficial advocacy of the maintenance of the nuclear deterrent appears to take the 'Britain alone' scenario more seriously, certainly lending little support to any European hope that, if necessary, Britain (with France) could step smartly into a slot vacated by the United States as nuclear guarantor of the Continent's security.[7] Few incentives can be imagined for a nuclear strike while Soviet conventional forces forge their way through Europe. Nor has it proved easy to construct plausible scenarios in which the United States agrees to do what is necessary to keep the British nuclear force operational but declines to play any other significant role in the defence of Europe, or in which the Soviet Union picks out Britain for special treatment.

An awkward conclusion is that the most likely advantage of the possession of a nuclear arsenal is the possibility of emerging relatively unscathed from a major confrontation over Europe rather than freedom to raise the stakes. If the USSR were to attempt to divide the Alliance through selective nuclear strikes, the most likely victims would be countries unable to retaliate. An independent arsenal might thus confer a sanctuary status. Dwelling on this point in public, however, would not assist in projecting images of either national muscularity or Alliance solidarity.

By the nature of her military position, Britain must come down firmly on the side of deterrence through uncertainty rather than through credible military response. The best available rationale was identified by the previous Government as 'providing a second centre of nuclear decision-making within the Alliance' to 'complicate the calculations of a potential adversary when contemplating aggression'. Mr Mulley, when Secretary of State for Defence, took the need to preserve uncertainty in an aggressor's mind very seriously. He explained to the Parliamentary

47

Committee the difficulty of discussing such matters as 'who is to be deterred from doing what by what kind of threat, and whether we should pose a deterrent threat together with our allies or on our own, or both'. The reason:

> [I]n relations to any possible aggressor, we do not want to be too precise about the circumstances in which our nuclear forces might have to be used were he to embark on aggression. This is because flexibility for ourselves, and uncertainty for the aggressor, are important factors in preserving a deterrent effect.[8]

I submit this invocation of 'deterrence through enigma' as evidence of the workings of the law of diminishing rationales.

France

The early development of France's nuclear capabilities took place in the context of a growing nuclear bias within NATO to which she wished to contribute. Confinement to conventional weapons would relegate France to second-class political status and a secondary military role. The effort to join the nuclear powers became identified with recovery from the humiliations of the 1940s and 1950s, essential to the destiny of the nation.

The United States put pressure on France in the early 1960s not to 'go nuclear' (her first test was in 1960). This threat to national pride accentuated suspicions of American motives. In Europe generally McNamara's approach was seen as an attempt to reduce the threat to the United States by increasing that to Europe, treating Soviet aggression with conventional arms as a 'limited matter', not necessarily deserving a nuclear response. The weaker link between Europe's security and American strategic forces would leave the European states badly placed to withstand Soviet nuclear blackmail, particularly if they were also to be prevented from having their own nuclear capabilities.

Two retired generals, Gallois and Beaufre, challenged the American strategic perspective. Gallois did not believe that conventional Soviet forces could be held back without nuclear threats. The problem was one of credibility. Unlike the United States, he saw this as a matter of *will* rather than of military capability. Sufficient determination on the part of the United States to

employ nuclear weapons in a conflict of secondary importance to herself would solve all NATO's problems, but her policies were creating entirely the wrong image. The best hope for the Western democracies was therefore to rely on the most credible threats – those made by nation states in defence of primary interests. To meet the criticism that threats by small nuclear powers could never be credible against a super-power he introduced the concept of 'proportionality', according to which what mattered was not absolute size but the threat posed in relation to the value of the stake it was defending.[9]

Gallois advocated decentralization of nuclear capabilities within the Alliance, not just to France. In fact, the argument was strongest if applied to West Germany, the most probable victim of aggression and therefore most in need of her own nuclear response. Because of her past and the 1954 Paris Agreement, this was not a practical option.

André Beaufre provided the most convincing argument for small nuclear forces in describing multiple decision centres as an added source of uncertainty for the aggressor. He argued that it was necessary to destabilize a strategic balance that the United States was allowing to become too stable: 'everything possible should be done to ensure that the threat should retain that minimum of spontaneous risk which leads to that prudence indispensable to the maintenance of the risk.'[10]

It is indisputable that an extra decision centre added an increment of risk, but less easy to demonstrate that this increment would be large, especially if the decision centre's occupants were subject to pressures similar to those on Washington. Unless the centre were situated in Bonn, there was no reason why the same inhibitions preventing a nuclear response in the event of a conventional attack on West Germany should not apply. This was also true with respect to the 'detonator' theory, according to which French nuclear use would trigger American use. The cause-and-effect relationship was difficult to establish (which was always the case with American use of nuclear weapons). It was just as difficult to explain why France (or Britain) would actually want to trigger nuclear use.

What these theories indicated was a general preference for policies that accentuated the risk to the adversary by threatening a nuclear crisis that could get wholly out of control, rather than the American search for ways to keep crises under control.

De Gaulle adopted the concept of 'proportionality' but in general expressed scant interest in detailed strategic analysis. His main objective for an independent nuclear force was to stake out an independent political position, encouraging Europe to escape from dependence on the super-powers. General Charles Ailleret set out the strategic rationale. It was assumed, first, that the world was developing in such a chaotic and unpredictable manner that one could not plan against 'a single, well-defined, possible enemy' and, second, that the flexibility necessary to cope with a wide range of possible contingencies could be provided by 'megaton ballistic missiles of a world-wide range, capable of intervening *tous azimuts*'.[11]

However, while other regions did exhibit growing disorder, Europe demonstrated remarkably stability, despite French attempts at disruption. Meanwhile, France could only develop a regional force (unless her SSBNs strayed far from home). With the rest of the Continent proceeding as before, this force appeared militarily marginal and irritating to allies because it encouraged delusions of grandeur.

At first there had been a suggestion that the *force de frappe* would only be invoked in the event of a direct threat to France, which would be deterred by the knowledge of virtually automatic retaliation. After De Gaulle's departure in 1969 French planners were soon contemplating the traditional NATO contingencies. The problems with the independent *force de frappe* were exposed in connection with the *Pluton* short-range missile. The requirement was explained by the need to avoid a rush into strategic nuclear use. Thus nuclear retaliation to *any* threat would be less than automatic; phenomena such as 'thresholds of credibility' were discerned. Deploying *Pluton* on the French border indicated a willingness to bombard German territory that was not wholly appreciated in Bonn. Of course, it was explained, France could not be indifferent to a battle raging on West Germany's eastern border, so the possibility of early participation in the defence of Europe had to be admitted. Finally, if the old scenario remained the most worrisome, then American assistance would still be vital, so it was necessary to play down the theme of the incredibility of the United States' commitment to Europe.

These trends in French thought became quite clear in 1976. Conventional forces were recognized as indispensable to *dissuasion*. The need to prepare 'to intervene with the whole or a part of our forces throughout the entire zone where the security of this territory may be most immediately threatened' was made explicit, acknowledging some dependence on the military prowess of allies. Surreptitiously, the French began moving back to those strategies of Alliance dependence and flexible response to which they had once taken such exception.[12] It can be argued that this constitutes further evidence of the law of diminishing rationales.

Diminishing Critiques

Specific criticisms of independent but small nuclear forces were most rigorously expressed by the Kennedy Administration and were summed up by Robert McNamara's description of them as 'dangerous, expensive, prone to obsolescence and lacking in credibility'.

In Britain the cost of the *Polaris* fleet has been small – around 2 per cent of the annual Defence Budget. The economic burden of the French force has been much larger but not (self-evidently) prohibitive. More relevant criticisms were made of two features: the vulnerability of such forces to first strikes, possibly leading to hair-trigger response systems and so to premature use, and their restriction to counter-city attacks, which would render them useless in the execution of limited and controlled strikes.

Dependence on counter-city threats was never denied by the European states. They might counter that American strategists, most notably McNamara himself, found if difficult to avoid threatening cities. The vulnerability problem proved to be less acute than envisaged because of the move to SSBNs, normally considered paragons of second-strike virtues. However, as the reduction in the danger of a premature detonation made these forces less worrisome to the United States, they became of less concern to the USSR. In becoming 'safe', they ceased to act as a major source of risk and uncertainty. The laws of diminishing critiques and diminishing rationales are linked, because the amount of real uncertainty these forces add to the strategic environment is minimal (if not zero).

49

Conclusion

This historical analysis has demonstrated that the strategic rationales for medium-range nuclear forces have become less compelling over time, and it has noted that the critiques are also being undermined as the issue becomes the removal of an established and reasonably tame capability instead of the abortion of one under development. The rationales attached to these forces now tend to stress the world's manifold uncertainties; all sorts of as yet unimaginable things might happen that would make one very grateful to have a handy nuclear arsenal.[13] More specifically, the virtues of multiple decision centres have been settled upon as the most convincing contribution to NATO. Partly out of necessity, but also out of conviction, Britain and France remain wedded to old-style notions of deterrence, according to which an adversary could never be sure of getting away with aggression without facing destructive retaliation. There has been little inclination to follow the 'Schlesinger doctrine' – to attempt to construct a force that could be employed with something approaching equanimity and so threaten with something approaching credibility.[14]

All things being equal, the case for small and independent forces might be expected to weaken in the future. To retain credibility, they require that there should be no dramatic breakthroughs in anti-submarine warfare technology (the lack of which cannot be taken for granted over the natural life-span of the next crop of SSBNs) and non-abrogation of the Anti-Ballistic Missile Treaty. Meanwhile, cruise missiles, not long ago considered the saviour of medium-range forces, have steadily come to appear less attractive because of development costs, the need for numerous launch platforms and the problem of penetrating Soviet defences.

A more immediate problem is the future funding of these forces. As existing systems get older, their operation and maintenance become more expensive; the procurement of the next (and presumably more sophisticated) generation of forces will impose an added budgetary burden.[15] If the 1980s turn out to be a decade of low economic growth, the expense may prove more irksome than it has in the past. Without steady growth in the real value of defence budgets, it will be difficult to maintain conventional military establishments of today's size. There have been a number of French hints of concern over the lack of a conventional force comparable with that of Germany. In Britain the thinning out of the British Army of the Rhine is one available option when the next economic crisis prompts a Defence Review. So the real question may not be the definition of strategic rationales for the British and French forces in isolation, but the issue of what priority they enjoy over conventional forces. The suspicion remains that the distinctiveness of the assets purchased for what will remain only moderate costs will ensure priority for the nuclear forces. But it should be recognized that this can only come at the expense of NATO's conventional strength.

The nuclear cause may be strengthened because of a number of recent developments that have conspired to draw attention to the British and French forces, suggesting that their hour has come and reversing the law of diminishing rationales.

These developments are, first, the age of visible parity and the imposing strength of Soviet strategic forces. This, it is argued, renders the American nuclear guarantee to Europe less credible than ever before. Europeans will have to look to their own devices.

Second, SALT codifies parity and reminds Europe of the extent to which its future can be determined by the super-powers. Both greater comity and greater hostility between the United States and the Soviet Union are feared. SALT may encourage the view that Washington will sacrifice European interests (failing to reduce Soviet M/IRBM forces while removing its own options for the modernization of theatre forces and, through non-circumvention clauses, those of its allies).[16] Thus the expectation that SALT III will deal with European-based forces lends weight to the impression of British and French forces as European bargaining chips in dealings with the super-powers. SALT has a sort of Midas touch; anything in danger of being affected by the negotiations is soon represented as particularly precious and requiring special protection.

Third, because of both parity and SALT, and as a result of the modernization of Soviet medium- to intermediate-range forces (*Backfire*/SS-20), attention has been directed to the whole gamut of forces (even the aged *Vulcan* and *Mirage IV*) that help to balance Soviet nuclear forces. The United States already classes the

British forces as part of NATO's theatre capabilities.

Fourth, the 'neutron bomb episode' has indicated the problems that arise from the introduction of new types of nuclear weapon into Europe without careful diplomatic co-ordination and preparation of public opinion. This is much easier when augmenting an existing capability than when creating a new one.

All this suggests a possible new rationale for the British and French forces as a European resource able to back up European interests. They can provide a serious and expert European contribution to deliberations on all nuclear matters and ensure direct involvement in decisions on nuclear employment by those sensitive to any menace to the Continent. A European-owned component of NATO's theatre forces could demonstrate to the United States that the Allies were doing their bit or else, if the worst came to the worst and the Americans withdrew, could provide the foundation for a new security system.

While not denying that the non-nuclear Europeans can derive some benefit and satisfaction from the nuclear forces of their neighbours, this argument can be taken too far. Its strength resides more in disenchantment with the United States than in confidence in Britain and France.

Expressions of doubt about the American guarantee are hardly a novelty in NATO, but they have increased noticeably in recent years. Many put this down to anticipation of a definite tilt in the strategic balance in favour of the USSR.

The pessimism seems to be overdone. The more dogmatic European theorists have assumed the untrustworthiness of the United States because of her self-interest in a crisis, believed to be only marginally affected by shifts in the military situation. France was at her most forthright on this matter during a period which appears, in retrospect, to have been a golden age of American superiority. More significant as sources of recent concern have been the lingering after-effects of Vietnam and Watergate and doubts over the aptitude of President Carter. The decline of the image of the United States, therefore, need not be a secular trend. Finally, it would be difficult to use concern over Soviet counter-force capabilities to justify greater reliance on Europe's counter-city capabilities.

The most problematic assumption is a deep sense of responsibility in London and Paris for the European 'interest'. This is not the normal view of either British instincts or French philosophy; it would require a degree of political union in Europe that, for the moment, seems beyond the realm of possibility. The most ardent proponents of Franco–British co-operation envisage little more than a sharing of some development and production costs, and even this is probably wishful thinking. Even with such a modest measure as the improvement of NATO's long-range theatre forces, British and French forces will not be presented as an explicit contribution to the force. While Britain sees *Tornado* and *Vulcan* (or some new American missile) as suitable for attacks on rear-echelon targets under the Supreme Allied Commander, her SSBNS, along with those of France, are considered quite separately as a strategic force, resolutely counter-city and under national control.

Without greater European unity, there seems little reason why West Germany, for example, should feel greater confidence in France and Britain than in the United States. In fact, the sort of circumstances that would prompt (and follow) American withdrawal might see a general collapse of Western solidarity rather than European co-operation. If we are about to enter a period of radical change in European affairs, (which is by no means self-evident) then it cannot be assumed that West Germany will remain non-nuclear. The thought of Germany, disillusioned with the EEC and NATO, throwing her weight about in the centre of Europe already animates a number of Frenchmen (among others), to whom this threat provides a more realistic rationale for the *force de frappe* than does the USSR. Even without excessive political turbulence in Europe, the more moderate of the arguments for a more prominent European force outlined above could be seen to apply to Germany more than to France and Britain. As already indicated, Germany is the state whose territory is most likely to be violated first in any Soviet act of aggression, and strategic rationales for a German nuclear force as a contribution to NATO's deterrent are more cogent than those for other countries. Politically, of course, as West Germany is the first to recognize, this would be a dangerous and disruptive move at the moment. If the next decades are full of chronic disorder,

51

however, the proper inhibitions *vis-à-vis* this matter in Bonn could well slacken.

As for the existing European forces, the conclusion of this Paper is to doubt the possibility of any startling new rationales for medium-sized forces. That they have any rationale at all is the result of the concept of deterrence, a gift to strategists in that its nature and workings remain so elusive and so imperfectly understood as to permit endless speculation with little danger of empirical refutation, and justifying the maintenance of almost any military capability on the grounds that it might be doing good and we could well be worse off without it.

NOTES

[1] Sixth Report from the Expenditure Committee, *The Future of the United Kingdom's Nuclear Weapons Policy*, Session 1978–9 (3 April 1979) contains a useful compilation of evidence on factors pertaining to the British decision. Typically, it was ignored by the British Press, a fact which bodes ill for any 'great debate'.

[2] North Atlantic Council, *Declarations on Alliance Relations* (Ottawa, 19 June 1974).

[3] A rare case of an American Secretary of Defense acknowledging that British and French forces might fit in with the strategic nuclear, rather than theatre nuclear, component of NATO's nuclear triad was that of James Schlesinger in 1975. However, he also described these forces as 'dwarfed by the immensity of the Soviet strategic and peripheral nuclear attack forces'. *Report of the Secretary of Defense to Congress on the FY1976 and Transition Budgets, FY1977 Authorization Request and FY1976–80 Defense Programs* (Washington DC: USGPO, 1975).

[4] The back-of-the-envelope calculation was that (1) it had been estimated that 25 bombs would knock out Britain; (2) the enemy area 'we have in mind' was 40 times this size; (3) 25 bombs multiplied by $40 = 1,000$ bombs, well beyond proposed production capabilities. Margaret Gowing, *Independence and Deterrence: Britain and Atomic Energy 1945–1952*, Vol. 1, *Policy Making* (London: Macmillan, 1974), pp. 188–9.

[5] In a defensive preface to *Limited Strategic War* (New York: Praeger, 1962), Klaus Knorr and Thornton Read noted that this sort of analysis could be criticized as 'abstruse theorizing', adding: 'This viewpoint is prevalent in England' (pp. v–vi).

[6] There is a lesser version of this argument, more powerful in practice, which recognizes the benefit to the United States (and the Alliance) of another country, familiar with the everyday running of a nuclear force and support facilities, as a second opinion.

[7] See some of the submissions by MPs to the Sixth Report from the Expenditure Committee, *op. cit.* Geoffrey Pattie (Conservative, now Minister for the Royal Air Force): 'The only really credible scenario is the threatened use of the strategic system in order to deter a nuclear attack on the United Kingdom itself. . . . British public opinion is most unlikely to approve the use of strategic weapons in response to a direct conventional attack on British interests and forces no matter where such an attack takes place' (p. 129). Robin Cook (Labour): 'It is inconceivable that a British Government would choose to respond to a conventional attack on Britain (and even more so to a conventional attack on West Germany) by escalating to a nuclear exchange with the Soviet Union' (p. 139).

[8] Testimony of the Secretary of State for Defence in *ibid.*, para. 2. For similar reference to multiple decision centres, see Memorandum by Ministry of Defence to Second Report from the Expenditure Committee, *Defence Expenditure, Government Observations on the Second Report from the Expenditure Committee*, Session 1975–6, paras 32–4.

[9] Pierre Gallois, *Stratégie de l'Age Nucléaire* (Paris: Calmann-Lévy, 1960); the English edition appeared as *The Balance of Terror*, trs. Richard Howard (Boston: Houghton Mifflin, 1961).

[10] André Beaufre, 'The Sharing of Nuclear Responsibilities: A Problem in Need of a Solution', *International Affairs*, Vol. 31, No. 3 (July 1965), p. 416.

[11] General Charles Ailleret, 'Directed Defence', *Survival*, Vol. X, No. 2 (February 1968), pp. 38–43.

[12] Speech by General Méry and comments by President Giscard d'Estaing, *Survival*, Vol. XVIII, No. 5 (September/October 1976), pp. 226–30. Prime Minister Barre has attempted to camouflage the trend by immersing it in Gaullist rhetoric. Speech of June 1977, *Survival*, Vol. XIX, No. 5 (September/October 1977), pp. 225–8. Collectors of euphemisms for the mass killing of human beings cannot miss the reference to attacks of the adversary's 'demographic' strength.

[13] This suffices as a last-resort rationale: as systems currently under development will remain operational until well into the next century, contingencies could arise for which the British and French forces would be uniquely suitable. The most popular such contingency involves extra nuclear powers. However, as actual and potential proliferators are regionally limited (China still does not threaten either the United States or Western Europe), clashes between Britain or France and a small nuclear power remain hard to envisage.

[14] For a rather futile attempt to demonstrate why and how they could seek this, see Graeme P. Auton, 'Nuclear Deterrence and the Medium Power: A Proposal for Doctrinal Change in the British and French Cases', *Orbis*, Vol. 20, No. 2, (Summer 1976), pp. 367–97. Presumably, both powers have flexibility of targeting options (excluding protected sites), but they are unlikely to be able to afford forces that could permit selective strikes that would be taken at all seriously while still leaving an invulnerable counter-city force in reserve.

[15] Ian Smart, *The Future of the British Nuclear Deterrent: Technical, Economic and Strategic Issues* (London: RIIA, 1977).

[16] The *Conservative Manifesto* for the 1979 General Election stated (without further explanation): 'The SALT discussion increases the importance of ensuring the continuing effectiveness of Britain's nuclear deterrent' (p. 29).

The Determinants of change: Deterrence and the Political Environment

CURT GASTEYGER

Deterrence has not prevented the world from changing.[1] We have gone a long way since the young and inexperienced nuclear powers tried to come to grips with the bomb, to integrate it into their strategy and to make it a persuasive tool not just for this strategy but also for their diplomacy. The early days of deterrence were characterized by four main features: an erstwhile predominance of military over civilian thinking about the bomb that postponed its 'politicization' and integration into a coherent policy; a feeling of total confrontation that was shared by the two opposing camps and left little, if any, room for dialogue and accommodation; a clear sense of the superiority of the United States that led to the belief that she had an educational mission *vis-à-vis* the Soviet Union; and a still unshattered trust in the benefits of technology, which more often than not saved the day by offering technological answers to political problems.

The Early Days of Deterrence

To make the bomb an instrument of diplomacy rather than military art turned out to be no easy task – and we still have some lingering doubts as to whether it was fully solved or even soluble. It was, therefore, no accident that in those early post-war years military thinking about nuclear weapons and their potential use prevailed both in the West and in the Soviet Union. Curiously enough, American generals largely shared Stalin's view that the A-bomb was not really something fundamentally different from 'traditional' weapons. The bomb would not therefore call for a basic change in strategy, let alone foreign policy. Stalin, for reasons of his own, steadfastly stuck to his 'five permanently operating factors', which no technological device could possibly upset. It was the Korean War, with its manifold politico-military ramifications, that really brought the civilians, the 'strategists', into play – and they in turn brought a growing sophistication to the thinking about deterrence. The lasting legacy of that war may well be that it forced politicians, for the first time, to think not just about the potential and the limitations of the nuclear weapon but also about its power to shape international politics.

As a policy of deterrence emerged in the wake of the Korean War, it became, in a way, the nuclear component of the (conventionally based) containment policy. As Robert Jervis rightly observes, the policy was as much a child of the cold war as it, in turn, supported many cold war policies.[2] It was an outgrowth of what might be called an 'absolutist trend' in American political behaviour, which swung from one extreme to the other, from alliance during World War II to total opposition. It postulated little other than complete confrontation; the Soviet Union was considered to be, to all intents and purposes, in complete control of the Communist Bloc. Hence a threat to the centre was thought to be sufficient to deter any action on the periphery, including that of a conventional kind. Conversely, a crisis provoked by this centre anywhere on the globe was seen to put the central balance itself into jeopardy: when North Korea crossed the 38th Parallel in 1950 troops were mobilized in Western Europe.

Deterrence policy thus originated and developed in a hostile world that left little, if any, room for accommodation. It could thrive in an unequivocal climate that helped to build alliances, to legitimize the undisputed leadership of the super-powers, to cement alliances into coherent and loyal units and eventually to silence ethical protests over the bomb.

With hindsight, it is a matter of conjecture who at the time felt more threatened, the United States or the Soviet Union. There is, however, no doubt that the United States was immensely more powerful and self-assured. The fact that she felt threatened by expansionist Soviet Communism did little to affect her sense of both moral and political superiority. Such superiority, after all, was only natural because democracy was by definition pacific, and its leaders, particularly those in the United States, were reasonable people. For the United States there was no question that she alone could control her destiny. Any idea of strategic parity or equality implied interaction with the adversary and consequently a sharing of responsibilities with him. In other words, it seemed tantamount to a diminution of the United States' own independence and freedom of action. It was therefore unacceptable.

The Coming of Bipolarity

In a way, this feeling of lonely greatness and almost total invulnerability reflected the reality of the 1950s and, nascent strategic vulnerability aside, much of the 1960s. Bipolarity (in the sense of two more or less equal powers facing each other throughout the world) may have existed in the minds of many people and may have influenced their behaviour, but in actual fact it did not exist, even in the northern hemisphere, in anything more than a narrow strategic sense. The United States was the only global power in political, economic and strategic terms, a power no doubt supported and amplified by, but quite frequently also in conflict with, the retreating European colonial powers.

The image, then, of a political bipolarity, projected and blown up by the Soviet Union's impressive military might, was certainly wrong in the 1950s and hardly less so in the 1960s after the Soviet split with China. Strategic bipolarity was in practice limited to the Atlantic–European region (with some unspecified ramifications in the Middle East), while the Pacific region, with Japan at its centre, always remained something *sui generis*. Contrary to Mr Dulles's prognostication, it was the *pax Americana* rather than the *pax Sovietica* that dominated the international scene for almost a quarter of a century. Consequently, it was the former that influenced perceptions of, and attitudes towards, the merits and credibility of concepts of deterrence evolved in, and offered by, the United States.

A sense of political mission, coupled with a technical superiority, could not but translate itself into what might be termed a kind of American 'doctrinal messianism': it was assumed that as containment was gradually 'mollifying' the aggressive Soviet system, the inevitable learning process would also convert Soviet strategists and induce them to espouse the inescapable logic of American strategic thinking. The 'balance of terror', epitomized by 'Mutual Assured Destruction' (MAD), made sense only if both sides accepted basically the same rules of the game. Deterrence, in short, pre-supposed two central actors with convergent notions. It was almost a matter of course that it was up to the more powerful and advanced to guide his weaker opponent, in both his own interest and that of mutual survival.

Finally, the concept of deterrence was not yet subject to the demands and potential restrictions of arms control. This is not to say that there were no ethical or political pressures to abandon the bomb altogether. Quite the contrary. Recent outcries over the neutron bomb reminded us of the violent anti-nuclear campaigns of the 1950s – which, strangely enough, have not been seen since. Deterrence policy may have had something to do with this, as it has helped to ensure some stability, which in turn has allowed for dialogue and some accommodation with the adversary. It was when people came to realize that there was no 'technological plateau' (beyond which further technological advances seemed impossible, or undesirable, or made no strategic sense) that the urge for arms control increased. That had not been the general view in the 1950s. As the Atoms for Peace Programme so clearly demonstrated, technology, including military technology, still seemed then to offer manifold promises, whose benefits for mankind as a whole were surely expected to outweigh by far its potential perils.

In sum, then, deterrence doctrines and policies as they developed in the 1950s rested on assumptions and beliefs that today seem both restricted and restrictive.[3] They were restrictive because they were evolved in, and applied to, a world that seemed relatively simple and unambiguous, with clear lines of demarcation and few centres of power, and a rather high level of confidence in what arms and technology could achieve if properly used.

The Determinants of Change

It seems surprising that the substance of deterrence, as developed in the 1950s, and refined in the 1960s, survived numerous changes in political circumstances and innovations in the technological field. In public perception at least, nuclear deterrence looks pretty much the same as it did 20 years ago. Ever since the United States became vulnerable to Soviet attack there have been lingering doubts in Europe about the credibility of American nuclear protection. These doubts notwithstanding, the official view was – and still is – that on the whole deterrence has worked and has spared us a nuclear holocaust. Most important, it has created a sense of stability that has helped to attenuate the rigidities of confrontation and has offered a framework for limited accommodation.

Measured by what at the time appeared to be an unending hostility, this is no mean achievement. And yet the limits of deterrence have become ever more visible as the international conditions in which it is supposed to operate have changed almost beyond recognition. To be sure, neither the horror nor the danger of a potential nuclear war has diminished – and in this sense deterrence, for lack of a realistic alternative, will remain a valid strategy. The question is therefore not so much whether deterrence is good or evil as whether, and under what conditions, it is still a useful instrument of policy, capable of dealing with a world that hardly resembles the one for which deterrence policy seemed both appropriate and efficient.

A major (if not the main) contrast with the world of the 1950s and even that of the 1960s lies in the fact that the international system has become, for the first time in human history, truly global. In political terms it has reached its outer limit, leaving the open sea – and perhaps space – as the only areas for further conquest. The rapid passage from some 50 states in the aftermath of World War II to about 150 today has not been without upheaval and conflict. But it has not led to a major conflagration, nor has it caused an irretrievable disruption of the system itself. It was not perhaps that first, post-war stage of almost uninterrupted expansion, accompanied by a widespread expectation of unlimited growth, which was particularly difficult and explosive. It could well be the present (second) stage of mutual adjustment with its multiple demands for a redistribution and fairer allocation of wealth, sharpened by a 'diffusion of power' on the one hand and a growing awareness of potential scarcity on the other, that contains the seeds of conflict.

This second stage is a world in which there is no longer a single power prepared, in the last resort, to act as 'policeman' in any one region. In almost every case there are at least two or three competing powers with global capabilities (but not global grasp). There is every indication that competition will grow rather than recede as the Soviet Union extends her global reach and China mounts the world stage. With more actors on that stage, with more potentially disruptive or divisive issues at hand and an ever wider spread of means for forceful action or influence, one can hardly remain sanguine about the future of international order.

A second major difference from those early days of deterrence lies in the fact that all countries, including the two super-powers, have become more vulnerable in many ways. Such increased vulnerability must make them think not only about the credibility and efficacy of deterrence but also about their attitudes and policies towards those countries whose resources or location have become essential (or even vital) to them. The spectacular enlargement of what we consider today to be the indispensable ingredients of national security is due to a great extent to this sense of increased vulnerability, which is often euphemistically called 'interdependence'. Probably the most dramatic change in the West's relationship with the so-called 'periphery' – primarily the Third World – has less to do with the prospect of its potential fragmentation and increasing military power than with the disturbing discovery that non-military issues are capable of tipping the scales of power or even affecting the strategic relationship between the super-powers. For the Western world in general, and for the United States in particular, the importance of the Middle East has been growing in proportion to its growing dependence on the oil this region supplies. Although this may be an extreme case, there are others that point in the same direction.

The Emergence of Mutual Vulnerability

There is no denying that the United States is much more exposed to such dependencies than the Soviet Union. What this amounts to is an *imbalance of vulnerability* between the two powers. While both have long been strategically vulnerable and may become even more so in the near future, the United States' vulnerability in non-military domains today far exceeds that of the Soviet Union. It inevitably influences the position of the United States as a world power and the way that position is perceived by others, including the Soviet Union. She may in turn become more vulnerable as she expands her external involvement and enlarges her economic commitments. Whether we should prefer a more vulnerable Soviet Union in exchange for her further global involvement is perhaps a theoretical question, but it is, of course, directly relevant to the way the strategic relationship between the two super-powers will develop and how it will affect the 'central balance'.

This relationship has undergone profound changes since the early days of deterrence. If the prevailing impression is that such change has favoured – and still favours – the Soviet Union, this is largely due to the fact that she is still at an acquisitive stage, with an unsatisfied imperial drive. The position of the Soviet Union contrasts sharply with that of the United States, which has passed the high point of saturation and is weary of shouldering global responsibilities that are scarcely appreciated abroad and jealously controlled by Congress at home. However imprecise and misleading this impression of a tilting balance may be, it nevertheless points to a fundamentally new development: strategic bipolarity in a global sense is much closer to reality today than it was 20 years ago.

It must be assumed that the 1980s will see even further Soviet engagement. In some parts of the world (such as the Middle East or South-east Asia) involvement may change from what now still looks more like fleeting commitments or insecure tenure into something more permanent, involving major interests and prestige. It seems very probable that the expansion of the Soviet Navy will have manifold strategic and political consequences, for this will affect both the credibility of Soviet engagements overseas and the power relationship with the American rival. It is not primarily the 'central balance' that is at stake, but the extent to which it can and should be isolated from major changes on the periphery. The problem of linkage between the two is likely to become more complex, as both the Soviet Union and the United States will have to weigh the advantages and risks of such linkage. As the Soviet Union's foreign engagements grow, her situation will come to resemble that of the United States today. In the days of total confrontation everything seemed linked to everything else. Now the super-powers are attempting to make the 'central balance' basically immune from other issues. For obvious reasons, it has been the Soviet Union that has consistently resisted any idea of linking strategic arms negotiations with her policies on human rights or in Angola or Ethiopia, for this would tie her hands or increase her risks in actions that, she claims, have nothing to do with detente or strategic deterrence.

This seems natural for a power that – unlike the United States – can only see gains in changing the *status quo* in regions where so far it had either few stakes or no stake at all; it seems even more natural if one remembers that the Soviet Union does not consider even the strategic balance (or, as she more appropriately puts it, the 'correlation of forces') to be immune to change. Irrespective of whether linkage is an operational concept, the fact remains that the United States has for a long time been able to move fairly freely wherever her intervention has been accepted and Soviet interests were not at stake. The same applies now to the Soviet Union.

The Definition of Interests

This may change. The Soviet Union's expansion is likely to intrude sooner or later into areas that the United States considers to be essential, if not vital, the first of which is almost bound to be the Middle East and, more specifically, the Gulf. Furthermore, she may assume engagements which, without loss of face or even loss of security, she will not be disposed to give up (Cuba has for many years been the sole example of such involvement). The world might then come close to the situation in which it believed itself to be 25 years ago, when events on the periphery were considered to pose a challenge to the 'central balance', thus invoking strategic deterrence. We may then expect either a further redefinition of vital interests or a renewed attempt to establish some 'rules of the game', however questionable and transitional they may be.

But perhaps the real problem with linkage lies elsewhere: to invoke linkage looks more often than not like an attempt to take refuge on the more familiar ground of the East–West context, where responsibilities are clear and culprits more easily identified than in those volatile areas over which one has little or no control. It appears easier to take the traditional adversary to task than to go to the roots of the trouble on the spot. Because local events are so complex, they hardly ever lend themselves to external influence and guidance, and yet they can have far-reaching political and strategic consequences. The collapse of the American system of containment outside the Western industrialized world certainly has something to do with the fact that traditional politico-military alliances were not helpful in solving internal problems. To countries like Thailand or Turkey, the Philippines or Greece, alliances have become something of a liability in domestic policy, while the link with deterrence, or the 'central balance', becomes increasingly doubtful, if not incredible.

It would seem that the Soviet Union, with her predilection for bilateral treaties of friendship and co-operation, is undergoing similar experiences. The neglect of the social dimension in foreign policy – Soviet claims to the contrary notwithstanding – may at least partly explain the present inability of the super-powers (as well as others) to shape and control events, not only 'in the unsettled regions of the Third World but even, to some extent, within their own alliances'.[4] However that may be, it could place the super-powers in a situation in which they feel increasingly torn between the temptation to exploit such fluidity and crises at each other's expense on the one hand, and the desire to control them jointly where they appear to jeopardize common interests on the other.

These are not necessarily mutually exclusive alternatives. Rather, they are the reflection of the dialectic relationship that has characterized Soviet–American policies ever since both powers accepted the prime facts of the nuclear age – namely, that rivalry does not exclude common responsibility, and that security has become something over which neither has independent and full control. If the SALT Treaties have any

lasting significance beyond their more immediate arms-control objectives, it lies in the formal acceptance of mutual interdependence at the strategic level. While in the context of their own security and that of their allies this community of interest between the super-powers rarely posed serious problems, the spectre of nuclear proliferation has awakened universal suspicion as to how far it would go. The dividing line between co-operation and confrontation, collision and collusion, so comfortably clear-cut during the cold war, has become blurred – and it may become further obscured as the likelihood of proliferation grows.

The Limits to Co-operation
Indeed, a more fragmented world in which military power (including, precisely, nuclear power) spreads may become less and less 'controllable', and the super-powers may perhaps agree to some more explicit concerting of action, if not action in common. The United States and the Soviet Union agree that they will remain, for the foreseeable future, in a class by themselves, with special responsibilities not only *vis-à-vis* each other but also towards the world as they see it. Not surprisingly, 'Soviet leaders, like their counter-parts in the United States, expect well-defined areas of co-operation and less clearly marked areas of conflict to characterize bilateral relations in the foreseeable future'.[5] The foremost area of co-operation has been, and is likely to remain, the nuclear field. As an American author asserts, 'a strategic multi-polar world could be anarchic if the major powers do not co-operate to prevent the realization of its latent instabilities'.[6]

So it may prove. Instability in the rest of the world, prompted and enhanced by nuclear spread, could in the end destabilize the 'central balance'. We must, in fact, expect in the coming years what could be termed a 'regionalization of deterrence', prompted by a further proliferation of both nuclear weapons and continental-strategic weapons (such as the cruise missile). The super-powers may then be faced with the question of how to reconcile such growing fragmentation or 'decentralization' with their own and other countries' interests in a more 'controllable' and stable order. However, in trying to solve this dilemma they will be caught almost fatally in the dialectical process by which more super-power co-operation and joint intervention will increase resentment and whet nuclear appetites – which in turn might give Washington and Moscow another reason for common action.

It is difficult to rate very highly the chances that this will happen: first, because the element of rivalry between the two super-powers is likely to outweigh that of common interest in all but a very few isolated cases; second, because the ways in which they see events and the future of the international system are still too far apart to permit anything other than transitory joint ventures; and third, because the effective prevention of nuclear proliferation requires much more than joint super-power action and does not rank first on the list of problems that bedevil our world and make it less and less manageable.

In any case, such an undertaking by the super-powers would have repercussions (as it already has) on their strategic relationship and their respective deterrence postures. Those most likely to be affected would probably be their allies, and Western allies in the first instance. The price to be paid for attempts to stabilize an increasingly turbulent periphery might be the erosion of trust in the inner core of the central balance, particularly if such action were either not successful or in conflict with the interests of those allies. Again, the question is whether there has to be a conflict between preserving the fairly stable alliance systems on the one hand and the need to prevent the further disintegration of the surrounding world on the other. Much depends on the way in which such options are handled. If such a dilemma does not exist, or poses no serious problems, for the Soviet Union (because she tends to act alone), it certainly does for the United States. The latter may find that perhaps the most cumbersome and time-consuming answer is, in the long run, the most satisfactory: namely, to persuade her allies that they should assume wider political responsibilities that would transcend the framework of the Western Alliance, although it is necessary to note that consensus will be difficult to reach.

Deterrence Revisited

The important conclusion to be drawn from all this may be that, despite various and significant adaptations, the military component in the American (or Western) concept of deterrence has remained unduly predominant. Deterrence revisited demonstrates a paucity of new ideas that, given the importance of the topic, is somewhat disturbing. It also shows, however, that some of its vital pre-conditions are better understood today. The outstanding importance of mutual perceptions or, rather, the need to learn more about the adversary is acknowledged; so also is the need for continuing communication and the political consistency that, more than mere military superiority, endows deterrence with its essential credibility.

Finally, we are in the process of learning that the American concept of 'mutual deterrence' may be nothing more than what John Erickson calls a 'chimera',[7] never really shared by the Soviet Union. While the West has stressed deterrence at the expense of defence, the Soviet Union has always seen the two as complementary elements of a comprehensive defence policy. In building up a capability for fighting a war, she has not indicated that she intends to unleash a war; she has merely demonstrated that she plans to minimize the losses should a war occur. She can never accept a mutuality of deterrence as long as she, unlike the United States, is confronted with more than just one major military adversary. It has not therefore simply been a traditional preference for over-insurance and large numbers that has led the Soviet Union to stress so firmly the military dimension of her policy, but rather a political environment fundamentally different from that of the United States.

The American educational drive was thus directed initially at an opponent who, for reasons of tradition, outlook and expediency, was unable and unwilling adequately to respond to it. It is not without irony (though it is symptomatic of the changing strategic setting) that the United States is beginning to learn some lessons from Soviet strategic thinking precisely at a time when Moscow may be discovering, in Africa and even in neighbouring Afghanistan, that excessive emphasis on military power will not by itself enable her to cope with the complexities of a world which the Soviet Union so desperately wants to influence.

How far can this learning process on both sides go? No doubt the United States' perception of herself, of her international role and her influence, has changed. There is greater reluctance to use force. There are, symbolized in the person of the President, renewed ethical qualms about the bomb, which translate themselves into a strong commitment to arms control and an even stricter non-proliferation policy. Both trends cannot but leave their mark on deterrence, its credibility and its consistency.

Yet on balance it would still seem that the far-reaching changes in the political environment have not altered fundamental attitudes, even if they have prompted some notable adjustments and reappraisals. The official consecration of strategic parity never fully eradicated the United States' innermost conviction about her superiority and the need to keep it, nor has it quite removed the Soviet inferiority complex. Both feelings still find their expression in the way the two superpowers conceive of deterrence and translate it into armament or, for that matter, define the finality of arms control.

Furthermore, neither the United States nor, to a lesser degree, the Soviet Union can resist the temptation to seek the answers to complex problems in technology rather than diplomacy. Ever since deterrence came upon us, technology has nearly always had the edge over argument or, more precisely, over a more fundamental reappraisal of the place of arms in international relations and a conceptual framework for their control. Whenever there has been an argument for change, new technology has proved, more often than not, that it was able to cope without change. The resort to technology has frequently been justified by an apparent need to improve one's bargaining position in arms-control negotiations. This was certainly true when the anti-ballistic missile and multiple independently targetable re-entry vehicle were introduced. It may again be true in the case of the 'Eurostrategic' weapons.

Anyone who follows the continuing SALT debate in Washington has therefore the awkward felling of *déjà vu*: the 'flight into technology' against which Dr Kissinger warned over 20 years ago[8] still seems irresistibly attractive. By offering facile answers which are at best temporary, it unfortunately distracts us from addressing the more fundamental and difficult questions: about the real value of technology and the future of arms control, about the relationship between technology, deterrence and security, and about the way in which deterrence can remain a viable policy in an increasingly complex and turbulent world. So while some of the continuing nuclear debate may be a transitory phenomenon, the task of mobilizing sufficient public support for deterrence policy at home and preserving its credibility abroad is not. It is a safe prediction that these things will be even more difficult to achieve tomorrow than they are today.

NOTES

[1] I am indebted to Mr Christian Leffler, Research Assistant with the Programme for Strategic and International Security Studies, Geneva, for valuable suggestions and assistance.
[2] Robert Jervis, 'Deterrence Theory Revisited', *World Politics*, Vol. 31, No. 2 (January 1979), pp. 289–324.
[3] Richard Rosecrance, *Strategic Deterrence Reconsidered*, Adelphi Paper No. 116 (London: IISS, 1975), p. 2.
[4] *Strategic Survey 1978* (London: IISS, 1979), p. 1.
[5] Nils H. Wessell, 'Soviet Views of Multipolarity and the Emerging Balance of Power', *Orbis*, Vol. 22, No. 4 (Winter 1979), pp. 786–813.
[6] Rosecrance, *op. cit.*, p. 37.
[7] John Erickson, 'The Chimera of Mutual Deterrence', *Strategic Review*, Vol. 11, No. 2 (Spring 1978), pp. 11–17.
[8] Henry A. Kissinger, *Nuclear Weapons and Foreign Policy* (New York: Harper & Row for Council on Foreign Relations, 1957), p. 4.

The Determinants of change: Deterrence and Technology

LAURENCE MARTIN

Deterrence is the characteristic strategic concept of the nuclear age. By no means new, it has been invested with fresh and central significance by the potential of nuclear weapons for producing a rapid and complete catastrophe, against which there is commonly assumed to be no defence. The technological breakthrough at the heart of this new military situation – the perfection of nuclear weapons – is unforgettable scientific and engineering knowledge; its consequences in strategic terms can never be wholly reversed, in the sense that the possibility of sudden and virtually complete destruction henceforth hangs over all potential victims of the leading military powers. In much strategic discussion, particularly that of a more popular nature, the problem of maintaining a secure retaliatory response to such a threat is the only subject of debate, currently exemplified by doubt about the continued viability of land-based strategic missile forces. This is, however, too narrow a definition of deterrence; in reality deterrence and even its sub-category, nuclear deterrence, is a much more complex affair, and this greatly complicates the task of evaluating likely future technological developments. This Paper avoids entering into such arcane but transitory disputes as those about hardening, circular error probable (CEP) and the compatibility of MAD with SALT; it attempts instead to outline a few more general, and perhaps more fundamental, relationships between technology and deterrence, drawing on some lessons from the past.

Even a brief attempt to do this engenders a salutory caution. It becomes apparent that, far from confidently predicting the future of deterrence in relation to technology, we are incapable of completely understanding even the past. Experts may comprehend the theories of strategy advanced by strategic publicists, though mutual accusations of misinterpretation are rife. We can be much less sure that we understand the deterrent policies actually pursued by nuclear powers in the past; even in the West, motives have frequently been obscure, while Soviet policy is wrapped in an enigma that affords ample scope for such current Western disputes as that concerning the concept of 'war-winning' in Soviet strategic doctrine. Least of all do we understand – indeed, in principle we cannot – whether or why past strategies of deterrence have been successful. Thus all assertions about the relationship between technology and deterrence in the past are in part speculative. We can explain what technology has done for strategic weapons and we can describe its impact on procurement and declaratory doctrine, but the effect of these developments on deterrence, in the future as well as the past, depends on how they are filtered through the perceptions and assumptions of the protagonists.

The Early Doctrines

The idea that deterrence was the appropriate strategic motif for a nuclear world burgeoned very early in the nuclear age. It can be found fairly well developed in the writings of the nuclear scientists themselves and of such social scientists as Jacob Viner and Bernard Brodie during the first couple of years after Hiroshima. The source of the idea lay in the notion that, defence being thought impossible, only the threat of retaliation could afford security.[1] That this retaliation was always assumed to be of a 'counter-value', city-destroying kind seems to have been the result more of the technologically determined incapacity of strategic air forces to attempt anything else for most of World War II than of any rational effort to relate atomic weapons to the psycho-political requirements of deterrence. It does not seem to have been perceived that the very way in which the limitations of available weapons systems had dictated strategy was a powerful argument for rethinking doctrine now that a technological revolution had occurred. The later distinction between deterrence by threat of punishment and deterrence by threat of effective defence and denial was not yet clearly drawn. Population and industry being the accepted targets, there was very little reference – and that probably incidental and unreflective – to the possibility of counter-force action as a source of security. The idea of striking first or second referred only to a sequence of inevitably associated events, not to the possible prevention of the riposte. Such reference as *was* made to preserving the security of the retaliatory force concerned the possibility of its accidental destruction as a by-product of urban-area bombing; the idea that an aggressor might turn counter-force into a strategy came much later. Nor was there any early speculation about whether a future great war might be fought without the new weapons, or about whether there was any middle way between universal peace and universal destruction.

On balance, we should probably be impressed by the speed with which these early analysts recognized the implications of the nuclear technological revolution for the place of deterrence in strategy. What was missing, however, was any serious debate over what it was that was to be deterred. Those who acknowledged the revolutionary impact of nuclear weapons seemed to assume – as the devotees of MAD do today – that the task of nuclear forces was merely to deter a nuclear attack on cities, admittedly the worst prospect the new strategic world afforded. Scant attention was paid to the question of whether nuclear weapons might be harnessed to protecting a nation against the more familiar, limited threats to its interests and security, to dealing with which military policy had traditionally been directed. Perhaps the fact that speculation about nuclear strategy began in a country that had only a few years previously pursued an isolationist foreign policy helped to foster this neglect. In such a context it is not surprising that there was a similar neglect of debate about what the relationships might be between nuclear

weapons and the conventional armed forces on which the military burdens of foreign policy must fall if doctrine confined nuclear weapons solely to the task of deterring nuclear attacks on the homeland.

Ironically, while strategic theorists were devising this specialized role for the nuclear weapon, the actual limited power of the fission weapon and the sparse quantities in which it was available had led the American military to build it into their war plans as mere added firepower for the tasks of attrition bombing in a prospective familiar and prolonged war of industrial mobilization.

The Dawn of Counter-force
The punctuation of the new cold war by the Soviet acquisition of nuclear weapons demonstrated, however, that a prime technological feature of the nuclear world was to be the steady proliferation of nuclear weapons and the achievement in reality of the two-way strategic balance that the early theorists had predicted. Now that the erstwhile isolationist United States was entangled in a widening network of alliances and local military commitments, the problem of reconciling extended interests (short of national survival) with incipient vulnerability to nuclear attack prompted further inspired strategic speculation. The famous American National Security Study, NSC 68, suggested that the imminent mutual neutralization of nuclear forces would render them less and less relevant to deterring anything but each other, and pointed to the consequent need to deter lesser threats by more conventional preparations for direct defence. In practice, the unwelcome economic and diplomatic implications of this prescription led the Eisenhower Administration to go in the opposite direction and, with the doctrine of Massive Retaliation, to seek to couple the strategic nuclear forces to the deterrence of lesser as well as mortal threats. In some versions of this never wholly clarified doctrine emerging nuclear plenty would permit the application of nuclear weapons to tactical as well as homeland targets, not merely to bolster conventional forces but also to present the enemy with the daunting prospect of escalation. This theoretical refinement was introduced only after a wave of scepticism about the plausibility of using the strategic nuclear threat to deter lesser aggressions

61

had bred the literature of limited war that still constitutes the primary source for our present-day debates about extended deterrence.

Simultaneously with the critique of Massive Retaliation, the famous Rand Corporation 'basing study'[2] was compelling recognition that maintaining the nuclear retaliatory force for any purpose was more than a simple matter of acquiring nuclear weapons. This was the problem that gave rise to the idea of a 'delicate' balance of terror. The undoubted delicacy lay in the newly appreciated fact that retaliatory forces could be vulnerable to pre-emption. Whether the overall balance of deterrence was delicate depended, of course, as it still does, on a much wider set of considerations, including the political purposes and risk-taking propensity of opponents. There is no public evidence that any nuclear power has ever seriously considered an attack to exploit the vulnerability of deterrent nuclear forces.

Nevertheless, the 'basing studies' were the dawn of counter-force. Already, it is true, the United States Air Force had added Soviet nuclear forces to its target lists as an adjunct to attacks on Soviet cities, but formerly there does not seem to have been any serious thought of making attacks on enemy retaliatory forces the centre-piece of strategy and thus a possible escape from the retaliatory danger. Once the retaliatory second strike came to be thought of not as an inevitable sequence but as a capability that could be preserved only with great care, ingenuity and expense, the relationship between technology and deterrence had decisively changed. A vulnerable force posed the danger both that it might be eliminated and that it might consequently be prematurely used and thus engender 'crisis instability'. The preferred solutions were partly doctrinal – dispersal, for example – and partly technological, with the new long-range missiles, which had exacerbated (though they had not created) the vulnerability problem, lending themselves well to hardening and concealment.

The difficulty of determining what the technical vulnerability of retaliatory forces to pre-emptive strikes means for the stability of the deterrent balance in the broader sense illustrates how uncertain is our understanding of the links between the strictly military equations and the overall framework of deterrence. We must accept the validity of the Rand study in so far as it demonstrated that a pre-emptive strike might well deprive one of the nuclear powers of its long-range arsenal. We cannot go on to infer that aggression has therefore become probable. A power believing itself, on technical calculations, to have a fairly clean first-strike capability may well refrain from implementing this capability because of moral considerations, because it must always have residual doubts about the calculations and about the operational uncertainties of even the most meticulous force analysis, or (perhaps most fundamentally) because it may lack the political will or compulsion to act even when the risks are low. Moreover, viewing an opponent with a vulnerable strategic force that might consequently be prone to precipitate use, a nuclear power may well be tempted to move in contradictory directions. The pure strategic analyst might advocate pre-emption; the statesman might prefer to behave with extreme caution, keeping political conflict and confrontation below the level at which the question of war ever arises. In general, the record of the nuclear age suggests that the latter tendency is the prevailing one, and that the great nuclear powers have responded to nuclear danger not by clever and adventurous strategies, but by simply avoiding all semblance of open military confrontation.[3] Admittedly, it is doubtful whether the Soviet Union has ever enjoyed a real, as distinct from a potential, first strike; it is noteworthy, however, that she long displayed surprisingly little concern about the vulnerability of her own forces to attack by those of the United States. In other words, we must not confuse technical calculations about the strategic balance with broader conclusions about the likelihood of war and aggression. Caution about getting into war with a nuclear power at any state of the technical balance may well be a more potent deterrent than a particular force posture.

Assured Destruction

Nevertheless, it is very reasonable to suppose that the possibility of a successful pre-emptive first strike – the criteria for success being determined by the political imperatives bearing on the potential attacker – might well increase the incentives to opt for war. The mere fact that no such war has occurred and that it scarcely seems likely ever to be an attractive option in absolute terms does not constitute a very convincing argument for neglecting the problem of the vulnerability of retaliatory forces. This was certainly the reaction of the United States in the early 1960s as she hastened to rectify the delicacy of the balance by deploying *Minuteman* and *Polaris*.

The whole of this episode, from the 'basing study' to the missile deployment, is a landmark in thinking about the relation between technology and deterrence. This adaptation of technology to preserve the invulnerability of retaliatory forces and thus, it was thought, effective deterrence, demonstrated that the balance could be maintained, but that it was not a God-given reward simply for acquiring nuclear weapons. Instead, maintaining the balance requires the constant adjustment of a dynamic system. Moreover, the stimulus for American technological evolution was not merely the appearance of a new threat in the form of long-range Soviet missiles; the mere acquisition of nuclear weapons by any new power, even with the established equipment of bomber aircraft, required fundamental responses. In other words, the extensive spread, as well as the intensive development, of strategic weapons provides incentives for qualitative improvement and the pursuit of so-called crisis stability is frequently at the expense of arms-race stability.

Despite the fact that they were themselves evidence of the rapid and radical evolution possible in nuclear weapons, the second generation of hardened or concealed long-range missiles led many to anticipate a technological plateau on which invulnerable retaliatory forces would be poised to attack indefensible urban targets. This would permit finite forces to be 'enough' and would allow a ceiling to be set on deployment, irrespective of the forces acquired by opponents. From the deficiencies of this outlook flow much subsequent strategic nuclear history and many of the West's current dilemmas about the future relationship between technology, strategy and deterrence.

On the technological side, the optimistic hopes for assured destruction based on finite, stable forces were destroyed by the collapse of their basic assumptions. Anti-ballistic missile defences, if not yet adequate to afford economical protection for populations, at least revealed that defence was not beyond aspiration. Increasing missile accuracy and the multiple warhead opened up renewed possibilities of defence by offensive action. Thus the dynamic nature of the technological framework was confirmed, and the second-generation missiles were revealed not as quasi-permanent solutions to the problem of force vulnerability, but as mere way-stations along the inexorable route of innovation.

Unhappiness about the speedy demise of a hoped-for 'natural' technical stability prompted a flurry of efforts to reach political agreements designed to halt the pace of evolution. Coming on top of the 'surprise attack' talks that had followed the original discovery of the 'delicacy' problem, efforts to freeze the nuclear balance into a more static mould, compatible with finite, counter-urban forces, may well have conferred undue sanctity on arms-control concepts appropriate only to a passing technological moment, partially obscuring the more important lesson that security depends on flexible adaptation to a dynamic technological milieu. In the event, the success of the arms-control effort, which evolved into SALT, has been severely limited by the propensity of technology to escape simple, negotiable categories and by the scale of Soviet military programmes. Soviet efforts remind us that 'deterrence' in the broader sense is not a universal goal if it entails stabilizing the arms race and strategic nuclear balance within a relatively stable political *status quo*. This in turn illustrates the second, and perhaps more radical, defect of stable deterrence based on MAD: namely, that in principle such a deterrent deters only assured destruction. It is sometimes true, as has been pointed out above, that the mere existence of nuclear forces seems to infuse the world with a good deal of caution. But, in theory at least, stabilization of the strategic balance on MAD principles greatly increases the risk that nothing less than a nuclear attack on a nuclear power's homeland will provoke a strategic nuclear response, and thus the dilemma faced by the authors of NSC 68 persists: the question of what deters lesser attacks on the extended national interests. MAD is thus open to the fundamental objection raised against Massive Retaliation: that it offers no options for lesser contingencies. The only difference is that Massive Retaliation was associated with a rhetoric of confrontation, so that the contradiction was blatant, whereas

MAD is usually coupled to an arms-control rhetoric of accommodation.

It is not easy to cite instances of aggressive behaviour that have occurred because of this potential paralysis in nuclear strategy, but the possibility of such aggression clearly exists in theory, and American leaders in particular have been repeatedly disturbed by the 'humiliation or holocaust' dilemma. The theoretical solutions are, first, the proliferation of national nuclear forces on Gaullist lines and the further 'extensive' application of technology to deterrence; second, the potential Finlandization of nations accessible to hostile military influence, if the opponent so wishes; third, the pursuit, as in the 1950s and 1960s, of philosophies of limited war (one such limited strategy is the flexible response of the graduated countering and hence, it is hoped, the deterrence of limited aggressions by conventional and nuclear forces confined to the theatre of action; another is limited use of the strategic nuclear forces themselves).

Towards Flexible Nuclear Responses
The idea of the limited use of strategic forces arose in the 1950s and played an initial, if diminishing, part in the McNamara strategy, for finite assured destruction was originally more a way of constraining procurement than an operational strategy clearly thought through and actually intended for execution. Somewhat paradoxically, the advent of technology designed to give strategic forces substantial assurance against pre-emption by a first strike also opened up the possibility of using some of them in measured ways, in the confidence that no retaliation could eliminate the withheld residue. Limited uses might be linked to limited stakes. Thus anticipations of what was later to emerge as Limited Strategic Options (LSO) were perceptible in McNamara's talk of controlled response and damage limitation. The scale of operation envisaged was apparently much larger than the selective strikes later proposed in the Schlesinger era, and political and technical difficulties drove McNamara increasingly to the declaratory rhetoric of assured destruction. But the underlying principle was similar: technology could facilitate controlled ways of using strategic nuclear weapons and thereby keep them coupled to the deterrence of threats less sweeping than all-out national destruction.

This idea remains with us today as both a hope and a fear. The hope is of more effective extended deterrence; the fear is that the expedient may be used by enemies too. By far the most extreme form of this fear is concern that rapidly improving accuracy would permit a large-scale but restricted attack on retaliatory forces, putting the victim in a position in which he would be the loser in all subsequent exchanges and would thus be effectively, though not literally, disarmed. It is this theoretical possibility that underlies today's anxiety about the vulnerability of fixed land-based missiles.

There is no need to pursue this particular debate here to see that the possibility of controlled nuclear strikes – not necessarily limited to counter-force exchanges, but always held below the level at which the victim loses his motives for restraint – opens up once again all the complex comparisons of the opposing orders of battle (both qualitative and quantitative) that the proponents of finite assured destruction hoped had been laid to rest. There can be no easy talk of 'overkill'. If nuclear forces can be used by each super-power against the other, or in other ways in which relative capabilities make a difference, then the details of such characteristics as accuracy, hardening and control become, once again, of consuming interest. Active defence again becomes worth debating because the strategy of limited options may demand less from a defensive system than would the goal of population defence. Accuracy may serve not merely to dig out silos, but also to permit greater confidence in the execution of any strike with a minimum of unintended effects. Communication, command, control and intelligence (C^3I) and retargeting capability become important variables. True, some degree of controlled response would be possible with any strategic technology, if appropriate doctrine were mutually observed. But clearly the very limited target sets deemed appropriate to the support of extended deterrence by latter-day LSO doctrine would be greatly facilitated by highly discriminatory capabilities.

It is not surprising, then, that once the doctrine had been conceived, suitable technologies proliferated, despite the assurance of the original advocates of LSO that little more than paperwork was required. The most general lesson, however, is that when strategists can conceive of less than total attacks or responses, and technology makes possible such long-range accuracy that strategic missions with conventional warheads are once again discussed, the problem of strategic deterrence is returned to the traditional military calculus in which the details of the offensive and defensive orders of battle cannot be ignored. Once the genie of limited options is out of the doctrinal bottle, it can never be wholly returned Nations may eschew the strategy and the weapons, but the possibility exists, and potential enemies will henceforth scrutinize each other's forces for signs of the appropriate capability, while feeling compelled to increase the invulnerability of their own weapons to it. It was the essence of the pure golden days of nuclear deterrence theory that no degree of ingenuity, whether in technology or in operational planning, could purchase immunity from retribution; this certainly is now shaken.

What do these developments mean for deterrence? Clearly, it all depends on how the word is used. If what is to be deterred is all-out nuclear attack, an undifferentiated riposte may be the ideal deterrent, although it opens up unpleasant prospects if statesmen do not behave rationally. But only a set of limited options, leaving the enemy ample incentive to restrain his own response, can plausibly be presented as a deterrent against lesser aggressions (particularly against third parties), thereby permitting the continuation of extended deterrence and possibly reducing the incentives for proliferation. This may be described pejoratively as 'making the world safe for nuclear war' or, more generously, as preserving the stabilizing possibility of introducing a deterrent nuclear note into a wider range of confrontations that might otherwise escalate to the point at which the 'humiliation or holocaust' dilemma arises. To be credible, any first use of nuclear weapons against a substantial nuclear power must be limited. In the most general terms, nuclear weapons above all must conform to a principle of measured action that ought to inform all military action against a nuclear power – namely, to select means that, as threats or deeds, leave the enemy continued grounds for restraint, while outweighing the political stake he has at issue. It will not, of course, always be possible to find such a fortunate level of action, but the increased possibilities for discrimination and control offered by modern

technology ought, in principle, to improve the odds. In the European theatre NATO would presumably try to threaten restricted targets, in or outside the Soviet Union, that were either relevant to the conventional or nuclear battlefield or simply hurtful to the aggressor. The installation of new theatre nuclear systems capable of striking Soviet territory is testimony to the supposed usefulness of limited action that the Soviet Union would certainly regard as 'strategic'. Since the arsenal for executing such a strategy includes dedicated submarine-launched ballistic missiles (SLBMs), and since these forces cap a declared strategy of escalation to nuclear action if the lesser, conventional responses prove inadequate, limited strategic strikes seem to have been explicitly related to the deterrence of limited and conventional aggression. Many may regard such a strategy as implausible and unnecessary, given the general deterrent aura of nuclear weapons, but experience suggests that simple reliance on this aura, without provision for specific limited action, creates great strains within an alliance, driving it towards the unpleasant alternatives of Finlandization or proliferation mentioned above. Elements of both tendencies are clearly discernible in the current debate over NATO nuclear policy.

It is not necessary to conclude such a debate here. Whatever the merits of a limited-options strategy, the point for the present discussion is that once it becomes widely believed that nuclear war might take forms other than that of a once-for-all spasmodic exchange and could range from large-scale disarming but city-sparing attacks, through limited punitive attacks (strikes in direct support of theatre operations), to mere demonstrations, it becomes necessary to measure force design against a complex range of political and military scenarios. Preparations could be made, for example, for limited, pre-emptive attacks on the forces with which the opponent might intend to execute his own limited strategies. Selectivity as a technological capability can respond to political purpose. Moreover, since such capabilities are designed to deal with limited (possibly initially conventional) contingencies, the problems of deterrence become affected not merely by the evolution of strategic nuclear technology, but also by the technological trends affecting capabilities at the lower levels of conflict. It is, indeed, the essence of flexible response that capabilities at the lower level may relax the demands made on the strategic forces.

The whole of this line of thought, which greatly complicates the problems of force design and arms control, is given added interest by our imperfect understanding of Soviet strategic thought. While, once again, there is no space here to enter into the 'why the Soviet Union thinks she could fight and win a nuclear war' controversy, it can at least be said that Soviet strategists do not seem to favour deterrence conceived as assigning a tolerance for damage to an enemy and then designing a force to exceed it. Rather, it seems to be the Soviet view that war might occur and that it would be desirable to have the capacity to prevail at any particular level of hostilities. It is not easy to identify a level of warfare for which the Soviet Union feels she need not seriously prepare. We do not need to evaluate Soviet prospects of success at every level to note that, with whatever theoretical justification, the result of strategic debates in the Soviet Union is to provide herself with forces that could acquit themselves well in a wide variety of circumstances. Moreover, unlike some Westerners, the Soviet Union does not seem to regard arms-control negotiations as being about the identification and restriction of bad technologies that might lead to 'instability'. Rather, she seems to seek a pragmatic series of trade-offs against specific systems that might favour the West more than herself. Whatever its roots, the doctrine of the Soviet Union seems to compel her both to regard all weapons as potentially usable and to strive persistently for quantitative and qualitative advantage.[4]

This political and technological background makes the business of striking a strategic balance increasingly complex. To the task of preserving an ultimate retaliatory force against all-out attack is added that of exploiting and countering the potential for limited nuclear action. Technical evaluations of force balances may give an idea of likely military outcomes; they cannot confirm that the psycho-political requirements for deterrence have been met. Nevertheless, at the purely technical level there is no reason to doubt that each super-power can ensure that all-out nuclear attack remains a poor option for the other. Inter-continental ballistic missile (ICBM) vulnerability, advances in anti-submarine warfare and other such developments will keep the balance shifting, but mobility, maritime sanctuaries (whether in territorial waters or negotiated) and many other expedients should suffice. Only a technological breakthrough negating the original nuclear revolution could wholly undermine the inhibitions against attacks and leave a victim no incentive for restraint. Indeed, even such a breakthrough may be insufficient, given the impossibility of full-systems tests of nuclear weapons and the consequent inevitability of residual uncertainties.

Doubtful Stability

It is consequently in the area of less-than-total nuclear strategies that technological evolution seems likely to keep the stability of the balance in doubt. The difficulty of regulating the relationship between strategic forces to achieve desired strategic ends is, in many respects, the same, whether approached by negotiated arms control or by unilateral efforts.

For a start, the arsenal of weapons grows ever more complicated. Since the simple day of the manned bomber and fission bomb, the ICBM, SLBM, cruise missile, multiple warhead, degrees of C^3I, 'fratricide', 'pin-down', the progression of accuracy, retargeting and reloading capability have combined to produce a dizzy matrix of possibilities.

In the second place, some of the most crucial characteristics of weapons are increasingly difficult to ascertain, whether for national intelligence or arms-control verification. Yet these characteristics may be more important than crude numbers for the subtler strategies of use. Indeed, because of practical as well as legal limitations on testing, even the proprietors may not have a perfect understanding of their own arsenals.

Third, technological evolution, especially the enhancement of accuracy over longer ranges, to the point at which not merely smaller nuclear yields but even conventional explosives are re-entering the possible category of 'strategic weapons', is blurring the definition of what we mean by 'strategic'. Similarly, such development as the re-emergence of air-breathing missiles for long-range delivery makes anti-aircraft technology, once thought relevant only to the battlefield, a contender for a role in strategic defence.

Fourth, many technological developments are highly ambiguous in their strategic significance.

66

The H-bomb itself, for example, was seen primarily, at the outset, as a simple magnification of the potential for city-busting. As the light-weight basis for the long-range ballistic missile warhead, however, it facilitated the hardening and dispersal on which invulnerability depended. Ballistic missile defence (BMD), once feared as a 'destabilizing' escape from deterrent vulnerability, became promising as a way of preserving the invulnerability of retaliatory forces. The multiple independently targetable re-entry vehicle (MIRV) can be the 'stabilizing' answer to city-defending BMD or the 'destabilizing' route to effective counter-force.

It may be that the mere fact that the technological context of deterrence is continually changing creates an element of international tension. But it may equally be argued, on the principle that qualitative arms competition is less dangerous than quantitative,[5] that a process of continual innovation postpones indefinitely the appropriate occasion for war. In practice, research and development runs along almost parallel lines in several countries. The scale of necessary developments, the lead-time involved, the need to offer publicly some proof of capability if it is to have a deterrent effect,[6] even perhaps the fact that so far the fastest innovation comes in the open societies, all suggest that trends become known in time for opponents to take counter-measures adequate to sustain a rough sufficiency so far as cruder, counter-value deterrence is concerned. Given the difficulty of devising, even conceptually, diplomatic and legal frameworks to embrace the rich detail of this dynamic technological environment and the consequent slowness with which arms-control negotiations proceed, it is probable that the chief burden of equilibrating adjustments will continue to fall on unilateral adaptations of national policy rather than on explicitly agreed formulae. The observed tendency of negotiations so far has been an attempt to force the technology into the over-simplified categories that are all the diplomatic process can master. Not surprisingly, one of the more striking results has been the speed with which technology has flowed into the still unrestricted channels, transforming the strategic situation with which the agreements were intended to deal.

There is fairly general agreement that both research and development are virtually uncontrollable; test quotas and other second-order restrictions promise only meagre results. Indeed, it may well be that drastic efforts to curb development – the Comprehensive Test Ban Treaty may be an extreme example – endanger the adaptability that sustains the equilibrium. Debate over such basic questions as the merits of a strategic triad over a dyad suggests that deterrence may be better maintained by variegated rather than by simplified force structures. Variety reduces the chance that adversaries may acquire a decisive advantage in either balance of forces or operational strategy – an example of the operational point being the well-known problem of synchronizing attacks on both bomber and missile forces. Arguably, the tendency of arms-control negotiations to find simple formulae is perverse in this respect also. The adoption of agreed 'freedom to mix' is both a concession to this difficulty and a confession of partial inadequacy.

Certainly there seems to be an unhelpful Western tendency, encouraged both by arms control and by military bureaucratic politics, to organize strategic debate around an erratic series of controversies over particular pieces of hardware that are characterized as inherently good or bad according to the critic's prejudices. At best, this increases the political cost of adopting a new strategy; at worst, it drives strategy into erroneous courses: the enhanced radiation weapon and the cruise missile look like providing contemporary examples. It might be healthier if the notion of an overall functional capability and balance, incrementally adjusted, prevailed over the image of the technological turning-point. Possibly the safest world would be one in which highly variegated but limited offensive forces were deployed by nations also possessing a degree of active and passive defence. These might both confer a plausible capability for limited options (thus preserving a salutary degree of extended deterrence) and provide for relatively low expectations of damage in major hostilities, while surely perpetuating more than enough uncertainty and residual horror to inspire the kind of overall caution that has hitherto characterized the behaviour of the nuclear powers.

Without much doubt, with due care and attention the super-powers will be able to ensure, by their own autonomous efforts, that a full-scale nuclear attack on them will remain an unattractive option for potential foes. It may be regrettable, therefore, that in recent years arms-control philosophy has directed strategic analysis much more towards averting this unlikely catastrophe than to considering the even more difficult and relevant task of ensuring that military policy extends a deterrent influence over lesser but more likely – and, by way of escalation, perhaps more ultimately dangerous – aggressions. The effective discharge of this task may require, at the technical level, a capacity for the limited use of strategic forces; whether this capacity constitutes an effective deterrent depends on political imperatives and judgment. Purely technological-military analysis cannot determine which technological-military postures are adequate. Military requirements should be derived from political purposes, which is a further reason for regret that SALT is being presented as a pre-requisite for detente rather than *vice versa*. Arms-control agreements might more safely be regarded as a part, and that a subordinate one, of a wider process of reconciling technological developments with strategic and, ultimately, political purposes.

This process is probably too complex to be embraced in a formally agreed framework, even between two actors. It may well be, however, that the chief disruptive effect of technological development on the familiar strategic scene will be the multiplication of sovereign participants in the balance. Current theories of deterrence and arms control are essentially bilateral. The future will probably complicate this scene in two ways. First, the spread of peaceful nuclear technology will increase the potential for the proliferation of nuclear weapons. Second, the existing lesser nuclear forces, although perhaps doomed for the indefinite future to remain qualitatively and quantitatively inferior to the super-powers, will be perpetuated and will rise to absolute levels of destructive power at which it will be increasingly difficult to leave them out of calculations: the projected French SLBM force-loading of over 700 warheads is a case in point.

It has been common to discount the significance of 'Nth' forces on grounds of numerical and technical inferiority. This has always been plausible only so far as forces needing to challenge the super-powers have been concerned, although even the most modest candidate for nuclear status is now well aware that far more than the mere acquisition of nuclear explosives is required. For those aspiring or already pretending to a role in the central nuclear balance, technology is at least ambiguous. The conception of limited nuclear options suggests that crude notions of achieving an equalizer by 'tearing off an arm' are less plausible than their proponents once believed. The possessor of a capability for graduated nuclear action could surely devise ways of prevailing over a much lesser nuclear power while still inhibiting the latter from delivering the final suicidal spasm. Nevertheless, recalling the earlier point about the cautionary effect of the suffused sense of danger that arises from the mere existence of nuclear weapons, it is hard to dismiss altogether the feeling that any country acquiring even a modest nuclear capability gains a scorpion-like status that must thenceforth be a major consideration in political calculation. To go to war with such a nation would be a grave step, given all the inescapable uncertainties about rationality, C^3 and the actual operational performance of systems that can never have been fully tested – not to mention the imponderable ecological consequences. Moreover, as the number and size of Nth forces increases, the 'Tirpitz factor' – the effect engagement with a lesser force may have on the larger power's position in the overall balance – becomes more relevant.

As an influence on the potential proliferators' decision about whether to acquire nuclear weapons or not, the concept and technological wherewithal for limited options is ambiguous. On the one hand, by offering would-be nuclear guarantors a more plausible instrument for extended deterrence, the technology for controlled use may diminish incentives for self-reliance; on the other hand, the possibility that major nuclear powers might find in limited options a way to use nuclear weapons without bringing disaster on themselves may encourage possible victims to seek some escalatory potential of their own to serve as a 'monitor' against escalation.

An alternative to limited strategic options as a way of trying to preserve the efficacy of extended deterrence in a state of ultimate mutual vulnerability is the well established doctrine of flexible response. In essence, this attempts to postpone the paralysis of strategic nuclear decisions by a substantial, if limited, capacity for direct defence. By preparing to make a stubborn defence against conventional aggression, it is to be hoped that the general danger of any kind of war between nuclear powers will engage the deterrent aura of the large nuclear weapons, even if the rationality of their ultimate use remains doubtful. The strategy can be criticized for merely postponing the strategic nuclear decision and for offering an aggressor a chance of limited liability if he tests the defender's will. But experience in NATO suggests that few are willing to rely wholly on the trip-wire of Massive Retaliation or, indeed, any instant nuclear action; even France diversifies her doctrine as her forces grow. Moreover, as effective retaliatory forces continue to make a nuclear strike from the blue as unattractive a technical option as it was always an improbable political act, escalation from limited wars is the most plausible route by which the super-powers might ever come to major nuclear war. Thus, mechanisms for controlling lesser conflicts are primary instruments in the deterrence of all-out nuclear war.

As a consequence, it is of no little importance for the future relationship between technology and strategic nuclear deterrence that the technology of limited war is also changing very rapidly. To take but one example, the recent evolution of precision-guided munitions for both conventional and tactical nuclear application has raised high, not to say extravagant, hopes of fundamentally reinforcing the defensive. If this were to increase the chances of presenting an effective defence, and hence 'deterrence by denial', it might ease the doctrinal burden on strategic nuclear forces. In particular, the limited nuclear option could perhaps be postponed in both its war-fighting-support and its retaliatory-punishment role. There is thus a synergistic relationship between forces designed for strategic deterrence and those designed for local defence, a relationship further complicated, as the grey-area systems illustrate, by the inter-changeability of much of the actual technology employed at either level of conflict. Once again, it becomes clear that the doctrine and technology of deterrence form an integrated and dynamic whole, to be harnessed pragmatically to foreign policy rather than scrutinized, weapon by weapon, for the 'bad ones'. The same point could be illustrated in terms of developing techniques for 'power-projection', the increased licence that may be given to would-be expansionist expeditionary forces under the 'undeterrent' umbrella of nuclear parity, and the consequent importance of the balance of capability for action-at-a-distance. In this case also, the issues are conditioned by the growing technological capability of lesser local powers to seek their own nuclear solutions.

Conclusion

From all of this it seems clear that in the light of technological change the future of deterrence must be discussed in terms much wider than the most commonly debated question of whether the super-powers can continue to maintain invulnerable counter-city forces as a basis for assured destruction. Admittedly, there are many problems besetting even that limited task. But to concentrate exclusively on it could be counter-productive for both the understanding of, and the perpetuation of, the wider stabilizing role of nuclear weapons and thus could even undermine the primary purpose of assured destruction – the avoidance of large-scale nuclear war.

The problems associated with designing nuclear strategy to do more than deter a major nuclear strike calls for a more complex system than simple assured destruction but may offer correspondingly greater reward, by way of leverage on world politics. Certainly, the sources of innovation in the field of nuclear weapons are so varied and so closely linked with other military technology, and are exploited by so many nations with such divergent interests, that the one-time hope of basing stability on relatively permanent force postures is no longer tenable. The nuclear balance will continue to be formed by rapidly changing technology and determined chiefly by autonomous national decisions, moderated occasionally, partially and usually only temporarily by explicit international agreement. In such a world the idea – suggested by the present Director of the International Institute for Strategic Studies[7] – that arms control must work in terms more of missions than of specific weapons is a judicious response to the nature of the problem, though opinions may differ on how far even such a sensitive approach will take us along the road to effective agreements.

Fundamentally, future developments seem likely to resemble very closely those of the recent past: rapid change in the technological components of the strategic balance, but effective functional deterrence of major war between the advanced nations. Negligence or a failure of political will might upset this prediction; it seems unlikely that any technological determinant need do so given the expectation that neither super-power can outwit the other.

NOTES

[1] The early history of nuclear strategic thought has yet to be systematically recorded but is sketched in many places. I have found especially useful and interesting an unpublished memorandum written in May 1968 by Albert Wohlstetter, and Bernard Brodie's own *War and Politics* (New York: Macmillan, 1973), ch. 9.

[2] The early version was A. J. Wohlstetter, F. S. Hoffman, R. J. Lutz and H. S. Rowen, *Selection and Use of Strategic Air Bases* (Santa Monica, Cal.: Rand Corporation, R-266, April 1954); Wohlstetter's later 'The Delicate Balance of Terror', *Foreign Affairs*, Vol. 37, No. 2, (January 1959), pp. 211–234 was a revised public version.

[3] As Raymond Aron put it at the IISS Fourth Annual Conference in 1968, 'so far, in their relations with each other these two states, these duopolists, have stuck firmly to the most elementary role of prudence: they have steered clear of all armed confrontation', *Problems of Modern Strategy*, Part I, Adelphi Paper No. 54 (London: IISS, 1969), p. 5.

[4] An interesting, recent and judicious addition to the vast literature on this topic is Helmut Sonnenfeldt's and William Hyland's *Soviet Perspectives on Security*, Adelphi Paper No. 150 (London: IISS, 1979).

[5] I have in mind the well-known distinction made by Samuel Huntington many years ago: 'Arms Races: Prerequisites and Results', *Public Policy* (Cambridge, Mass.: Graduate School of Public Administration, Harvard University, 1958), pp. 41–86.

[6] This is a consolation only so far as pre-war diplomacy is concerned; if war occurs, secret capabilities take full effect.

[7] Christoph Bertram, *Arms Control and Technological Change*, Adelphi Paper No. 146 (London: IISS, 1978).

Deterrence and SALT

MICHEL TATU

'SALT II provides an increasing stability and predictability in a world of uncertainty . . . It restrains the competition and makes the challenge more manageable and predictable.'[1]

This statement of President Carter's National Security Adviser provides the official answer to the question this paper is supposed to address: is the SALT process useful to deterrence and, more precisely, has it become a part of deterrence itself? While there is no question that the SALT process has made the bilateral competition more manageable and is, therefore, warranted *per se*, it is not so clear that this will result in more stability in this 'world of uncertainty'.

SALT has been helpful in two ways – in some of its results as well as in the process itself. Whatever may be said about some specific weaknesses, the SALT I and II agreements have produced definite results, which have stabilized the arms race in important areas. The Anti-Ballistic Missile (ABM) Treaty in 1972 closed the path to one important destabilizing development. Even if this Treaty seems to be in danger in the foreseeable future and has pushed the arms race in other directions (had it not existed, there would probably be no need at the present time for mobile missiles), it did contribute to a more stable relationship between the super-powers for more than a decade.

In the same way, the most important single achievement of SALT II is the 'fractionation' limit imposed on both sides. The agreement on this point not only helps to compensate the United States for the throw-weight advantage granted by the Soviet Union, it also frees strategic planning of one of its biggest uncertainties. For the first time planners on each side will have a finite number of warheads to deal with in the arsenal of the other. Though this number is very high, there is still a much better prospect of solving the problem of ICBM vulnerability in the 1980s and 1990s than would be the case if warheads were not constrained.

What further SALT agreements could achieve is not yet clear. We can expect that even if ceilings are not lowered, they will not be increased, thereby allowing the strategic planning to go on relatively undisturbed as far as numbers are concerned. New technological developments might be curbed too – for example in the area of anti-satellite warfare.

Last but not least, the talks have produced agreement on verification. Certainly, these agreements have not been perfect: the opportunities for cheating – especially in relation to the encryption clause in SALT II – will continue to be the centre of heated debate. But, as most military experts in the United States have pointed out, cheating and concealment would be much more widespread without SALT and would, indeed, become the rule and not the exception. On the whole, and given the progress of National Technical Means of Verification, the two SALT agreements have produced a reasonable balance between the level of verification and the high numbers of arms involved. This situation might be upset only if serious misunderstandings were to appear in the management of the agreements, or if a dramatic decrease in the numbers of arms allowed to each power made any cheating potentially much more dangerous than it is now. As an extreme example, an agreement banning all nuclear weapons would make each side highly vulnerable to *any* kind of cheating by the other, since a very few concealed launchers in the possession of one would totally change the picture. In fact, such an agreement could not be verified in a reliable way.

71

The SALT process itself contributes to stability by giving each side a clearer (though still dim) view of the other's intentions. The United States knows very little about Soviet arms programmes until new hardware is actually deployed, but each agreement tells her at least what the Soviet Union will *not* do in a certain period of time; furthermore, the emphasis placed by Soviet negotiators on certain arguments during the talks often gives the United States a better idea of what they would like to do. For example, their demand, put forward in 1977–8, to be able to deploy one new type of single-warhead ICBM (the so-called 'monobloc' missile) was interesting mainly as a sign of their desire to maintain a strong counter-value deterrent force.

This incentive does not exist for the Soviet Union, since all important American arms programmes are known well in advance through open information. But, like the United States, she now has the advantage of knowing exactly what her partner in the talks will *not* do during the period of an agreement and, more important, she can use her fuller knowledge of American plans to try to orientate the arms competition in a direction favourable to herself. Though the Soviet Union is better informed, however, she also has her problems. While the United States may not know exactly what Moscow is up to in terms of missile deployment and numbers, she does not expect to be surprised by Soviet technology, nor confronted by new and imaginative types of Soviet weapons. The USSR, on the other hand, can be confronted with what certainly appears to her to be American technological breakthroughs. It was so with the MIRV development in 1968 and with the strategic cruise missile in 1975. Even though the deployment of such systems does not take place for some years after announcement, even the announcement often comes as an unpleasant surprise for Moscow, since the corresponding technology is not available to the Soviet Union at the time. The only solution for her is then to embark upon a crash programme to catch up, but this in turn upsets her plans and diverts resources from other defence needs. Furthermore, the time it takes her to catch up with the technology is usually longer than the time-lag between the American decision to implement a new system and its deployment. For example, it took more than five years for the Soviet Union

to develop a MIRV, and the American MIRV was deployed long before the first Soviet MIRVs.

The disparity in the information available to each side about the other's intentions nevertheless puts them at odds as far as bargaining positions are concerned. The United States is more interested in overall cuts in numbers and in reversing those *past* Soviet deployments that are of concern. The American negotiators were happy to freeze Soviet ICBMS in SALT II at the level of numbers reached at the end of the 1970s, but it can be argued that a pause would have come about anyway after 15 years of continuous build-up. As far as *future* Soviet programmes are concerned, the United States is in the dark, and American bargaining positions cannot be worked out. Which types of weapons does Moscow plan to deploy after 1985, and what should be the American demands in SALT III? To guess is risky, especially as the Soviet Union may press certain demands to create the impression that she is interested in one system of weapons, while actually planning and working on another.

The important point in this context is that because of Soviet secrecy, the United States is much more vulnerable to a technological breakthrough that might be achieved by her negotiating opponent than the other way around. If the Soviet Union were ahead in technology, she would give the United States a much shorter time in which to catch up – only the period between testing in flight and deployment: in effect, confronting her with a *fait accompli*. This in turn implies that there must be a strong and continuing American research and development effort.

Moscow's bargaining position is much easier to define. Given the fact that the Soviet Union knows about both the American programmes and her own, Soviet aims can consist only in eliminating any possible obstacle to her own deployments, curtailing possible American efforts to counter these deployments and, generally speaking, trying to suppress or limit those American deployments that are of concern to her. This will not be easily achieved, however. SALT I and SALT II did nothing to prevent the ambitious Soviet strategic build-up of those years (with the exception of the SS-16), but then neither did the agreements prevent the United States from going ahead with programmes highly unpleasant for Soviet planners – the MIRV in the early 1970s and the strategic cruise missile, two systems that were judged too promising in Washington to be discarded. Nevertheless, the Soviet Union was able to obtain some important constraints on the cruise missile in SALT II before any missiles were deployed, just because she knew very precisely what American plans were in this area. The Soviet prospects for limiting the MX are less promising, if only because this system is a late imitation of previous Soviet weapons, and Moscow would have to give away a large portion of its forces in exchange for an American undertaking not to deploy this new mobile – and so less vulnerable – system.

SALT and the Strategic Balance

Two general observations can be made in this connection, since SALT is a continuous process, having a value recognized by both sides as the legitimate framework for the discussion of bilateral strategic matters. Such discussions should in turn relate to decisions about strategic weapons. Each side, before embarking on a new arms programme, should consult the other to see if concessions on his part could make the programme unnecessary. But even if this does not work (and we must acknowledge that it is too much to expect from the Soviet Union at the moment), it would be equally legitimate to claim that any renunciation of a new strategic system should become part of the bargaining process. The unilateral cancellation of the B-1 programme by the United States in 1977 was, from this point of view, highly regrettable. It might have been negotiated against a similar Soviet weapon (why not the *Backfire?*); and even if this attempt failed, the United States might have used it as a bargaining chip to get better terms in other areas, especially after the sharp reaction of Moscow to the earlier American proposals for 'deep cuts' in March 1977.

This is not to say that the principle of using bargaining chips should become systematic. An arms programme that was promoted only for the sake of negotiation would not be credible, and the other side would not feel it necessary to make reciprocal concessions. To be 'exchange-able', an arms programme must be technically credible and must have acquired a momentum of its own. That was so in the case of the B-1,

as it was with the *Sentinel* ABM system in the early 1970s, although Richard Nixon confesses in his memoirs that he considered it to be a bargaining chip from the very beginning.[2]

At the same time the SALT process should never be considered an end in itself, nor as a sort of 'good' counter-weight to a 'bad' arms race. The effect of SALT is not to stop the arms race; it is a part of it. In the present circumstances its aims can only be to contribute to channelling that race in a desirable direction and to make the situation less uncertain. This is true irrespective of doctrines, but it is even more true in the light of what can be guessed about Soviet intentions. Assuming the worst – which is probably safer and closer to reality – the Soviet posture is based on three principles. First, deterrence should be replaced by a capacity for coercion. In other words, American nuclear power should be neutralized in order that Moscow should have a freer hand in military and political manipulation outside Soviet borders. Second, for the purpose of neutralizing the American deterrent, the Soviet Union must have a nuclear war-fighting capability. A nuclear war must be considered a possibility, and Moscow has to be prepared to fight it and win it. Third, military spending in the Soviet Union is not contingent on SALT. More precisely, although a SALT agreement can permit a reallocation of resources from one weapons programme to another, it will not affect overall spending, which is already close to the maximum.

Given these three assumptions, the choices that face American planners are more easily defined. It should be remembered that SALT should be secondary to strategic planning including weapons development and deployment (it is clear, by the way, that the Soviet Union regards SALT in this light). For example, a B-1 programme would have added little to the American retaliatory force by comparison with other means of delivery, especially the air-launched cruise missile. But it would have diversified the American Triad by adding a new penetrating bomber to stand-off bombers equipped with cruise missiles, and this would have compelled the Soviet Union to add to her air defences. Assuming that Soviet defence spending is already near its maximum and cannot be substantially increased in peacetime, it should be considered an advantage that she should spend more money on defence than on offence.

A similar analysis can be made with regard to the MX. There are two parts to this programme. As a counter-force, anti-silo weapon, it is destabilizing, in the sense that the Soviet Union could become nervous that, with the deployment of substantial numbers, all her land-based systems, accounting for 70 per cent of her warheads, would become vulnerable to a first strike. The alternatives for her are either to 'go to sea', an option that is considered desirable by high planners in the White House as the most stabilizing, or to switch to a mobile basing mode for her own ICBMS. Assuming that this latter option does not make verification impossible, it would be favourable for the United States, since it would again compel the Soviet Union to divert military allocations to defensive measures rather than the construction of new weapons. There is, of course, a third option: she can decide to do nothing, assuming quite reasonably that an American President will never launch a first strike. After all, an officially posted 'launch on warning' doctrine would be sufficient to deter the use of American nuclear power against the Soviet Union, even in the context of a Soviet-made international crisis.

The other feature of the MX system (which need not be tied to a new missile and could apply to *Minuteman*) is the mobile basing mode. The horizontal multiple protective shelter (MPS) system that seems about to be adopted will mean that some 4,000 to 5,000 high-precision warheads will be needed to destroy the 200 ICBMS deployed this way – and more than that if a light ABM defence, compatible with the ABM treaty, is built around them. Since the total number of warheads in the Soviet arsenal seems likely to be limited by the fractionation limit in SALT II, it is to be considered desirable that a large portion of this arsenal (about half of the warheads supposedly available to the USSR in 1985) will be devoted to the neutralization of only 200 ICBMS, instead of being targeted at thousands of unpredictable, softer targets.

This should not preclude a move to sea – or to the coastal waters – at a later stage: after all, nothing has yet been said about the future of the 1,000 *Minutemen*, whose vulnerability problem might have to be solved by other means. In the long run there might be a redistribution of forces within the Triad, with a limited land-based leg used mainly to 'fix' the maximum number of the most accurate enemy warheads and with a redundancy of more diversified forces in the two other legs: deep-sea *and* coastal-water submarines, air-launched cruise missiles *and* penetrating bombers. This situation would be more stable than that which obtains now and could form the basis on which more significant decreases in numbers could be agreed.

Can SALT be used to press these ideas on the Soviet Union? The answer should be yes, if only because SALT has produced the two key elements which make the management of the arms race possible: a commitment not to hamper verification by national technical means and an overall limit on numbers. Without these features the arms race would look like an uncontrolled push in many directions at the same time, without any guarantee that the chosen counter-measure (for example, MPS) will be adequate to check the threat. The negotiators should consequently see to it that these elements are maintained and, if possible, reinforced in future agreements.

In this connection there is a strong possibility that a mobile Soviet ICBM system will be less verifiable than its American counterpart: that is why common rules should be adopted on the basing mode of mobile ICBMS. Beyond that, however, it is hard to see how the United States could, by talking, persuade the Soviet Union to adopt more peaceful doctrines and more stabilizing weapons programmes. This can be done only by other weapons programmes tailored to ensure greater stability even if adopted by the other side.

In this respect, although Soviet arms programmes are wrapped in secrecy, their pattern is not particularly mysterious. Moscow's priorities may differ from those of Washington; some Soviet sectors may be developed earlier and more fully than in the United States; but, broadly speaking, they are the same. The Soviet Union has not introduced any innovative nuclear delivery system since the first ICBM in 1957; she has substituted Soviet quantity for American quality – more launchers, bigger missiles and more powerful warheads – and has tried to catch up with new American deployments. That is why she can be expected to build and deploy mobile ICBMS, a strategic cruise missile and possibly a modern long-range bomber in the years ahead. The airborne leg of her Triad has been neglected so far, but probably more by necessity than by choice. The need to be perceived as equal (or superior) to the United States, or, more simply, bureaucratic inertia will compel the Soviet Union to catch up in those areas too.

To sum up, assuming that the vulnerability problem of ICBMS can be solved satisfactorily (and in ways consistent with the needs of verification), we can anticipate a situation in which the Soviet and American nuclear arsenals may be more similar than they are now. That will in turn add another element of stability to the strategic competition.

The Problem of Alliance

But SALT brings stability only between the two super-powers and only in regard to the use of their strategic nuclear arsenals. If it introduces 'more predictability in a world of uncertainty', as Mr Brzezinski puts it, it is only in the sense that the use of those arsenals to solve crises is less likely. SALT does not prevent crises, nor does it prevent the Soviet Union from taking advantage of them whenever possible. Indeed, there were as many international crises after SALT began as before, and probably more Soviet gains, at least in Africa and Asia. Furthermore, the fact that none of those crises escalated into a nuclear confrontation must be attributed more to the frightening power of nuclear arms and to the achievement of parity than to the SALT process itself, although SALT has made it possible for each side to know more about the other's power and doctrine and has probably encouraged a more cautious approach.

But the real problem with SALT, as with nuclear deterrence in general, is the problem of the alliances. The achievement of parity between the United States and the Soviet Union could not but raise doubts in the mind of friends and foes alike about the will of the American President – and of his people – to risk nuclear war to defend any other country. SALT did not create this situation but, by cultivating and con-secrating the notion of parity, it has strengthened that perception. In other words, more certainty and safety for the two super-powers means less certainty and less security for their allies, at least on the Western side. (Curiously enough,

doubts have never been raised about the Soviet will to 'defend' Eastern Europe, and this is presumably because not only has the Soviet Union stated that she would do so, but also because she already uses force to keep her bloc together. The alliance is artificial but the com-mitment more credible.)

Trouble with allies was probably unavoidable, but the way out of this dilemma is not an extension of the bilateral tranquillity achieved by SALT to all alliance-related matters. What is needed is *more*, not less, uncertainty in Soviet minds about allied reactions in case of aggres-sion, and that can be achieved only by more diversification and pluralism in the nuclear decision-making process. Broadly speaking, the answer to the Soviet military build-up is not the continuous reinforcement of one 'camp' under American leadership, but the addition of new independent but friendly centres of power in order to complicate the task of Soviet planners.

As far as SALT is concerned, the inclusion of Britain and France in the negotiation would mean little in terms of numbers (in fact, the nuclear forces of these two countries are too small to be negotiable), yet it would tend to diminish Soviet uncertainties as far as their use is concerned. Furthermore, it could sustain the *status quo* and preclude the options both of Western European nuclear co-operation and of further build-up, options which must be kept open for the future.

For the same reason, the inclusion in SALT III of all American nuclear systems in Europe – even after the deployment of new NATO 'Euro-strategic' weapons – can only freeze Europe in its present position, with all the implied frustra-tions and quarrels. It would also feed suspicions of a bilateral American–Soviet tutelage imposed on Europe. The idea that such an inclusion will extend to Europe the stability that the two super-powers enjoy in their nuclear bilateral relationship is not convincing, since SALT deals only with the deployment of forces and does not solve the problem of the use of those forces for the promotion of peripheral interests. In fact, it makes the situation worse by reducing the credibility of the perceived commitment. That is why the United States should resist Soviet – and allied – pressure in this direction and should postpone once more the introduction of theatre nuclear forces in SALT.

Guidelines for American Negotiators

There are three other things that the United States could do to alleviate allied fears and limit the dangers of excessively 'bilateral' management and stability.

— *The United States could refrain from conducting any discussion with the Soviet Union about nuclear strategic doctrines.* She could also limit pronouncements on such matters in order to maintain the highest possible level of uncertainty in Soviet minds. This is the easiest thing for her to do. The extreme redundancy of nuclear forces on both sides leaves an American President with a large number of options when faced with aggression against an ally – and the Soviet Union is aware of this. This also gives the impression that the President actually does not know what he will do in such a case. It would be better in this respect that the Soviet Union should know as little as she does now about these intentions and the American President a little more.

— *The United States should consider linking SALT to other issues.* Linkage should not be proclaimed as official 'doctrine' because any 'doctrine' put forward for managing the Soviet–American relationship would make American policy more predictable in Soviet eyes and, consequently, easier to overcome or circumscribe. Furthermore, a 'doctrine' is inevitably a subject of contest, both inside as well as outside the negotiations. Unless it fitted Soviet purposes, linkage would immediately become the target of Moscow propaganda, which would make its use more difficult. But since SALT (and American policy behind it) aims at introducing more stability in international relations, it seems reasonable that any significant lack of restraint by Moscow in an international crisis should be penalized through SALT. For example, Soviet involvement in Angola should have been 'punished' by the postponement of SALT negotiations in January 1976 (postponement came later and for domestic reasons, so that the point was lost on the USSR). The USSR has used the same method when, in January 1979, she postponed the talks for a few months because of Deng Xiaoping's visit to Washington. It is true that linkage should only be used for international matters of great concern for the US. SALT is too important to be linked, for example, to domestic repression in the Soviet Union, unless this were to appear to constitute an open challenge to American policy and prestige. It means also that the Soviet Union must continue to have an incentive to pursue SALT. American arms programmes and technological developments must remain a matter of concern to her.

— *The United States should look at SALT as only a part of the overall strategic picture.* She should examine carefully *all* the consequences of the decisions made in SALT. It is safe to assume that overall Soviet defence spending is, and will remain for the foreseeable future, at its maximum peacetime level. This level will not be substantially reduced by SALT. The resources released as a consequence of an agreed limitation in one area will not go towards butter and consumer goods for the citizen, whatever the Soviet leaders say, but to other areas of military procurement. But, by the same token, overall defence spending cannot be substantially increased. That is why it is important and worth while to try to influence this spending in order to divert it into less dangerous channels.

Conclusion

SALT and American arms programmes should be used to compel or induce the Soviet Union to spend more on defensive than on offensive strategic weapons and, in the latter category, to choose less destabilizing systems. Since what the Soviet Union does not spend on central strategic arms deployment will go to her European theatre forces, or to the anti-Chinese deployment, or to conventional forces, it might be unwise to encourage or allow a major diversion of funds from central systems.

It has been already observed that the *Backfire* quarrel with the Soviet Union has had the effect of appearing to divert the threat to the European allies: the less this aircraft is 'anti-American', the more it is 'anti-European'. This point is secondary in the present circumstances, but the idea can be extended. In the long run, it may seem wiser to let the Soviet Union develop a new long-range bomber, or strategic cruise missile, or any other second-strike nuclear system than to force her to concentrate on conventional weapons, an area in which the West has no decisive technological edge and cannot compete successfully. If by chance the Soviet Union gets what she wants in SALT (complete stability of nuclear central systems, with equal or superior numbers on her side, equal quality and no scope for American innovation), she will have achieved what is assumed here to be her first aim in SALT – the neutralization of American nuclear power. Conditions will then be better suited to the exploitation of conventional superiority. Even if the Soviet Union were effectively deterred from using conventional power by the threat of American nuclear retaliation, the very fact that she could concentrate her resources on conventional defence, and further tip the conventional balance in her own favour, would be unattractive to the West.

In other words, we should not wish the SALT negotiations too much success. If complete success meant the end of the nuclear arms race, it could be counter-productive, given the high levels already achieved and the trend of the Soviet leadership to push other forms of militarization. If it made for stability in the nuclear relationship between the super-powers, it would be interpreted as a further erosion of American commitment to allies and friends. Finally, the extension of SALT to the European theatre nuclear forces will not solve the problems of the alliance; it will aggravate those problems by increasing the basic inequality within the alliance and by allowing the Soviet Union to meddle in alliance politics. The best is the enemy of the good.

NOTES

[1] Zbigniew Brzezinski, speech at the International Platform Association, Washington, 2 August 1979.

[2] Richard Nixon, *Memoirs* (New York: Grosset & Dunlap, 1978), p. 416.

Soviet Strategic Conduct and the Prospects for Stability

BENJAMIN S. LAMBETH

Throughout the nuclear age American defence planners have had ample exposure to the broad essentials of Soviet military thought, including its stress on the operational virtues of strategic superiority and its persistent advocacy of forces capable of fighting to meaningful victory in the event of war. Until recently, however, American officials tended to dismiss these views as merely the parochial axe-grindings of the General Staff and to profess confidence that those civilians on the Politburo 'who really mattered' had the inherent good sense to appreciate the superior wisdom of prevailing Western strategic logic.[1]

As long as the United States remained comfortably ahead of the Soviet Union in the quality and numerical strength of her strategic forces, this sort of ethnocentric hubris could be indulged in with little immediate consequence to Western security. Even sceptics concerned about the thrust of the Soviet build-up that first became apparent around 1966 could, at least during the early stages of SALT I, temporarily suspend disbelief and voice reasonable hope that, once the Soviet Union attained strategic parity with the United States, she might discover substantial merit in moderating her subsequent deployments and in continuing to pursue her global interests within a deterrence environment, spared from significant risk of war by the stabilizing influence of 'assured destruction' capabilities on both sides.

In the light of the repeated frustrations encountered throughout SALT II and the growing evidence of Soviet determination to acquire forces well beyond those required to support a simple 'assured destruction' policy, however, it has now become clear to all but the most hopeless romantics that the time for such optimism has long since passed and that a considerably more sober appraisal of Soviet motivations and goals is in order. From every indication that one can gather from its uninterrupted record of force enhancement since the conclusion of SALT I seven years ago, the Soviet leadership has signalled its unambiguous commitment to the accretion of a credible war-fighting capability in all bands of the conflict spectrum in total disregard of, if not outright contempt for, repeatedly articulated Western security sensitivities. Although this commitment does not mean that the Soviet Union is any less interested than her Western counterparts in the continued avoidance of nuclear war, it does suggest an underlying Soviet conception of deterrence quite unlike that which has traditionally held sway in the United States. Accordingly, the American defence community has found itself increasingly driven to base its future planning on the discomfiting reality of demonstrated Soviet performance rather than on the evanescent hope of the eventual convergence of Soviet and American strategic values.

Of course, how this growing appreciation of Soviet doctrinal dissimilarity will ultimately affect the complexion of American strategic programmes remains far from self-evident and will depend heavily on the results of the 1980 Presidential election campaign. Already, however, the battle lines are forming over the matter in a fashion that suggests that the mere fact of consensus on the broad nature of Soviet strategic philosophy in no way implies any unanimity of opinion about what the United States ought to do in order to accommodate it. This is not the place for a detailed review of the various points of contention currently prevalent on the issue of American force requirements for the coming decade, let alone any attempt to join the debate with specific programme recommendations for addressing the Soviet strategic challenge. It is, however, an appropriate forum for exploring some of the aspects of Soviet behaviour that have given rise to the problem in the first place, the understanding of which will be critically important to any rational consideration of policy options that will be available to the United States in the years ahead.

The Sources of Soviet Strategic Intractability

Although ideological imperatives and traditional great-power ambitions obviously account for a great deal of the adversarial nature of Moscow's strategic comportment in recent years, much of the difficulty the United States has encountered in trying to elicit a measure of co-operative Soviet behaviour in SALT can be explained simply by the fact that the Soviet Union approaches her national security problem in a way fundamentally unlike that characteristic of most Western defence-planning processes. The distinctive aspects of the Soviet strategic style are not, in themselves, the outgrowths of conscious malevolent intent so much as merely the natural products of a unique political culture and historical tradition.[2] Nevertheless, they have had the effect of reinforcing the inherent competitive tendencies of the Soviet leadership and exacerbating the problem faced by American negotiators in their efforts to induce the Soviet Union to agree to a common code of strategic conduct which might be expected to stabilize the super-power relationship.

Perceptions of the Deterrence Problem

To begin with, the Soviet Union defines the nuclear dilemma and the force requirements she sees as dictated by it using an intellectual approach quite alien to the concepts that have largely informed the strategic policies of the United States over the past two decades. To put the point of critical difference in a nutshell, the American propensity – running as far back as the formative works of Bernard Brodie in the late 1940s – has been to regard nuclear weapons as fundamentally different from all other forms of military fire-power because of their unique potential for inflicting truly catastrophic damage in a single blow. Naturally, flowing from this appreciation has been a consuming American belief that any widespread employment of these weapons would call down such unmitigated calamity on all participants as to make a mockery of the traditional Clausewitzian portrayal of war as a purposeful tool of national policy.[3] As a consequence of this pervasive disbelief in the practical attainability of meaningful victory by either side in a nuclear war, the American defence community has come to embrace the notion of deterrence based on the certainty of mutual societal annihilation in the event of nuclear war as, *faute de mieux*, the only workable solution to the problem of ensuring Western security in the modern era.[4] Without being diverted into a detailed review of the numerous American policy choices that have emanated from this concept in recent years, we may simply list the more notable among them: the rejection of strategic superiority as an American force-posture goal; the abandonment of efforts to provide for significant active and passive defences against a concerted Soviet attack on the United States; the conscious refusal (at least up to now) to seek comprehensive hard-target capabilities that might threaten the survivability of Soviet strategic retaliatory forces; and the persistent effort, through SALT, to preserve and bolster the long-term stability of the nuclear balance by ensuring that mutual societal vulnerability remains the central regulating mechanism of the East–West deterrence relationship.

The Soviet Union, for her part, fully shares this American appreciation of the awesome destructiveness of nuclear weaponry and equally elevates deterrence to a level of pre-eminent importance in her hierarchy of security concerns.[5] Beyond these elementary and obvious points, however, any significant similarities between Soviet and American strategic theory are hard to come by. Perhaps most important, Soviet political-military decision-makers reject the notion that the security of the Soviet state should be entrusted to any autonomous and allegedly self-sustaining 'system' of nuclear deterrence, such as that envisaged by the Western concept of Mutual Assured Destruction.[6] In their view, while nuclear war may remain highly remote, it is far from inconceivable and could prove gravely detrimental to Soviet interests, to say the least, in the absence of adequate preparations to minimize its effects should it occur.

From this premise unfolds a logical chain of reasoning and goal-setting entirely at odds with the approach hitherto pursued by mainstream American defence analysts and policy-makers. For one thing, Soviet recognition that nuclear war is a possibility that might some day have to be confronted and dealt with has led to a perceived obligation on the part of the leadership to undertake every feasible measure to mitigate its destructive impact so that the Soviet state might emerge in the least impaired condition permissible under the circumstances. For another, it has inspired the development and systematic refinement of a military doctrine concerned less with manipulating the peacetime perceptions of potential adversaries than with accumulating the operational concepts and repertoires necessary for assuring the effective combat employment of Soviet forces should the ultimate day of strategic reckoning ever come. What it boils down to essentially is an approach to deterrence based not on acceptance of a mutual suicide pact but on an abiding belief in the plausibility of achieving recognizable victory in strategic nuclear war.[7]

To be sure, this Soviet doctrinal certitude regarding the theoretical 'winability' of a nuclear exchange hardly implies that Soviet leaders regard the prospect of such an exchange lightly or harbour confident expectations that any victory worth having would inexorably be theirs even in the best circumstances of war initiation, let alone the worst case. It does, however, attest to an attitude towards the role of strategic power heavily informed by classical principles of military thought and reinforced by a pervasive fear that denial of the possibility of victory would entail a fundamental rejection of the legitimacy of military institutions of which eventual defeatism and moral decay would be the inevitable results. More important, it also dictates guidelines for Soviet force development quite inconsistent with the reasoning typically invoked in support of the annual strategic programme proposals of the United States.

Because of its orientation towards the amassing of credible war-waging options rather than the mere preservation of deterrence through punitive retaliatory capabilities, Soviet doctrine calls for force quantities and characteristics well in excess of what would be regarded as adequate for underwriting a simple assured destruction

policy. In practical terms, this involves, among other things, a requirement for such inter-related strategic assets as comprehensive counter-military targeting capabilities; a surveillance and warning network capable of supporting timely intra-crisis pre-emption; substantial, secure reserve forces for trans-war escalation control and contingency employment; and a command and control system configured to provide sustained leadership direction of Soviet force operations throughout the duration of a war. It would require a thick catalogue to document the numerous activities of this sort that have been steadily under way in the Soviet Union in recent years. Suffice to say here that virtually nothing about any of them gives substantial ground for questioning the central role played by the basic premises of Soviet doctrine in lending organization and coherent purpose to Soviet military construction efforts.

Two broad implications of this Soviet 'deterrence through denial' fixation for the long-term prospects for East–West stability warrant emphasis. Neither of them, sad to say, offers encouragement. The first of these is the Soviet leadership's staunch refusal to have any traffic whatever with bilateral arms-control schemes that require the Soviet Union to be an active partner in the enhancement of her own strategic vulnerabilities. Although the Soviet concept of security stresses the importance of avoiding nuclear war at all reasonable costs, it contains not a shred of evidence to indicate any Soviet belief that the deterrence enforcing that imperative ought in any way to be 'mutual'. Even though the Soviet leaders recognize and acknowledge the *existence* of mutual deterrence (if only because, at least for the moment, it constitutes an inescapable fact of strategic life), they scarcely consider it a desirable situation to be continued into perpetuity, and indeed have directed much of their strategic investments, since the conclusion of SALT I, precisely towards doing away with it at the earliest possible opportunity. It is one of the more notable ironies of the modern era that despite a decade of superficially tranquillizing detente politics, the pre-launch survivability of American land-based ICBMs is now substantially less than it was when the SALT process first began and faces the almost certain prospect of disappearing altogether by the mid-1980s as a result of projected accuracy improvements in the Soviet SS-18 and SS-19 missile forces.

Although to a considerable degree the United States has no one but herself to blame for this looming unpleasantness, because of her unilateral choice not to proceed earlier with such alternatives as MX, the fact remains that the impending threat to *Minuteman* was altogether foreordained, from the outset of SALT II, by the inexorable logic of Soviet strategic doctrine. Soviet military theory stresses the critical importance of minimizing *Soviet* susceptibilities to nuclear war through the vigorous pursuit of offensive and defensive damage-limiting capabilities. It says nothing, however, about co-operation in minimizing the susceptibilities of the adversary and quite a bit about the virtues of endeavouring to do precisely the opposite. From the Soviet viewpoint, as a Rand colleague has remarked, 'Minuteman vulnerability is *our* problem. That it happens to be *our* problem of *their* making . . . simply reflects the continuing competitive nature of detente'.[8] As long as the Soviet Union persists in her commitment to deterrence through damage limitation and the United States remains locked into Mutual Assured Destruction thinking, this sort of calculated Soviet insensitivity to Western security concerns will remain a fundamental impediment on the path towards achieving a common strategic language in the arms-control arena.

The second problem posed for stability by Soviet doctrinal imperatives concerns the immoderate force-acquisition goals that Moscow's pursuit of comprehensive war-waging options naturally implies. Traditionally, Soviet military spokesmen have been emphatic in their insistence on the importance of what they have termed 'military-technological superiority'.[9] Throughout the SALT experience, however, such injunctions have become progressively muted over time, to the point where Mr Brezhnev has now made it one of the central themes of his public-relations posturing towards the West that the Soviet Union lacks even the slightest interest in, let alone ambition towards, pursuit of such superiority.[10] With all due respect for the personal rectitude of the Soviet President, it must be said that a great deal of disingenuousness lies behind such professions of innocent Soviet intent. It would be difficult, of course, to refute the argument that the Soviet Union is genuinely

committed to the principles of 'essential equivalence' and 'equal security', in so far as such commitment entails little more than mere agreement to comply with the precise letter of verifiable SALT restrictions and ceilings. To extend such an argument to the point of maintaining that the Soviet leadership has abandoned its traditional belief in the value of tangible military advantages in deterrence and conflict management, however, would be to misread fundamentally the underlying purposes of current Soviet force modernization activities.

Whether or not one elects to call it 'strategic superiority', the central goal of the Soviet military investment effort of the past decade has consistently been the acquisition of an overall force posture of sufficient strength and versatility to enable the Soviet Union to command the initiative in any determined nuclear showdown with the West.[11] There is every reason to believe that the Soviet Union considers this goal to lie well within her grasp. Aside from activities expressly prohibited by SALT, she will almost certainly continue to make every possible effort towards bringing it about. Should the net result prove to be a further exacerbation of the already considerable 'arms-race instabilities' inherent in the present super-power relationship, it will merely stand as yet another reminder that the Soviet Union has never accepted 'stability' as an appropriate goal of strategic planning to begin with, and has never given the slightest indication of interest in considering unilateral restraints whose sole objective was merely to help the Western powers solve their security problems.

Decision-making and Weapons-Acquisition Processes

Although the detailed workings of Soviet strategic programme formulation and implementation are poorly understood, what needs to be noted, for the purposes of this discussion, is simply that the distinctive style of Soviet military research and development and weapons procurement, with its relative insulation from disruptive outside influences, constitutes an almost natural institutional handmaiden in the service of the systematic (if not always efficient) implementation of the broad force-structure directives provided by Soviet doctrine and leadership choice.[12]

81

Here again it may be instructive to examine the Soviet arms-acquisition process from the perspective of the various ways in which it differs from that of the United States. In the American case, to note perhaps the most fundamental point of divergence, there has tended to be little more than the most superficial correlation between 'doctrine' and the actual complexion of American strategic force characteristics in recent years. Indeed, given the almost obligatory determination of each successive Administration to dismantle the conceptual architecture left by the previous incumbents and to reformulate the defence policy of the United States in a fashion more congenial to its own liking, it is not unreasonable to ask whether the United States has even *had* a strategic doctrine worthy of the name in recent memory.[13] For the most part, American defence procurements essentially constitute recurrent short-term sub-optimizations based more on considerations of cost-effectiveness and the exigencies of budgetary politics than on any coherent effort to relate military capability to broad strategic concepts and goals. Development proposals and deployment options are invariably subjected to the most rigorous technical and economic scrutiny and, as often as not, end up being rejected on grounds of excessive cost, quite irrespective of whatever contribution they might make toward enhancing American preparedness.[14] In so far as 'doctrine' (if one can call MAD a 'doctrine') has shown any direct bearing on the character of the US strategic posture at all, it has tended to have an inhibiting rather than an invigorating effect by restraining programme initiatives that, in the view of prevailing American deterrence theory, would threaten to destabilize the strategic balance.

In sharp contrast to this virtual flea market of conflicting influences and pressures that affect American defence decision-making, the Soviet system of force-planning and implementation is almost pristine in its simplicity. Unlike the case of the United States, where it frequently seems that everybody is a strategic expert after a fashion, the process of establishing force requirements and determining implementation schedules in the Soviet Union is an exclusive prerogative of the General Staff. As far as we can gather, the civilian leadership (at least throughout the Brezhnev era) has tended to keep the activities of its military research and development and planning communities on a fairly loose rein and to restrict its own role largely to the determination of broad policy goals and budgetary allocations.[15] As a consequence, Soviet military programme management tends to involve an extremely routine pattern, wherein Defence Ministry and General Staff officials lay down specific procurement needs based on available fiscal authorizations, the Military-Industrial Commission assigns various design bureaus and production entities appropriate implementation responsibilities, and the various armed services oversee the ultimate deployment of new systems – all with the relentless regularity of a Swiss watch.[16]

Obviously, of course, this is a grossly over-simplified encapsulation of what is doubtless a highly complex and bureaucratized military decision-making world in actuality, and it is scarcely intended to leave the impression that the institutional machinery of Soviet defence planning is devoid of significant internal frictions and corporate rivalries. The disagreements that may arise, however, typically tend to be over matters of detail rather than substance and are ultimately adjudicated within the family, as it were, rather than through external intervention. As a consequence, it is hardly surprising that Soviet military programmes should show such close congruence with the formal precepts of Soviet military doctrine. There is no legislative agency to subject them to disruptive line-item scrutiny and amendment, no independent 'arms-control' constituency to challenge their premises or to wage obstructionist rear-guard campaigns against them, and a sufficiently entrenched leadership structure to obviate tendencies towards the sort of erratic and costly programme starts, stops and delays that have often afflicted the orderly implementation of American defence plans in recent years as a result of frequent personnel turnover.

As for the weapons acquisition process itself, what matters ultimately for the behaviour of the Soviet Union as a strategic competitor is that the inherent dynamism and inertia of research, development and production processes, once commitments to commence work have been authorized, tend to have a snowballing effect to Soviet programmes that renders them extremely resistant to modification or termination. Given the pervasive Soviet doctrinal belief in the operational virtues of military abundance, there is typically little disposition in Soviet defence circles to turn the machine off once it starts producing and a whole cornucopia of bureaucratic incentives to keep it going. In the United States there are all varieties of institutional constraint on the numerical levels which American forces can attain, quite apart from the formal limitations imposed by SALT. In the Soviet Union there are no known strictures on such force expansion other than absolute budgetary ceilings and the military's capacity to assimilate new hardware in a controlled manner. Leaving aside those systems governed by SALT, one must search far and wide for any evidence that the overall Soviet military expansion effort – whether in tanks, tactical fighter aircraft or elsewhere – has any clearly defined end-point in sight. The system simply keeps developing them and pumping them out like a perpetual motion machine.

If it is the case, as one must suppose, that this all but self-energizing mode of arms accumulation is the product of a conscious leadership choice (or at least acquiescence) rather than merely the manifestation of a mindless military bureaucracy rolling about like a loose cannon without rational purpose or political discipline, one can hardly escape the conclusion that the Soviet concept of deterrence is likely to remain dominated by a preference for unilateral investment rather than bilateral agreement for the indefinite future, making continued Western matching efforts in comparable equities the inevitable price for staying in the game. What renders the prospect of such efforts so problematic in this troubled era is the West's lack, for better or worse, of the advantages afforded the Soviet Union by her largely unfettered institutional mechanisms and political environment in the singleminded pursuit of her defence business, unhampered by the need constantly to check over her shoulder for the political opposition.

Unilateral Exploitation of SALT

Finally, at least passing reference must be made to the important role SALT itself has played as a source of Soviet strategic intractability. Here the root causes and resultant manifestations of Soviet conduct becomes blurred, for the SALT experience can be interpreted as reflecting ample

elements of both. On the one hand, the repeated let-downs encountered by the United States throughout the protracted history of SALT II – most dramatically represented by the brusque Soviet refusal even to entertain the 1977 Carter proposal for comprehensive ICBM force reductions – may be said collectively to have provided a fairly definitive litmus test of Soviet strategic intentions by confirming the worst suspicions of those who had always argued that Moscow was trafficking in the SALT trade solely for the purpose of looking after its own parochial interests.[17] On the other hand, one can argue that SALT (at least since the signing of the initial accords in 1972) has also been a major consideration directly affecting the character of Soviet conduct as a result of the opportunities with which it has provided the Soviet Union to participate in the joint legislation, as it were, of constraints on American technological advances, while at the same time offering not merely licence but positive encouragement for the unilateral pursuit of Soviet strategic gains within an explicit framework of American acquiescence.

Since it has now become one of the more fashionable enterprises to point out the various ways in which Moscow has manipulated SALT to the detriment of Western security, it would serve little purpose to review the evidence bearing on that theme at any length here. Simply to illustrate the sort of advantages the Soviet Union has accrued as a result of her societal closure and the disposition of the United States to give her the benefit of the doubt during the initial round of SALT, we may cite as a representative case in point the SALT I provision granting the Soviet Union a roughly three-to-two numerical advantage in ballistic missile submarines. At that time, one may recall, the Soviet argument justifying the need for this numerical edge stressed the longer transit times required for Soviet nuclear ballistic missile submarines (SSBNs) to reach their patrolling stations compared with those of the United States because of unfavourable geographic circumstances, necessitating a margin of Soviet superiority in submarine strength in order to provide Moscow with the capability to match the number of American boats on operational deployment at any given time. Yet scarcely had the ink on the Interim Agreement dried when the Soviet Union flight-tested her new SS-N-8 submarine-launched ballistic missile to inter-continental range for the first time, confirming its capacity (known all along by Soviet planners) for covering most American targets from Soviet territorial waters and thereby making a silent mockery of the whole 'geographic liability' argument used to such successful effect in SALT I. One is tempted to suspect in this instance that the Soviet Union had long before made up her mind about how many SSBNs she wanted and simply capitalized on SALT for assuring a level of Soviet superiority that might not have been allowed to go uncontested by the United States in other circumstances.[18]

Before the accretion of such examples sobered those who had professed to see Soviet participation in SALT as a genuine indication of Moscow's interest in seeking a solution to the deterrence dilemma through co-operative stabilizing measures, the American tendency was to approach SALT on the well intentioned assumption that, under the best of circumstances, it might eventually evolve into an effective *substitute* for unilateral defence planning by bringing the strategic programmes of both super-powers into an explicit negotiating context. As the record now shows, things have scarcely worked out that way. The Soviet Union has done nicely in gaining a measure of indirect influence over the complexion of the strategic activities of the United States, as perhaps best attested by her success in forcing the Carter Administration to forgo deployment of the MX ICBM in the vertical-shelter scheme originally preferred by the Defense Department because of apparent ambiguities regarding that scheme's compatibility with SALT restrictions on silo launchers, thus obliging the American research and development community to turn to the less ideal and substantially more expensive hori-zontal-shelter concept now under public discussion.[19] One would be hard put to find an example of American success in achieving any comparable degree of leverage over the technical characteristics of Soviet strategic programmes.

For the Soviet Union, SALT has been approached from the outset as a direct adjunct of her military planning rather than as an alternative means of addressing the problem of Soviet security. Her most authoritative nego-tiators have been senior representatives of the military-industrial community, with collateral responsibilities in the arena of Soviet defence policy formulation.[20] For her, SALT has tended to be employed quite purposefully as a means of attempting to secure at the bargaining table unilateral advantages that might prove less easy to come by on the technological battlefield of unrestrained arms competition. The hard-headed self-interest that has substantially moti-vated Soviet participation in SALT lies at the heart of the difficulties the United States has long encountered in reconciling her own idealistic expectations with the disappointing returns the SALT process has actually served up thus far.

To help clarify this problem, we can perhaps usefully portray the Soviet construction of SALT as an approximate analogue of the manner in which the Soviet Union has long formulated her domestic constitutions and laws. She has directed meticulous attention towards the careful drafting of language within whose broad framework she can comfortably demonstrate literal compliance, while at the same time exerting studious effort to imbue that language with sufficient ambiguity to permit her to do essentially whatever she would have done in any event, even in the absence of the formal protocol in question. One need only recall the almost casebook cleverness of Moscow's handling of the controversial silo-expansion provision of the SALT I Interim Agreement (which ultimately led to the SS-19, the now-impending Soviet threat to *Minuteman*, and the recent highly publicized *mea culpa* of Henry Kissinger) to appreciate the benefits this negotiatory approach has bestowed on the Soviet Union in the arms-control arena.[21] One increasingly hears laments and protests from commentators of diverse persuasions that even though the Soviet Union may be observing the precise letter of SALT I, her strategic comportment has consistently represented a thoroughgoing affront to the 'spirit' of arms control. People who express such indignation should know better. Arms control has little to do with Soviet involvement in SALT. The Soviet Union is there to enhance her own strategic capabilities to the maximum possible extent, ideally deriving the coin of such enhancement at the unilateral expense of the United States. Her negotiators, and their political superiors at home, devote a great deal of thought to the language of the agreements they sign – and for a purpose.

For them, the concept of the 'spirit' of SALT is purely an artifact of the creative Western imagination.

Implications for the Long-term Competition

It is now generally agreed among most American analysts and planners that regardless of whether or not SALT II is ultimately ratified by the Senate, the survivability of the land-based missile force of the United States will come under a growing threat within the next few years as a result of impending improvements in the hard-target capability of Soviet fourth-generation ICBMs. Whether or not this prospect would have been permitted to arise in the absence of the Vietnam war and its pernicious effect of distracting American attention from strategic nuclear matters is a fascinating but moot question. The fact is that as a consequence of unilateral American decisions not to invest in significant efforts to deal with the silo vulnerability issue over the past decade, the Soviet Union has succeeded in gaining prospective access to a significant component of the American deterrent triad for a window of at least several years in the early to mid-1980s, during which time the United States will have virtually no options for implementing effective offsetting measures.[22] Even in the best of circumstances, the repeatedly delayed MX is not now anticipated to reach initial operational capability until 1986, a year after the SALT II Treaty is scheduled to expire.

A proper appreciation of Soviet strategic motivations and objectives on the part of American decision-makers at the time the SALT dialogue first got under way might have permitted an anticipation of this unfortunate development and the undertaking of appropriate moves to accommodate it in an orderly fashion. Instead the American national security community studiously elected to observe restraint in strategic research and force development in the hope that the Soviet Union, seeing that cue, would reciprocate and join in a mutual effort, through SALT, to introduce an element of quiescence and order into the super-power nuclear competition. We now know, of course, that this early anticipation was doomed from the outset by the truculent Soviet refusal to view the strategic deterrence problem in terms consistent with the premises and assumptions of Western stability theory. As this Paper has

sought to argue, the divergent Soviet conception of the deterrence dilemma and the natural tendency of the Soviet military decision-making and arms-acquisition processes to support that conception have constituted systematic obstacles blocking the achievement of the sort of co-operative super-power arrangement designed to moderate the dynamism and dangers of the nuclear stand-off that has been advanced by Western arms-control theorists as the preferred end-point of the detente process. Given this lack of interest in the attractions of Western strategic logic and Moscow's entrenched resistance to being 'educated' towards a recognition that those attractions might entail benefits for Soviet security, one may even go so far as to express reasonable doubt whether what Thomas W. Wolfe has called 'the arms-control vision of the strategic future' ever constituted a realistically attainable goal of American foreign policy and diplomacy.[23]

A great deal of emphasis has been placed in recent SALT debate on the 'war-fighting' focus of Soviet doctrine, and on the implication that this might reflect an underlying Soviet disposition to think the unthinkable in a manner that threatens grave consequences for Western security in the event of a nuclear confrontation. Yet ironically, for all its rhetorical toughness, it is not the combat orientation of Soviet military thinking *per se* that creates the principal grounds for legitimate Western concern. Despite its evident possession of force-employment options configured towards the achievement of some identifiable form of military victory should nuclear war prove unavoidable, the Soviet leadership has long been highly circumspect in its global strategic comportment and fully appreciates the compound uncertainties – about enemy rationality under pressure, about the technical capabilities of its own forces, about the probable performance of its commanders in the swirling confusion of a massive nuclear exchange, and so on – that collectively constitute the important 'other side of the coin' of Soviet force-application planning and tend to place the superficially ominous language of Soviet doctrine in a rather less alarming light.[24] Moreover, the contingency plans and targeting concepts (though not yet the strategic forces themselves) of the United States have, in recent years, been undergoing some highly publicized changes; attention has turned from the simple-minded criteria of 'assured destruction' towards a more traditional and realistic pursuit of military options associated with goals involving some sense of rational political purpose.[25] Surely none of this has been lost on the Kremlin.

What does warrant reasoned concern about the 'war-fighting' proclivities of Soviet strategic thought and the image of victory inspired by it is the practical impact which that doctrinal concept has had in governing the intensity and scope of actual Soviet military investment. Even here, it is essential to view the tangible outgrowths of Soviet military expenditure in proper perspective – something many Western observers have failed to do in their narrow infatuation with the technical aspects of Soviet strategic activities. It is not the *Backfire* by itself, nor the SS-18, nor any other combination of Soviet weapons that lies at the root of the current Western security predicament. Given the will and the necessary countervailing investments, these sorts of problems can be dealt with. What ultimately matters about Soviet behaviour, as far as the broader East–West competition is concerned, is the overarching philosophical orientation that lies behind it and gives it direction and vitality. It is an orientation firmly wedded to a commitment to security through ever-increasing strength, and as long as the Soviet Union remains under its influence, it will continue to set the ground rules for East–West strategic interaction. For Soviet leaders and planners, the nuclear environment is almost literally perceived as a modern-day Hobbesian 'state of nature', in which mere 'sufficiency' of armaments can never be enough.

Increasingly, American and West European authorities of diverse outlooks are coming to appreciate this fact and to recognize its practical bearing on the character of Soviet conduct. Despite this promising development, however, there continues to be considerable reluctance within official American and NATO European circles to undertake the necessary conceptual leap towards the more responsive force-development policy dictated by this recognition of Soviet reality. Although awareness of Soviet doctrinal and operational uniqueness is now widespread throughout Western intelligence and defence agencies, and has even begun to make its influence felt in certain marginal areas of

contingency planning and military training,[26] it still figures only remotely, at best, in the formal processes of actual force-structure development and implementation. This is an unfortunate circumstance, which will need to be rectified before any significant progress can be made towards undoing the cumulative ills that have beset the strategic posture of the United States and the NATO military balance since the Soviet force-expansion programme first began. There is ample room for differing views about the specific Western declaratory policies and programme decisions that might be best suited to dealing with the challenge posed by the Soviet strategic threat. If there is any message here that might help to inform the drawing of the appropriate outer boundaries for such contention, it is simply that endeavours such as SALT will never provide more than peripheral instruments for attempting to modulate the East–West strategic competition and thereby enhance international security at the margins. If the West is to remain a respectable player in this competition, it will have to begin imposing measures conducive to stability, in spite of Soviet strategic intractability, rather than persist in continued adherence to the elusive hope of eliciting Soviet co-operation on the cheap.

Whether this gloomy verdict means that SALT and detente have become hollow goals without promise or prospect will depend heavily on how the United States elects to reconfigure her foreign and strategic policies over the coming decade. It would be wrong, at least for the moment, to conclude that the United States has been reduced to emulating the worst features of Soviet behaviour simply for lack of more imaginative alternatives. At the same time, it seems increasingly clear that the optimistic assumptions underlying American detente diplomacy in recent years have been proved to be roundly ineffective in eliciting the sort of Soviet reciprocity that any stable ordering of East–West relations must require. This is not to say that Moscow is not susceptible to arms-control agreements that coincidentally happen to serve Western interests, or that SALT should be summarily abandoned simply because of past American disappointments and frustrations. As the Anti-Ballistic Missile (ABM) Treaty of 1972 demonstrated, the Soviet leadership has shown itself to be quite capable of accepting self-denying strategic ordinances when the alternative to doing so has appeared decidedly less attractive. SALT I was a noble experiment aimed at testing the Soviet Union's willingness to work towards a bilateral relationship disciplined by a common commitment to mutual deterrence and moderated arms competition. By her persistent refusal to accommodate to this expectation in SALT II, however, the Soviet Union failed that test and revealed her abiding disdain for Western notions about the strategic world.

The imperative facing the United States in the immediate years ahead, therefore, is the forging of a new approach to stability that appeals to Soviet strategic sensitivities and insecurities; reliance on the dubious prospect of Soviet empathy with the preferred concepts and goals of the West should be discarded. This will require, at the least, a continuation of the current American effort to project a refurbished image of strategic seriousness through such programmes as MX and NATO nuclear force modernization. Given the profound concern and ill will generated by the recent Soviet invasion and occupation of Afghanistan, it may also require an end to SALT as it has been approached and conducted thus far. In time, however, there is every reason to believe that a resurgent mobilization of American industrial and technological assets will work to circumscribe Soviet expectations about the limits of the possible. Notwithstanding the nominal strictures of SALT, the Soviet Union has been working at close to maximum capacity in her military investment for more than 15 years. Much of her resultant success in improving her strategic posture, moreover, has been directly attributable to the comparative slackening of countervailing American investment over the same period. The Soviet Union deeply respects Western technological prowess and would have good reason to wonder how long she could maintain her present rate of military growth without the buffering influence of some SALT-like governing mechanism, should the United States credibly decide to run the gauntlet of serious arms competition once again. Whatever the outcome, such an effort would at least promise to present a new test, couched in more familiar terms, which the Soviet Union would be less likely to fail again. Between the two undesirables of business as usual and a return to outright international jungle warfare, it is hard to imagine any other acceptable American alternative.

NOTES

[1] Apart from intelligence information, details on Soviet military thought have been available in a substantial body of scholarly analysis running back for more than two decades, beginning with Raymond Garthoff's *Soviet Strategy in the Nuclear Age* (New York: Praeger, 1958). As Colin Gray has observed, 'most American strategic thinkers have always *known* that there was a uniquely "Soviet way" in military affairs, but somehow that realization was never translated from insight into constituting a serious and enduring factor influencing analysis, policy recommendation, and war planning'. 'Nuclear Strategy: The Case for a Theory of Victory', *International Security*, Vol. 4, No. 1 (Summer 1979), p. 60.

[2] For an interesting elaboration on this point, see Robert Conquest, 'Why the Soviet Elite is Different from Us', *Policy Review*, No. 2 (Fall 1977), pp. 67–72.

[3] In his first major statement of this thesis, which set the intellectual tone for more than three decades of subsequent American strategic theorizing, Brodie asserted: 'Thus far the chief purpose of our military establishment has been to win wars. From now on its chief purpose must be to avert them. It can have almost no other useful purpose.' *The Absolute Weapon* (New York: Harcourt, Brace, 1946), p. 76. By 1955 Brodie had gone so far as to conclude that because of the destructiveness of nuclear weapons and the loss of the post-war American nuclear monopoly, the world had fully come 'to the end of strategy as we have known it'. 'Strategy Hits a Dead End', *Harper's*, Vol. 211 (October 1955), p. 37.

[4] This conviction was most recently reaffirmed in a high-level strategic balance assessment produced by the Carter Administration in 1977. See Richard Burt, 'U.S. Analysis Doubts There Can Be a Victor in Major Atomic War', *New York Times*, 6 January 1978.

[5] This point has been missed by many observers of the Soviet military scene. There has been a tendency in recent American strategic debate, particularly on the conservative side, to contrast the American orientation towards 'deterrence' with the Soviet doctrinal fixation on 'warfighting', as though the two approaches were somehow aimed at diametrically opposed objectives. This distinction misunderstands the essence of Soviet political–military thinking.

[6] This point was succinctly expressed by one of the erstwhile 'moderates' in the internal Soviet defence debate during the mid-1960s: 'When the security of a state is based only on mutual deterrence with the aid of powerful nuclear rockets, it is directly dependent on the good will and designs of the other side, which is a highly subjective and indefinite factor . . . It would hardly be in the interests of any peace-loving state to forgo the creation of its own effective means of defence against nuclear-rocket aggression and make its security dependent only on deterrence, that is, on whether the other side

will refrain from attacking.' Major General N. Talenskii, 'Antimissile Systems and Disarmament', in John Erickson, ed., *The Military-Technical Revolution* (New York: Praeger, 1966), pp. 225, 227. The same philosophy was echoed by Premier Kosygin at the Glassboro summit in 1967, when he reportedly told President Johnson that giving up defensive weapons was 'the most absurd proposition he had ever heard'. Henry Kissinger, *White House Years* (Boston: Little, Brown, 1979), p. 208.

[7] As one Soviet military commentator has put it, 'there is profound error and harm in the disorienting claims of bourgeois ideologues that there will be no victor in a thermonuclear world war. The peoples of the world will put an end to imperialism, which is causing mankind incalculable suffering'. Major General A. Milovidov and Colonel V. Kozlov, eds, *The Philosophical Heritage of V. I. Lenin and Problems of Contemporary War* (Moscow: Voenizdat, 1972), p. 24.

[8] W. E. Hoehn, Jr, *Outlasting SALT II and Preparing for SALT III* (Santa Monica, Cal.: Rand Corporation, R-2528-AF, November 1979), p. 21.

[9] See, in particular, Lieutenant Colonel V. Bondarenko, 'Military–Technological Superiority–The Most Important Factor in the Reliable Defence of the Country', *Kommunist Vooruzhenykh Sil*, No. 17 (September 1966), pp. 7–14.

[10] In a representative pronouncement Brezhnev claimed in 1978 that 'the Soviet Union considers that approximate equilibrium and parity are enough for defence requirements. We do not set ourselves the objective of gaining military superiority. We also know that this very concept loses its meaning with the existence of the present enormous stockpiles of accumulated nuclear weapons and means of their delivery'. *New Times*, No. 19 (May 1978), p. 7. More recently, Brezhnev also asserted: 'I should like to emphasize again what I have repeatedly said of late. We are not seeking superiority over the West. We do not need it. All we need is reliable security'. *Time*, 22 January 1979, p. 22. The problem with the 'reliable security' formula, of course, is that it is open-ended and does not recognize any natural stopping points for Soviet weapons acquisition. In effect, given the uninterrupted pace of recent Soviet force modernization, it amounts to little more than a case for superiority by another name. For further discussion of this point, see Benjamin S. Lambeth, 'The Political Potential of Soviet Equivalance', *International Security*, Vol. 4, No. 2 (Fall 1979), pp. 26–32.

[11] Contrast Brezhnev's assurances, for example, with this injunction attributed to Marshal Nikolai Ogarkov, Chief of the Soviet General Staff, following a meeting in Moscow in 1978 with members of the House Armed Services Committee: 'Today the Soviet Union has military superiority over the United States and henceforth the United States will be threatened. You had better get used to it'. 'Sounding Brass and Tinkling Symbols', *Air Force Magazine*, July 1978, p. 6.

[12] One example of the inefficiency produced by this system may be seen in the extreme diversity of the Soviet ICBM posture. As a consequence of the Soviet practice of multiple prototyping and concurrent deployment of complementary systems, the Soviet ICBM inventory includes at least six distinctive missile types and more than twice as many variations or 'mods'. (By contrast, the American ICBM force consists of just two *Minuteman* variants, with 54 additional *Titans* held over from the 1960s.) However impressive the overall capability afforded by this non-standardized Soviet ICBM posture may be, it almost certainly comes at a high price in terms of associated problems of maintenance support, launch crew training and operational readiness. Such a differentiated force structure would probably be regarded by American planners, with good reason, as needlessly and unacceptably complicated.

[13] This absence of an enduring vision in the strategic policy of the United States has scarcely escaped Soviet notice. As one Soviet military theoretician remarked, with almost embarrassing incisiveness, the term 'military doctrine' has been employed in Western parlance 'in so many and varied ways that it has virtually lost its true meaning. It is frequently identified with strategy or understood in a narrow sense, connected only with ... certain tasks the state is resolving or plans to resolve through military means at a particular time ... Let us just take U.S. military doctrine. How many names it has been given! All these names, of course, reflect their authors' aspirations to adapt to changing conditions, but they confuse a correct understanding of military doctrine'. Lieutenant General I. Zavialov, 'The Creative Nature of Soviet Military Doctrine', *Krasnaia Zvezda*, 19 April 1973, p. 2.

[14] The cancellation of the B-1 bomber by President Carter in 1977 after over $3 billion of development investment is only the most dramatic recent example of this tendency. Whatever the underlying political and strategic wisdom of that decision may have been, it stemmed in considerable part from what must be recognized as an unusually extravagant American style of advanced weapons development. Over the past two decades the American military R&D community has been so driven by the assumed promise of high technology that it has insisted on producing successive generations of weapons incorporating simultaneous advances across the entire spectrum of system characteristics. As a result, it has tended to produce dream machines of undeniable technical elegance (as supremely typified by the B-1), yet with performance gains of frequently questionable operational need and design features of such sophistication as to render the overall procurement package either unaffordable or excessively costly for production and deployment in operationally sufficient strength. The Soviet Union, by contrast, has tended to follow a more conservative philosophy of incremental product improvement, motivated by the conviction that the best is the worst enemy of good enough. Although this practice has yielded Soviet innovations of rather modest quality as measured by prevailing American technological standards, it has also facilitated the steady Soviet accumulation of large numbers of weapons adequate for fighting the war that could occur tomorrow morning. In the United States the preferred course has been the more ambitious one of concentrating on highly refined and expensive systems that might or might not (because of the vagaries of domestic budgetary politics) be deployed to fight the war that could occur ten years down

the road. The consequence of the latter approach has all too often been lots of impressive R&D but little ultimate contribution to the strategic posture of the United States.

[15] For a detailed analysis of the key organizational features of the Soviet weapons acquisition process, see Arthur J. Alexander, *Decision-making in Soviet Weapons Procurement*, Adelphi Papers Nos. 147–148 (London: IISS, 1978).

[16] There is evidence, for example, that Soviet missile design bureaus are authorized to generate successions of prototypes as a standard practice without having to wait for the Defence Ministry to issue formal requirements for new systems. These prototypes are then tested and routinely served up for production and deployment decisions at periodic intervals in the development cycle. There is also evidence that the leadership frequently approves simultaneous deployment of competing proto- types for little reason other than to hedge against tech- nological risk and to maintain adequate work pro- grammes for all major design and production entities. The net result is a Soviet missile industry which, in one graphic description, 'for years has been grinding out new ICBM models like Ford and General Motors put out cars'. Walter Pincus, 'Soviets Seek SALT Change To Keep Missile Developers Busy', *Washington Post*, 7 January 1979.

[17] For an informed account of this episode, see Strobe Talbott, *Endgame: The Inside Story of SALT II* (New York: Harper & Row, 1979), pp. 38–67.

[18] Further development of this point is offered in David S. Sullivan, 'The Legacy of SALT I: Soviet Deception and U.S. Retreat', *Strategic Review*, Vol. 7, No. 1 (Winter 1979), pp. 26–41. In a rejoinder to the Sullivan article, Defense Department SALT Task Force Director Walter Slocombe has strenuously challenged the allegation that the Soviet Union actively 'deceived' the United States in gaining this and other advantages in SALT I. 'A SALT Debate: Hard But Fair Bargaining', *Strategic Review*, Vol. 7, No. 4 (Fall 1979), pp. 22–28. The argument, however, is academic. Whether the Soviet Union was guilty of 'deception' or simply withheld disclosure of her deployment plans from American negotiators, as Slocombe more correctly maintains, there is no denying that she exploited her societal closure to achieve a satisfactory SALT I arrangement whose attainment would have been far more problematic in the absence of iron- clad Soviet secrecy. That the United States has her own naiveté rather than the Soviet Union to blame scarcely vitiates the independent importance of the Soviet accomplishment.

[19] In explaining the difficulties encountered in settling on a politically acceptable MX basing mode, Lieutenant General Kelly Burke, then Director of Operational Requirements for the United States Air Force, noted that 'this is the first time we've built a strategic system and married it with the arms-control process . . . We're building a system to accommodate SALT as it is and as it may be'. 'MX Basing Approval Expected', *Aviation Week and Space Technology*, 30 July 1979, p. 12.

[20] See Igor S. Glagolev, 'The Soviet Decision-making

Process in Arms Control Negotiations', *Orbis*, Vol. 21, No. 4 (Winter 1978), pp. 767–776.

[21] In a *post hoc* effort to rationalize the technical surprise wrought by the SS-19, Kissinger conceded to a State Department press gathering in December 1975 that 'we obviously did not know in 1972 what missiles the Soviet Union would be testing in 1974'. Rowland Evans and Robert Novak, 'The SS-19 Loophole', *Washington Post*, 27 July 1979.

[22] The *reductio ad absurdum* occasioned by this failure to begin attending to the silo vulnerability issue once it became undeniable has been the recent spectacle of senior American defence officials lending official support to the threat of 'launch on warning' as a last-ditch deterrent option in deep crises. See Charles Corddry, 'U.S. Debates Launch Time for ICBMs', *Baltimore Sun*, 11 February 1979. This affront to every sensible principle of strategy falls barely short of scandalous in view of the far more rational alternatives that could have been pursued with greater forethought and willingness to act accordingly. The Soviet threat to *Minuteman*, after all, scarcely materialized overnight.

[23] Thomas W. Wolfe, *The SALT Experience* (Cambridge, Mass.: Ballinger, 1979), p. 263.

[24] Elaboration of these and other potential Soviet sources of caution may be found in Benjamin S. Lambeth, *Uncertainty in Soviet Deliberations About Deterrence and War* (Santa Monica, Cal.: Rand Corporation, forth- coming).

[25] This trend began with the quest for greater targeting flexibility promoted by Secretary Schlesinger during the Nixon incumbency and has continued, with much less public fanfare, throughout the period of the Carter Administration. On the origins and early content of this effort, see Benjamin S. Lambeth, *Selective Nuclear Options in American and Soviet Strategic Policy* (Santa Monica, Cal.: Rand Corporation, R-2034-DDRE, December 1976). For subsequent developments since President Carter's arrival in office, see also Richard Burt, 'U.S. Moving Toward Vast Revision Of Its Strategy on Nuclear Warfare', *New York Times*, 30 November 1978 and Robert Kaylor, 'Brown Would Widen Range of Russian Military-Targets', *Washington Post*, 14 January 1979.

[26] Particularly notable in this regard has been the USAF's effort to provide realistic air-to-air training for its tactical fighter crews through the use of aggressor squadrons flying the F-5E as a MiG-21 surrogate simu- lating known Soviet aerial combat techniques. Also notable is Project *Checkmate*, a headquarters-level Air Force programme intended to enhance USAF tactical air employment planning in Europe by contributing informed insights into Soviet operational styles and illuminating potentially exploitable Soviet vulnerabilities. See Captain Don Carson, USAF, 'Teaching Tactics in TAC's Migs', *Air Force Magazine*, March 1974, pp. 44–7, and Phillipe Grasset, 'Dissimilar Air Combat Training–A Revolution in Realism', *International Defense Review*, Vol. 8, No. 6 (December 1975), pp. 823–7. See also Captain James Lawrence, USAF, 'Readiness: Project Checkmate', *Aerospace Safety*, September 1978, pp. 1–5.

Perceptions of the Strategic Balance and Third-World Conflicts

THIERRY DE MONTBRIAL

While the gradual evolution of the world towards multi-polarity is being increasingly taken into account by politicians and experts with respect to economic and energy problems, at the strategic level the main point of the discussion remains the East–West balance, and especially the balance between the United States and the Soviet Union. To be sure, the notion of the 'diffusion of power' is widely debated. Nevertheless, the consequences of this diffusion for the relationship between the 'central' strategic balance (that between the United States and the Soviet Union) and the rest of the world, in particular the Third World, have not yet been seriously studied. And it must be emphasized, of course, that reference to the strategic balance between the super-powers implies perceptions of that balance as much as its actual quantitative and qualitative aspects.

This paper will address two symmetrical questions: what is the impact of the strategic balance between the two super-powers on Third-world conflicts, and what is the impact of Third-world conflicts on the strategic balance that exists between the two super-powers? These issues will certainly be discussed more and more thoroughly in the 1980s. As the problems to be tackled are very complex, I propose to raise questions rather than provide definitive answers.

Super-power Strategic Balance and Third-world Conflicts

Let us start with the generally held view that nuclear weapons have resulted in an 'enforced peace' between the industrialized countries by freezing the *status quo* in Europe. In other words, nuclear weapons have contributed to stability. This stability is, of course, fragile, as it is constantly exposed to political and technological development. Outside the central region, however, nuclear weapons have not led to universal peace – indeed, they have probably encouraged, indirectly, the multiplication of limited conventional wars. Blechman and Kaplan[1] have shown that the gains made by the two super-powers in these conflicts since the 1950s have had little to do with the state of their nuclear strategic relationship. In particular, the United States was not able to take advantage in the Third World of her strategic superiority at the time when it was unquestionable. However, it does not follow from this that, were the strategic balance to clearly shift in favour of the Soviet Union, Moscow would not behave in a more aggressive way in the Third World, although cases in which a direct link between the central balance and super-power interests in the Third World can be seriously demonstrated are few. For the United States today only the Middle East (because of Israel and the oil question) and Latin America (because of the Monroe Doctrine) can be considered to be critical areas in this respect, and this explains the caution that the Soviet Union is exhibiting there. Other examples, such as Korea, are border-line cases. In most other situations the super-powers find it difficult to define the risks that they could allow themselves to run. Moreover, as a result of decolonization and socio-economic factors, most regional crises have local origins. Iran is a case in point. Be that as it may, it would seem that for one super-power to have 200 more or 200 fewer ICBMs than the other would *not* be a determining factor in either the origin or the outcome of a regional conflict.

Beyond these general observations, the question of the influence of the central strategic balance on Third-world conflicts is logically inseparable from the global strategies of the two super-powers. Soviet strategy towards the West can be formulated in the following way:

— maintenance of the *status quo* in Europe, to be nudged, by way of very small steps, towards the 'neutralization' of Western Europe. The policy is best summarized by the concept of a 'dynamic *status quo*'.

— 'revolutionary' and 'imperial' behaviour in the Third World, through the cautious but systematic exploitation of all opportunities, to ensure, at the least, a say in regional affairs (which the USSR clearly did not have in the colonial era). The Soviet Union also maintains strategic objectives (such as the acquisition of air and naval facilities) and economic objectives (such as access to raw materials that might well be required some day – for example, oil from the Persian Gulf). She also wishes, more generally, to weaken the West.

The United States, on the other hand, with no clearly defined strategy in the Third World, is oscillating between a global approach, which led as early as 1975 to the forging of a link between the SALT negotiations and Soviet activities in Africa, and a regional approach, which leaves the Soviet Union unchallenged directly, while depending upon local forces to expel her. The latter might be called the 'Vietnam syndrome': because the United States was defeated in Vietnam, many Americans imagine that the Soviet Union will not win a war in a Third-world country. However, precisely as a consequence of the American defeat in Vietnam, the Soviet Union may have come to believe that the way is clear to move ahead very fast (though with prudence) in the Third World, and she will do so as long as she does not come close to a major confrontation with the United States.

Today the only open challenge to the global strategy of the Soviet Union comes from China, which the USSR can hardly confront directly, in spite of a crushing disparity in military strength. Because of this, the Soviet Union is forced to adopt the indirect strategy of encircle-ment, which is illustrated by her actions in South-east Asia and, more recently, in Afghanistan (though, of course, the Soviet invasion of Afghanistan serves several other purposes).

The situation would be quite different if the United States Administration, strongly supported by the American public, were to resort to a general strategy of 'containment' *vis-à-vis* the Soviet Union. Any local Third-world conflict might then entail the risk of a major clash between the two super-powers. This in turn would immediately raise the possibility of a resort to nuclear weapons, and the state of the central strategic balance would clearly affect the crisis. If the United States felt strategically inferior to the Soviet Union, she might find herself incapable of resorting to a nuclear alert – as she did in October 1973, during the Arab–Israeli crisis – and this might be read as a sign of weakness that the Soviet Union could exploit to the full.

Two conditions must be fulfilled if the United States is to put a stop to Soviet activism in the Third World: she must be able, politically and militarily, to engage Soviet forces locally; and she must be backed by a favourable, or at least a not unfavourable nuclear balance. If these conditions are met, the global balance of power may then deter the Soviet Union from under-taking actions that could lead to a major confrontation. The experience of the last 30 years shows that the Soviet Union has been most anxious to avoid a direct military clash with the United States, precisely because of the fear that it might lead to nuclear escalation.

Certainly, the United States could not afford to place herself in a situation in which she was hampered both by strategic inferiority and by a refusal to countenance military intervention abroad. This would lead at first to a series of defeats without wars, but after a time the probability of a major confrontation would increase – a consequence of frustration or desperation. History offers a number of ex-amples to illustrate this dynamic, such as the chain of events that began with the accession of Hitler to the Chancellery in 1933 and cul-minated in the invasion of Poland in 1939, the latter being no more than the immediate cause of the war.

The Nixon-Kissinger notion that nuclear stability, consecrated in SALT, would lead to a 'structure of peace' for the whole world is obviously wrong. Similarly, the idea (put for-ward by the French government) that detente should be indivisible does not stand up to close analysis. This would apply only in the totally inconceivable case that all local interests were seen as equally vital by one or other of the super-powers. Then, and only then, would nuclear deterrence apply credibly everywhere: world order would be imposed by the threat of nuclear war; we would have general enforced peace; and the Soviet–American duopoly would prevail all over the planet.

In the real world, however, there are many areas in which the interests of the two super-powers are in flux and in which they will not be able to agree to maintain the *status quo*. The idea that regional stability can result from a satisfactory management of East–West relations by the United States and the Soviet Union is based on the implicit assumption that enforced peace already applies all over the world. However, in many troubled regions it is clear that harsh competition prevails, not co-operation or even negotiation. Nevertheless, there is scope for limited American–Soviet co-management, even when vital interests are not at stake, as long as the super-powers have a common interest (for example, nuclear non-proliferation) or when they sense that they might be drawn into a clash that neither is willing to face.

When the major interests of the super-powers are not involved, medium powers (for example, France in Africa) and some regional powers (sometimes called second-order powers) enjoy a significant margin of manoeuvre. These powers could either operate in some form of alliance or could lend a certain counter-weight to Third-world countries, thus allowing them to maintain a balance between the two super-powers. This is an interesting aspect of multi-polarity. (The super-powers are not usually pleased to see others complicate their affairs; it was not exactly with enthusiasm that the United States admitted the positive effect of the action taken by France in Zaïre in 1977 and 1978.) The Soviet Union, too, has to take account of the interests of some European countries in certain Third-world areas. (Again the example of French interests in Africa comes to mind.) She knows that she could not hurt such interests without damaging severely her relations with the powers concerned. Without doubt this consideration tends to promote stability, but the medium powers are unlikely to claim that such interests are 'vital'; they would not justify the extension of the French nuclear umbrella, for example, to an African country. In addition, it must be said that so far only very few medium powers have shown

a serious commitment to the stabilization of Third-world areas, and it is very probable that this situation will remain unchanged in the foreseeable future.

Third-world Conflicts and the Central Strategic Balance

Let us now examine the other side of the question. It is obvious that certain crises in the Third World, as soon as one of the two super-powers is involved, can affect the central balance, in terms of weapon systems and perceptions. The Cuban missile crisis was one of the causes of the Soviet strategic effort during the 1960s and the 1970s. An Arab occupation of Israel would have a considerable effect on the credibility of American commitments abroad, particularly in Europe, and thus on the central balance. However, the effect on the central strategic balance of a struggle in the Third World is essentially a function of the super-powers' delicate assessment of their own interests. Thus it seems unlikely that Soviet–Cuban intervention in Angola and in Ethiopia directly weakened 'central' American credibility, because the United States displayed a certain indifference towards the issue. Conversely, the outcome may turn out to be different in Afghanistan, given the importance Washington attached to this issue.

In this connection there is an indirect linkage that might become more and more important in the future. The Soviet involvement in crises such as Angola, Ethiopia, the Persian Gulf and South-east Asia has certainly contributed to produce in the United States and the West a political climate that is increasingly hostile to the Soviet Union, while at the same time reinforcing the image of a weakening American power. As a consequence, ratification of SALT II has been shelved because of events in Afghanistan, and a decision has been made to increase defence spending in the United States. While at one time it was supposed that this hostility might cause the Soviet Union to exercise a little more restraint in her involvement in Third-world conflicts, in order, for example, to secure SALT ratification, the Soviet invasion of Afghanistan at the end of 1979 shows that Moscow has chosen to exploit fully the opportunity created by the power vacuum in Iran, even at the cost of killing the ratification of SALT II. The Afghanistan operation aims to secure the Soviet borders, to bring the Soviet Union closer to the Indian Ocean and the Persian Gulf and to exploit instability in Iran. Thus the stakes are very high. After all, the Soviet leadership remembers that after the intervention of the Soviet Union in Czechoslovakia in 1968 it took less than a year to normalize relations with the West and to resume the detente process.

Ultimately, the problem may lie in the Soviet concept of security. Kissinger has already demonstrated that 'absolute security' for one actor means 'absolute insecurity' for the others.[2]

Conflict Escalation

The question of the influence of Third-world crises on the central strategic balance is usually raised in connection with the risk of conflict escalation: to what extent is there a risk that a local crisis will degenerate into a central crisis? This slide into central crisis is generally seen as an accidental development and does not apply to crises that, as a result of super-power commitment, entail the risk of escalation (for example, the Middle East).

The question for the super-powers is therefore whether the actions of third parties might drag them too far into conflicts in which the stakes *do not seem* vital for either of them. Future events in Iran will be very critical in this context. There the interests of both super-powers are very important, though not necessarily 'vital'. But where can one draw the line? At some point in the development of the crisis the Soviet Union might decide to launch in Iran an operation similar to that in Afghanistan. This would create the kind of situation discussed above. The Soviet Union would not make such a move unless she felt sure that the United States would only reply verbally but she could miscalculate, as she did in Cuba. The super-powers could then come close to a nuclear confrontation.

Another possibility is more directly related to the problems under consideration here. Iran might disintegrate into a civil war, and the oilfields and the Straits of Hormuz could be sabotaged. In such circumstances the super-powers could react in an unpredictable way; an 'undesired' nuclear escalation could very well occur. Should the crisis in Iran degenerate, however, the United States and the Soviet Union would probably resort to Article 4 of the Agreement on the Prevention of Nuclear War (22 June 1973), which provides for this contingency:

If at any time relations between the parties or between either party and other countries appear to involve the risk of a nuclear conflict, or if relations between countries not parties to this Agreement appear to involve the risk of nuclear war between the US and the USSR or between other party and other countries, the United States and the Soviet Union, acting in accordance with the provisions of this Agreement, shall immediately enter into urgent consultations with each other and make every effort to avert this risk.

A more general problem is that Third-world countries may become militarily more relevant – and not only with nuclear arms. The super-powers have a strong and common interest in controlling strictly the military capabilities of their clients. One of the reasons why the Middle East is such an unstable area today is that some countries in that region have a military capability that provides them with at least short-term independence from their respective protectors. From this perspective the Soviet–American negotiations on limiting the transfer of conventional weapons ought to be carried through.

Structures of Regional Stability

However, if the objective is to prevent more drastic local instabilities, what is needed is the emergence of structures of security in the Third World that exclude the super-powers. Such structures would therefore have to crystallize around 'second-order powers' or, in some cases, be based on alliance systems involving a medium power. (General de Gaulle, when proposing that some African countries should enter into 'defence agreements' after decolonization, had in mind that these countries could save on armaments through a common effort and would thus be better able to concentrate on the task of development. Today the fact that France honours her commitments has implications that far exceed her stake in the conflicts in which she intervenes, such as that in Chad.)

Yet the appearance of new structures of regional security (and even the maintenance of those that already exist) will depend to a large extent both on the strategy of the super-powers and on the willingness of the medium powers concerned to carry the burden of such structures

The present 'revolutionary' conduct of the Soviet Union in the Third World is enough to suggest that there is only a faint possibility of the rapid emergence of new structures of regional security that would *not* be controlled by the super-powers through rival, second-order 'blocs'. Similarly, the hope that significant results can be reached through efforts to limit conventional arms exports has little prospect of being realized at a time when one super-power is pursuing revolutionary aims and the other is indecisive. Disarmament (or, more precisely, arms limitation) is at best the product of a *status quo*. Arms control cannot precede establishment of a *status quo*. The best that might be hoped for is agreement on 'confidence-building measures' among regional powers, as well as among the super-powers, to limit the risks of conflict arising as a result of an accidental event.

The Spread of Nuclear Weapons

This leaves the question of nuclear arms in the Third World. The nuclear weapons in question are fission bombs – an obvious fact that is nevertheless worth stating. For some time to come fusion technology will remain the preserve of those countries that have highly developed and diversified industries and in which political purpose is both clearly expressed and sustained over several years. Testing and research are obviously indispensable for the acquisition of a hydrogen bomb. This is important, for if an *atomic* weapon were to be employed in the Third World, the physical consequences would be limited.

This is not the place to discuss whether a 'proliferated' world would be more or less stable than the present one, but even those who hold the view that the universal extension of the 'balance of terror' would promote greater stability are bound to admit that since all the states would not acquire nuclear weapons at the same time, the transitional phase would be highly unstable. No power has yet succumbed to the temptation to make a preventive strike, but this is no compelling proof for the future. There are many politically unstable countries whose leaders are not predictable by our standards and would not hesitate to use an atomic weapon, if they had one, against a neighbour or even a big power.

There are two basic reasons for super-power opposition to nuclear proliferation. First, the atom bomb is the only weapon of massive destructive power that can be obtained at the price of a limited industrial effort. And, second, the psychological barrier between nuclear and conventional arms remains immense, in spite of the growing destructive power of modern conventional weapons. The super-powers fear that the possession of nuclear arms by Third-world countries would increase the risk that hostilities would escalate to a very high level and would thus increase considerably the risk that they might be caught up against their will in events with unforeseeable consequences. The 1973 Agreement on the Prevention of Nuclear War limits these risks, at least at the central level, but the world of the 1980s seems likely to be one in which partial nuclear proliferation and the use of the atomic bomb in conflict will become more probable.

While it is difficult to construct a typology of possible scenarios, we can postulate a number of hypotheses. Is it realistic to expect a Third-world country to use (or threaten to use) a nuclear weapon against a super-power or a medium power? This contingency is not very likely as long as the potential target is situated within the national territory of the power in question, but a 'mad' Head of State might ignore the consequences of retaliation and thus, *ex ante*, increase the credibility of his threat. Such a case cannot therefore be totally excluded.

What about the use of nuclear weapons against a target (say an aircraft carrier) that is outside enemy territory? A country that took such action would almost certainly expose herself to retaliation, including nuclear retaliation that would ensure her defeat in the conflict. There would be little likelihood of protection from either super-power, since the punishment would be legitimized by the initial attack.

Indeed, a nuclear attack by a Third-world country against a developed country or another Third-world country is conceivable only in extreme situations of the 'Massada' type. For countries like Israel or South Africa, the use of nuclear weapons would make sense only in the last resort; consequently their deterrent value is not negligible. (As is often said, the problem for such countries is not that they have nuclear weapons but that others believe they do.)

The most likely scenario is the use of nuclear weapons by one country in the Third World against another. Although it is incautious to generalize, it seems likely that neither super-power would want to be seen to legitimize such an act, and the victim, whatever the rights and wrongs of the case (real or putative), might receive massive assistance from the Western world to compensate for its sufferings. Moreover, *all* forms of retaliation against the aggressor would be legitimized. Unfortunately, this scenario is not wholly improbable.

In any case, it is hard to envisage mechanisms of extreme crisis escalation that would lead automatically to a direct confrontation between the super-powers, unless the conflict involved stakes that they considered vital. Local nucleari-zation would not, therefore, radically change the causal link between Third-world conflict and the central strategic balance.

The objective of nuclear-free zones remains, of course, highly desirable; as is the case with conventional arms transfers, however, such zones will be viable only if they are based on a res-pected political *status quo*, and it is no coinci-dence that the only contemporary (though imperfect) example of a nuclear-free zone is Latin America which was brought about by the Treaty of Tlatelolco.

Conclusion

It seems that there are complex but very real links between the super-power strategic balanec and Third-world conflicts. A Third-world con-flict involving one of the super-powers directly could lead to nuclear escalation if it were seen by the opposing super-power as belonging to a sequence of events that threatened its vital interests at some point. Then the dialectic of deterrence will operate to the full. On the other hand, some Third-world conflicts could de-generate for local reasons and might also lead to nuclear escalation; then, because of the high degree of uncertainty, the risks would be very high. Nuclear proliferation, although it will probably create very unpleasant contingencies, does not seem likely to alter the problem in a fundamental way. These preliminary findings, while incomplete, do suggest that more con-ceptual work needs to be done in this area, in order to explore further the kind of questions broached in this Paper.

NOTES

[1] Barry M. Blechman and Stephan S. Kaplan, *Force Without War* (Washington DC: Brookings Institution, 1979).

[2] Henry A. Kissinger. *A World Restored.* Vol. II *Metternich, Castlereagh and the Problems of Peace 1812–22.* (London, Weidenfeld & Nicolson, 1957).

Nuclear Weapons in Third-world Conflict

YEHEZKEL DROR

The problems associated with nuclear proliferation suffer from much discussion and little
analysis. The number of articles and conferences
dealing with such problems[1] taxes the reading
and travelling capacity of anyone interested in
the subject, and the repetition of opinions and
prescriptions raises serious questions about the
possible exhaustion of the ideas, methods and
concepts of strategic studies. Although the technological and economic aspects of nuclear
proliferation are quite fully explored in the
literature,[2] the strategic and security dimensions
of nuclear weapons from a Third-world[3] perspective are neglected and distorted in many, and
perhaps most, of the relevant discussions.[4] There
is much that smacks of wishful thinking, distorted perceptions and analysis and attempts to
'sell' certain views, all of which tends to produce
quite mistaken theories about the possible uses
and misuses of nuclear weapons in Third-world
conflicts.[5] One conclusion that seems compelling
is that more perceptive and multi-dimensional
analysis of this subject is needed, analysis that
is more in tune with Third-world thinking and
realities.

It would be presumptuous to claim to have
reliable answers to the complex questions of the
strategic implications of nuclear weapons for
Third-world conflict. But what is required is the
destabilization of contemporary 'conventional
wisdom' and some innovative – even daring –
thinking on the subject.

This paper will therefore present a number of
clearly defined propositions in a *pointilliste* form.
I shall avoid concrete illustrations and references
to specific countries in order to try to push the
discussion towards a general and somewhat
abstract level rather than getting lost in the
particular. Complete analysis requires an itera-
tive movement between novel concepts and
interactive models on the one hand and reality
(concrete or simulated) on the other. But,
taking into account the present state of discussion
on the subject, the more urgent need seems to be
for improved assumptions, concepts, propositions and models as essential and urgent pre-
requisites for a more correct perception and
analysis of the unfolding reality. Hence the
argument of this Paper is in the form of ten
main propositions and some broad conclusions.
The propositions are deliberately somewhat one-
sided, so as to counter-balance the bias of most
Western literature on the subject.

When nuclear policies are arrived at via at
least quasi-rational decisions, some consideration
of benefits and costs constitutes the core of
decision-making. Certainly, 'going nuclear' involves any Third-world country in significant
costs, such as direct investment in nuclear
activities, super-power pressures and sanctions,
the increased risk that neighbours may also 'go
nuclear', with possible catastrophic results for
all, and many more.[6] But in the eyes of Third-
world countries a lot of Western strategic
literature appears to overestimate these costs.
This Paper, therefore, emphasizes the potential
benefits of 'going nuclear' from the subjective
perspective of Third-world countries. While it
is to be hoped that a reasonable view will prevail
and that proliferation will be avoided, in the
interest of the Third-world countries themselves
as well as of humanity as a whole, such hopes,
given present events and trends, seem somehow
unrealistic.

It is clearly the moral duty of strategic writers
to balance carefully the usefulness of realistic
analysis with the dangers of putting ideas into
the wrong heads. Thus some of the literature on

non-conventional terror does much more harm than good. But in respect of the nuclear policies of Third-world countries, the situation is quite different: these countries' own analysts know their business, whether or not decisions are affected by academic articles. On the other hand, Western countries and the super-powers seem often to misread potential developments and therefore fail to prevent them, or at least fail to reduce the damage caused by them.

The propositions presented here focus on the question of whether or not to build nuclear weapons. This is an oversimplification: the extremes of total abstention from any interest in nuclear weapons (and credible proof of such abstention) on the one hand, and demonstrated deployment of a nuclear arsenal on the other, permit the emergence of ambiguity. Thus a country may build up some nuclear research and development capacity, may engage in nuclear-related activities, or may explode a single nuclear device without proceeding to develop a weapons capability. Not only does such a wide range of less than clear-cut positions dominate actual nuclear policies, but the alternatives are multi-dimensional, permitting a complex mix of hardware and image-shaping policies.

For the exploratory purposes of this paper, such richness of variety is neglected: the propositions deal with yes or no decisions, in the sense of moving or not moving in the direction of a nuclear weapons capability (or even stepping back from such a decision). This is probably adequate to investigate why Third-world countries are more inclined to move towards nuclear weapons than is supposed in the majority of Western strategic reasoning. More advanced analysis would require careful consideration of graduated and multi-dimensional situations.

1. *There are situations in which possession of nuclear weapons would improve the security of some Third-world countries.*
When a Third-world country is seriously endangered by adversaries, and when conventional defence cannot be relied upon, nuclear weapons may enhance its security. Although the acquisition of nuclear weapons may create risks, those risks may be preferable to the alternatives. For example:
— Countries faced by conventionally superior adversaries, or 'pariah' countries facing adversaries supported by other countries and feeling abandoned by the world, or countries facing adversaries with nuclear weapons, may feel that the risks of unstable or quasi-stable nuclear confrontations are preferable to the possibility of non-nuclear defeat or unilateral nuclear pressure.
— A country faced by strong adversaries may try to 'buy' big-power support by threatening to 'go nuclear' if, for example, conventional weapons are not provided. She may also seek nuclear weapons as a way of putting pressure on adversaries to agree to a compromise solution to a conflict and thus forgo their reliance on conventional advantage.
— Countries that are confronted by diffuse threats – threats, perhaps, that are not even concrete – may also quite rationally (from their own perspective) move towards nuclear weapons as a kind of general insurance in a turbulent and quite violent world. This is especially true if such countries own valuable resources (for example, oil), for they may regard themselves as potential targets for seizure and believe that seizure could be deterred by nuclear weapons.

It is true that even endangered countries may – according to Western standards and values – be better off with conventional inferiority than with an unstable nuclear balance stimulated by their own active nuclear-weapons policy, but this perspective may not be shared by such Third-world countries. Their policy may be based on short-term perspectives, with immediate security concerns receiving priority over longer-term dangers.[7] They may prefer to adopt a posture that involves some risk of nuclear mutual destruction but may provide security, rather than one that entails a high risk of conventional defeat without any real risk of destruction.

Here one must also take into account the subjective nature of threat perceptions. There is a tendency in some Third-world countries to see dangers and enemies in exaggerated forms, as a result of domestic political needs and historic perceptions.[8] The 'objective' Western view that these are misperceptions is irrelevant, and indeed may sometimes be incorrect. If the world is seen, from the perspective of individual actors who regard themselves as incapable of influencing the general trend, as very threatening and as moving towards violent conflict and intense aggression against themselves, then the acquisition of nuclear weapons is quite rational.

2. *There are situations in which nuclear weapons will serve the external goals of some Third-world countries, even if their own security is not in danger.*

A mistake widespread in Western strategic literature is to consider the potential usefulness of nuclear weapons for Third-world countries from a purely defensive and *status quo* perspective. A number of Third-world countries have active external goals, which can range from relatively minor (but locally often intensely significant) border disputes to 'crusading' goals involving radical change in other countries. In such cases the following reasoning may in part apply:

— Nuclear weapons may help to achieve aggressive goals abroad in a variety of ways, ranging from delicate suasion and psycho-attrition to threat, compulsion and first-strike use. The aggressive country must, in any case, expect its target or targets to try to acquire nuclear weapons in response. Therefore, even though the aggressor might be better off if neither had nuclear weapons (especially if the aggressor were conventionally stronger or could become so), he could not rely on continuing dependence on conventional arsenals. A decision by such a country to 'go nuclear' may be very sensitive to the speed with which the target country or countries could also acquire nuclear weapons. There will be a strong temptation to use a temporary nuclear advantage to realize policy goals and to prevent the subsequent acquisition of nuclear weapons by the target countries concerned. Only if the aggressor thought that he could achieve his goals conventionally, *and* that he could not achieve them if the target also possessed nuclear weapons, *and* if there were no possibility of achieving a nuclear advantage which could be used to realize his goals, would an aggressor's decision to 'go nuclear' be considered to be counter-productive (and thus irrational) from his own point of view.

— A country might feel that it had a 'manifest destiny' or mission (with or without concrete aggressive designs) to become a global power, to lead and represent the Third World, or to spread a new version of some religion or ideology. Nuclear weapons might then be desired as a symbol and a basis for international power and prestige, even if there were no obvious sense of danger or clearly defined aggressive goals.

I elaborated these points some time ago in the context of the 'crazy state' concept.[9] Western thinking is still dominated by the implicit assumption of the 'end of ideologies', at least in respect of aggressive ideologies and expansionist religions. Such projections of some quite recent developments in Western countries on to the Third World may result in very serious strategic intelligence mistakes in appreciating probable developments. Correct analysis of socio-political and cultural-ideological dynamics in a number of Third-world countries may lead to quite different expectations, with a high probability of the emergence of 'crazy states'.[10] Such 'crazy states' will move towards nuclear weapons if they are technically able to do so. Going nuclear is to them quite rational and instrumental, according to their world view – both to fulfil a 'manifest destiny' and to protect themselves against their enemies, who are seen in exaggerated but self-fulfilling images.

3. *There are situations in which nuclear weapons may serve the domestic needs of Third-world countries, even when they may not be useful for any external function.*

There seems to be insufficient overlap between strategic analysis and study of the domestic political dynamics of Third-world countries, and inadequate teamwork between those involved. Much of the inadequacy of contemporary discussions of the nuclear policies of Third-world countries stems from this. Under some conditions the acquisition of nuclear weapons (including well publicized progress towards it) may fulfil important domestic functions. These could include:

— Helping with nation-building through the strategy of the 'heroic project', which strengthens solidarity and engenders feelings of pride and achievement.

— Diverting internal tensions.

— Increasing popular support for a government that succeeds in such a project.

In Western eyes and according to Western criteria, such considerations do not justify a step as radical as nuclear weapons acquisition, and the use of limited resources for such a purpose seems very wasteful. But this may not necessarily be the perspective of all Third-world leaders.

4. Some Third-world countries may move towards nuclear weapons even if they do not serve any discernible useful function.

Bureaucratic politics exists also in Third-world countries. Indeed, the power of technological and scientific elites may be considerable, leading to a slide into an active nuclear policy once a nuclear research establishment has been set up. The usefulness of nuclear energy to some Third-world countries may accelerate this process. Here earlier Western aid to Third-world countries may have played a critical role. Even if no weapons-grade material is made available (a doubtful proposition) and even if no direct weapons-relevant information is provided (even more doubtful), by helping in the creation of nuclear establishments the Western countries have sometimes created a political-bureaucratic force which wants to move in the direction of nuclear weapons production.

A different but equally important possibility is that a Third-world country may be dominated by a single ruler who, for idiosyncratic reasons and as a consequence of his own psychological needs, wants to move into nuclear weapons. If oil-rich, such a leader may be in a position to take a quite underdeveloped country along the road towards nuclear weapons, even if they do not seem to relate to specific goals (though, of course, some rationalization will always take place). It is a very disturbing feature of the contemporary world that such situations are possible.

5. Propositions 1 to 4 may converge to create very intense situations conditioning the acquisition and use of nuclear weapons.

This proposition has both an analytical and an empirical component. Analytically, some of the elements of the contexts mentioned above are identical or have a tendency to coexist and to reinforce one another. Empirically, in a number of Third-world countries many factors do, in fact, show a tendency to converge, so that nuclear weapons may appear to constitute effective, multi-purpose policy instruments and, at the same time, may satisfy domestic needs and functions.

If this is true and if Proposition 6 (which concerns mutual accelerator effects) is also true, then nuclear weapons may appear useful and necessary from the perspective of more Third-world countries than is often supposed in the literature, despite the fact that other factors may work in the opposite direction.

6. An 'accelerator effect' exists. Nuclear weapons in the hands of some Third-world countries increase the need for them in a growing number of other Third-world countries.

This point is well recognized, sometimes under the 'domino model' or related metaphors. Propositions 1 to 5 apply with growing intensity where other Third-world countries possess nuclear weapons, for they either increase the security risks or they create a situation of relative deprivation or inferiority. At the very least, they reduce the 'threshold' and stimulate irritation.

There are some *prima facie* exceptions to this generalization. For instance:
— If an allied country has nuclear weapons, her help may be relied on.
— If a hostile country has nuclear weapons and suspects an opponent of moving towards the acquisition of nuclear weapons of its own, that country may be tempted into pre-emptive use.
— A country frightened at the possibility that nuclear war may occur may decide that non-possession of nuclear weapons is the best way to evade involvement.

Some of these exceptions relate to acquisition strategy rather than to the ultimate desire to have nuclear weapons. Thus a country may try to hide production until ready for deployment in order to reduce the temptation to pre-empt. But in general the 'accelerator effect' seems stronger than any of the dampening effects listed here.

This may result in a catalytic process whereby a few proliferation events significantly accelerate nuclear weapon acquisition in a growing number of countries. Even if such a chain reaction has only a low probability (and who can be sure of that?), the possible consequences are disastrous enough to justify consideration and the preparation of preventive (or at least containing) measures.

7. Many factors that inhibit the acquisition of nuclear weapons in Western countries are less cogent in the Third World.

This proposition is largely empirical and therefore in the nature of a hypothesis. Some of the factors covered by the proposition are:

— In Western countries nuclear weapons provoke public odium and repugnance. It is doubtful whether this applies in Third-world countries.
— In Western countries the use of nuclear weapons is associated with holocaust, the end of mankind or, at the least, catastrophe for Western civilization. Third-world countries probably do not regard the consequences of their use in the same way.
— Western countries seek to maintain the *status quo*. They have a propensity for minimizing risks and are inward-looking. These tendencies are much less evident (sometimes not evident at all) in the Third World.

As a result of these and many other differences in perception and association (and significant differences in real conditions), analysis from a Western perspective may be quite distorted and may lead to incorrect predictions. This applies both to the broad framework of Western appreciations (to use military-staff terminology) that conditions the way we think and to explicit strategic concepts and models.

8. *Changes and innovations in strategic concepts and models are required to analyse the roles of nuclear weapons in Third-world conflicts.*

This is the central proposition. To explore the dimensions of the matter and indicate lines for further work, it is necessary to disaggregate the proposition and present briefly some relevant considerations.

The usual vocabulary of Western nuclear analysis does not apply to Third-world situations, or applies only with significant re-interpretations. 'Assured second strike', 'graduated response', 'sanctuary', etc., are terms that simply do not fit in any foreseeable Third-world conflict. They cannot be used, in considering Third-world situations, with the same meaning as they have acquired in big-power confrontations. Not only must the calibration be changed, but any strict application of them can be very misleading when considering interactions between adversaries with a very limited number of nuclear bombs and relatively simple delivery systems deployed in protected but unhardened facilities. There is, in most cases, much ambiguity. The facts about nuclear capabilities are uncertain, and a first strike with limited instruments against a Third-world adversary may or may not incapacitate the target, which may or

may not be able to retaliate with some remaining nuclear weapons. Unreliable intelligence, the propensity for risk-taking and many random factors may play a larger part in determining the results of nuclear exchanges between Third-world countries than they do in the rigorous calculations applied to super-power confrontations (which may also be doubtful).

Therefore any discussion of nuclear interactions among Third-world countries using the vocabulary of super-power confrontation ('balance of terror', 'deterrence stability', etc.) is more misleading than enlightening. Not only an 'assured second-strike capacity' but also 'graduated-response' capacities are likely to be absent (for reasons that are as much technical as political). The basic assumptions of shared logic, values and calculation must be taken much less for granted. This does not mean that nuclear confrontations may not, under some circumstances, result in quasi-stable balances in which both sides consider the risks of nuclear exchange too high, and in which, therefore, a situation of 'mutual deterrence' would exist. Pre-requisites for such a quasi-stable balance (the concept of 'mutual deterrence', which carries with it all the impedimenta of super-power interaction, is best avoided) seem to include: possession of nuclear weapons that, to the other side, seem capable of surviving a first strike: the expectations that such surviving weapons will be used in retaliation; a cost-benefit calculation that the chances of success are outweighed by the costs of a retaliatory strike; and two cultures that follow such kinds of calculation and logic.

The possibility of the 'irrational' and even 'counter-rational' use of nuclear weapons seems much higher among Third-world countries because of the characteristics of their political dynamics and the cultures of some of them. Third-world countries operate in an environment dominated (but not necessarily controlled) by the super-powers – an environment, therefore, radically different from that in which the super-powers themselves operate. This adds many complications. Possible intervention by the super-powers (and perhaps other nuclear powers) must be taken into account. These might include sanctions against first use, assurances to countries that forgo nuclear weapons and are endangered by other Third-world countries that possess them, and pressure to give up nuclear options. One could also envisage confrontations between Third-world countries and the super-powers in which the latter either operate together by agreement or work against each other. Strong pressure on 'pariah states' by both super-powers or super-power action to assure essential raw materials (for example, oil) serve as quite realistic illustrations of such possible situations.[11] Possession of nuclear weapons, accompanied by a 'Samson complex' (not a 'Massada complex', as stated in some fiction and analysis),[12] made credible by an image of some degree of fanaticism and 'craziness', could pose a threat even to a super-power and would constitute a challenge that a super-power might well try to avoid because of the costs involved in any result. France's discussion of her nuclear posture *vis-à-vis* the Soviet Union and some Swedish literature dealing with scenarios in which small nuclear powers are pitted against a super-power look similar, but the problem is really quite different because of the higher credibility of (by Western standards) 'irrational' or 'unreasonable' behaviour on the part of Third-world nuclear countries.[13]

Such complications need much more analysis and research, but *prima facie* they would seem capable of leading to situations quite different from those prevailing in the super-power nuclear interaction. Thus the possibilities of conventional conflicts below the threshold of nuclear weapons, as well as the distinction between 'strategic', 'theatre' and 'tactical' uses of nuclear weapons, must be completely reworked in the Third-world context. In the Third World there may be complex confrontations between a number of countries with nuclear weapons or nuclear weapon options, all of more or less the same order of magnitude. This is quite different from a multi-polar world with two super-powers and a small number of additional states with limited global nuclear capabilities. Again, innovative analysis is required.

The functions of nuclear weapons and related options in Third-world conflicts and interactions short of actual use are much more complex than those of weapons held by the Western nuclear powers. Suasion, threat, compulsion and conventional *fait accompli* under a nuclear threat are only a few illustrations of the potential uses of nuclear weapons in Third-world conflict, uses which go far beyond those present or foreseen in the Western world. Actual use could also take forms more diverse, in some respects, than those envisaged in the Western world. These could include anonymous strikes and the secret supply of nuclear weapons to other countries, or even to counter-elites or terrorist groups.

These points appear to justify the proposition that additional strategic concepts and models are needed to do justice to the potential uses of nuclear weapons in Third-world conflicts.

9. *Nuclear weapons reduce the aggregate security of Third-world countries, but this is irrelevant from the perspectives of individual countries.*
The proliferation of nuclear weapons among Third-world countries and their increasing use as policy instruments increase the probability that some nuclear wars will occur. These will be horrible for all involved and will have results that will be detrimental to the security of the Third World as a whole. However, this aggregate analysis may not seem convincing to those in the Third World who tend to regard such arguments as a smoke-screen put up by the present nuclear powers in order to preserve their privileged position and to keep open neo-colonial options.

Even if most Third-world countries were to agree that the aggregate costs to them all of the acquisition and possible use of nuclear weapons will be much higher than the benefits to individual countries, this would not be particularly helpful. Since no mechanisms exist to redistribute costs and benefits, it is hard to see how the Third World as a whole can act in such a way as to reach an optimal solution. Countries therefore seem certain to adopt their own policies regarding nuclear weapons, and some will see the acquisition of nuclear weapons as serving their individual needs and will disregard the common good. Some may even hope that nuclear weapons may actually deter conflicts and thus serve the common good, though this appears to be fallacious logic.

10. *Big powers will become involved in Third-world nuclear conflicts.*
Nuclear tensions in the Third World and the possibility that nuclear explosions may occur are bound to have consequences for the nuclear threshold in Europe. They will also affect

101

interests of the super-powers in large areas of the Third World and may lead to direct confrontations between Third-world countries and Western powers. It is therefore extremely unlikely that Third-world nuclear conflicts and super-power politics can be decoupled. An active nuclear policy in Third-world countries will constitute a substantial change in global politics, accelerating the movement towards what Guy Pauker has called a 'new barbarism'.[14]

It seems doubtful whether this conclusion is very sensitive to either a high or a low nuclear posture in super-power relations. It is also doubtful whether there are any realistic super-power alternatives that could influence the propositions presented here. This is not to say that nothing should be done. Attempts could be made to influence specific countries that seem close to becoming nuclear states, and various measures could be adopted to make the acquisition of nuclear weapons more difficult. Efforts to make groups of Third-world countries act collectively to prevent nuclear proliferation are obviously worthwhile. This kind of mixed strategy should delay and reduce the global costs of the acquisition of nuclear weapons and should lessen the chances of their use in the Third World. Time may thus be gained, which would undoubtedly be a benefit. But it is not easy to be optimistic that nuclear proliferation and the ultimate use of nuclear weapons in the Third World can be prevented in the long run without radical changes in the global order, such as an American–Soviet co-operative *diktat* inhibiting all proliferation and use and providing for enforced supervision and heavy sanctions. But it is doubtful whether such a change could come about without some shocks, including nuclear wars in the Third World.

Conclusion
Whether these somewhat pessimistic views are accepted or not, it seems possible to draw four main conclusions.

First, nuclear weapons have a variety of uses for Third-world countries. These include specific military and security uses, as well as a broader utility as a quite versatile policy instrument. Many such uses are quite rational from the perspective of the countries involved.

Second, Western concepts and models of deterrence stability (and Western strategic thinking in general) need to be adjusted – even substantially changed – in order to cover nuclear-weapons issues in Third-world countries. New concepts developed for analysing nuclear issues in the Third World may also throw new light on Western strategic issues that are sometimes analysed in much too simple and rationalistic a way.

Third, in the aggregate nuclear weapons will reduce the security of the Third World. This is not necessarily true for specific Third-world countries, however, and may not be true for Third-world blocs confronting shared dangers. In any case, aggregate benefits do not often provide the criteria on which individual countries are likely to base decisions.

Fourth, Third-world nuclear forces will influence the nuclear relationships of the super-powers, but in ways that will be diffuse and hard to predict. Trigger effects leading to super-power nuclear confrontation appear doubtful, and catalytic war seems far off, but global turbulence and the progressive erosion of nuclear thresholds may change accepted assumptions and lead to new super-power postures. Nuclear proliferation in Western countries and in modern Eastern Bloc countries may have a more direct impact on the main blocs and on relations between them, and it could be argued that such proliferation could in turn be accelerated by Third-world nuclear activity.

At the very least, the problems of Third-world nuclear politics illustrate the need for new strategic concepts and for improved methods of strategic analysis, thus constituting a professional challenge of much practical importance. That challenge involves serious intellectual difficulties, not least because of the need to shake off misleading Western precepts and assumptions.

NOTES

[1] See for example the interesting papers of the International Symposium on the Prospects for Nuclear Proliferation in Developing Countries, Institute for Far Eastern Studies, Kyung Nam University, Seoul, Korea, 22-24 January 1979.

[2] For a good overview, see Albert Wohlstetter *et al.*, *Moving Toward Life in a Nuclear Armed Crowd?* rev. edn. (Los Angeles: Panheuristics, 1976).

[3] I use the term 'Third World' as given, though I think it a misleading concept which aggregates what cannot be aggregated. The diversity included in the open-ended set of 'Third-world countries' renders almost meaningless most conclusions which are presumed to apply to all of them, and it is doubtful whether the 'Third World' is a useful unit for historical, comparative or analytical studies, in Toynbee's sense of that term. In this paper the term 'Third World' refers to a sub-set of such countries which meet the following criteria: possession of a technological and economic infrastructure or substitute economic resources which permit some nuclear activities; existence of a decision centre which deals with nuclear policies; and for most, but not all, of this analysis some degree of instrumental rationality (not to be confused with goal rationality – that is, 'reasonableness' in the Western sense).

[4] A good contemporary discussion is Enid C. B. Schoettle, *Postures for Non-Proliferation* (Stockholm: SIPRI; London: Taylor & Francis, 1979), which also includes an extensive bibliography. Some very good analysis is included in Lewis A. Dunn and Herman Kahn, *Trends in Nuclear Proliferation, 1975-1995* (Croton-on-Hudson: Hudson Institute, Report HI-2336/3-RR, May 1976), and Lewis A. Dunn *et al.*, *U.S. Defence Planning for a More Proliferated World* (Croton-on-Hudson: Hudson Institute, Report HI-2956/2-RR, April 1979).

[5] Well worth pondering in this context is Herbert Goldhamer, *Reality and Belief in Military Affairs: A First Draft* (Santa Monica, Cal.: Rand Corporation, R-2448-NA, February 1979). Urgently needed is a study on 'Reality and Belief in Western Thinking on the Third World': It may well be that misperception of Third-world processes and, even more, commitments to wrong policies *vis-à-vis* the Third World are built into contemporary Western appreciation and policy-making – *cf.* the findings in Leslie H. Gelb with Richard K. Betts, *The Irony of Vietnam: The System Worked* (Washington DC: Brookings Institution, 1979).

[6] For a rational-decision matrix applied to small countries, see Yehezkel Dror, 'Small Powers Nuclear Policy: Research Methodology and Exploratory Analysis' *Jerusalem Journal of International Relations*, Vol. I, No. 1 (Autumn 1975), pp. 29-49.

[7] This is true in Western countries too, as illustrated in the domestic field by the so-called 'political-economic cycle'. See Edward R. Tufte, *Political Control of the Economy* (Princeton: Princeton University Press, 1978), especially Ch. 2. Some study of comparable 'political-strategic cycles' in Western countries is needed to show the correlation between strategic policies and approaching or receding election dates. Indeed, there is some tendency in Western discourse to project on to other countries not Western realities, but Western idealized self-images, which are not valid even in so-called highly developed countries.

[8] The thinking of Carl Schmitt, who divides the world into friends and foes, may well fit the present and expected world views held by some Third-world countries. See C. Schmitt, *Der Begriff des Politischen* (reprinted Berlin, 1963). A short discussion of this perspective is included in Gianfranco Poggi, *The Development of the Modern State* (Stanford: Stanford University Press, 1978), pp. 5-9. The poverty of historical knowledge and comparative sociological perspective in modern strategic thinking makes a strong contribution to misperception of Third-world problems and situations, including nuclear issues.

[9] Yehezkel Dror, *Crazy States: A Counter-Conventional Strategic Issue* (Lexington, Mass.: Heath, 1971; New York: Kraus Reprints, 1980). The term 'crazy states' is a carefully defined concept composed of five main dimensions, goal aggressiveness, goal commitment, innovativeness of conflict style (that is, 'immorality'), instrumental rationality and action capabilities.

[10] One should warn against the assumption that only Third-world countries may become 'crazy': the most extreme recent case of a nation going 'crazy' is Nazi Germany – a fully developed Western country.

[11] A very important problem is the use by super-powers and other nuclear Western powers of their nuclear superiority in their interventions in the Third World, for instance by publicized movement of nuclear weapons. A recent study seems to indicate that such actions increase the successes of the political uses of armed forces. See Barry M. Blechman and Stephen S. Kaplan, *Force Without Wars: US Armed Forces as a Political Instrument* (Washington DC: Brookings Institution, 1978), especially p. 94ff. Whether in the longer run nuclear suasion against Third-world countries will accelerate their movement towards nuclear weapons is another question. It may well be that the super-powers face here two distinct strategies: either to avoid any nuclear threats (however indirect) in conflicts with Third-world countries or to use massive coercion to prevent nuclearization as a Third-world reaction against super-power intervention. Any in-between policy may be the worst because it will promote nuclear proliferation on the one hand and will not effectively prevent it on the other.

[12] See Leonard Harris, *The Massada Plan* (London: Sphere, 1978).

[13] A recent outstanding Swedish publication on defence planning illustrates the neglect of 'crazy' surprise events and the methodological difficulties of thinking about such possibilities which are compounded by the cultural barriers in highly 'normal' Western countries with rationality-dependent analytical approaches of the operation research type. See C. S. Jennergren *et al.* (eds). *Trends in Planning* (Stockholm: Swedish National Defense Research Institute, 1978). None of the chapters of this work faces such types of problem, even though they may appear in the Swedish context in a variety of forms.

[14] Guy J. Pauker, *Military Implications of a Possible World Order Crisis in the 1980s* (Santa Monica, Cal.: Rand Corporation, R-2003-AF, November 1977).

Index

106

functions, 101, 102; and general deterrence, 18, 90; and goals, achievement, 98; integration with conventional forces, 2, 5; irrational use, 98, 100–1; limited use, 101; modernization, 45, 46, 66; and non-nuclear attack, 35, 90; numerical sufficiency, 2–3, 9, 11, 12, 29, 31, 90; perceptions of, 99–100; and political advantage, 45; proliferation, 2, 3, 5, 16, 19–21, 57, 61, 94–5, 96–102; reluctance to use, 1, 11, 14; tactical, 5; testing, 66; use, conditions of, 18–19, 101; vulnerability, 1, 3, 17, 35; *see also* Arms control

Nunn, Senator, 11

Ohio-class submarines, 36
Open-ended nuclear philosophies, 2–3
Oppenheimer, Julius, R., 5
Options, nuclear, 2
Ottawa Declaration (1974), 45

Paris Agreement (1954), 48
Parity, strategic: and arms control, 21; decline of, 34; development of, 7, 17; early views of, 54; and reality of deterrence, 9, 17–18, 75; and SALT, 75; and small independent forces, 50
Pauker, Guy, 102
Peace: and crisis control, 18; and deterrence, 14, 15, 17, 18, 21
Perception: and nuclear weapons, differences, 99–100; of threat, subjectivity, 97
Periphery, and central balance, 55, 56, 58
Pershing depots, 35
Persian Gulf, 56, 91, 92, 93
Philippines, foreign alliances, 57
Philosophy of deterrence: and arms control, 21–2; and change, 53, 55; differences, East–West, 2; early, 7–8, 13–14, 15, 50, 53–4, 60–1; and extended deterrence, 2, 21, 31–2; high posture, 20; inconsistency, 16; limitations, 14–15, 21; low posture, 20; maximalist, 32; minimalist, 32; morality of, 16, 59; open-ended, 2–3; and technology, 59; United States, 2, 4, 8–9, 46–7, 48, 53–4, 58, 62, 64, 79, 82, 85–6; *see also* Rationales
Plateau, technological, 54, 63
Pluton missiles, 49
Poland, World War II, 26, 27, 28
Polaris, 45, 47, 49, 63
Politics, and extended deterrence, 31–2, 33; and military requirements, 68
Populations, target, *see* Cities
Poseidon, 36
Power, hierarchical, 20
Power-projection, 69
Proliferation, 2, 3, 5, 16, 19–21, 57, 61; and Third World, 94–5, 96–102
Psychological deterrence, 17, 18, 32, 34

Qualitative disarmament, 22
Quick Reaction Alert (QRA), bases, 35

Rand Corporation Basing Study, 62, 63
Rational action, conception of, 21, 86; *see also* Crazy states
Rationales for nuclear forces, 45–52; *see also* Philosophy of deterrence
Reality: and Mutual Assured Destruction, 32; and super-power balance, 92
Relative deterrence, 2, 3

Reluctance, and nuclear weapons, 1, 11, 14
Research and development, parallel, 67
Resources, and power, 55
Response to challenge, 33
Restraint, criteria of, 3
Retaliation, assured, *see* Mutual Assured Destruction; flexible, 64–6
Risks, alternative, 24, 25, 26, 27, 28, 29
Ritter, Gerhard, 25
Romania: foreign policy, 24, 25; and Germany, 26
Russia: and Austria, 24; and Germany, 24–6; *see also* Soviet Union

SA–5 missiles, 43
SALT (Strategic Arms Limitation Talks): achievements, 71–2; and allies, 75; bargaining process, 73; China's effect on, 43; and crises, 75; and detente, 68; and deterrence, 71–7; and European nuclear forces, 50, 75, 77; functions, 3, 9, 20, 57, 71–2, 73, 76; linkage of issues, 76; and technological change, 21; SALT I, 78, 80: ballistic missile submarines, 83–4, silo-expansion, 84, and Soviet Union, 87; SALT II: encryption clause, 71, expiry, 85, fractionation limit, 74, functions, 71, ICBM reductions, 83, numerical constraints, 5, and Soviet Union, 87, and United States, 11, 31, 32, 59, 92; SALT III: development, 20, and Europe, 50, 75, and Great Britain, 45
'Samson complex', 101
Sandys, Duncan, 46
Satellites, Chinese, 42
Schelling, Thomas, 12, 13
'Schlesinger doctrine', 50
Schlieffen Plan, 25
Second-strike retaliation, 8, 9; development of, 62; importance of, 9, 12; numerical significance, 9
Security, and nuclear weapons, 97, 101
Sentinel ABM system, 73
Silos: destruction, 22, 35, 64; launchers, 84; vulnerability, 85
Single Integrated Operational Plan (SIOP), 8
Skybolt missiles, 47
SLBMs (Submarine-launched ballistic missiles), 36, 47; and limited conflict, 65
Small nuclear forces: criticisms of, 49; funding of, 50; rationales for, 45, 48, 50, 51, 52; and Third World, 92, 93–4
Smoke, R., 15
South Africa, nuclear weapons, 20, 94
South-east Asia, Soviet intervention, 92
South Korea, nuclear weapons, 20, 43
Soviet Union: ABMs, 41, 43; and arms control, 80–1, 84; and China, 18, 38, 40–4, 91; conventional weapons, 18; culture, unique, 79; decision-making process, 82, 85; defence policy, 58, 73–4, 76, 78, 79; and Europe, 18, 34, 35–6, 50, 91; expansionism, 56; in Far East, 41; foreign policy, 56, 57; future conditions, 3, 56, 72, 85; and Germany, 27; global strategy, 91; ICBMs, 7, 35–6, 74, 85; imperial drives, 56, 91; intervention, 29, 56; and Japan, 34–5; law drafting, 84; military ascendancy, 21, 80, 81, 83, 87; nuclear weapons, integration, 2; open-ended policies, 3, 83; parity, 17–18, 19, 61, 78, 85; philosophy of deterrence, 2, 18, 58, 66, 78, 79–81, 85, 86; and SALT, 72–3, 74, 75, 76–7, 78, 83–5; secrecy, 72, 74; security, concept of, 93; strategic doctrine, 78–87; targets in, 41; and Third World countries, 3, 90, 91, 92,

93, 94; and United States, 7, 13, 15, 17–18, 40, 42–4, 57, 91; vulnerability, 56, 62; and war, 78, 80, 85, 86; weapons-acquisition process, 82–3, 85; and the West, 86–7, 91
SS-4s, 35, 41
SS-5s, 35
SS-12s, 41
SS-16s, 72
SS-18s, 81, 86
SS-19s, 81, 84
SS-20s, 10, 34, 35, 41, 43, 50
SSBNs, 49, 50, 51, 83, 84
SS-N-8 missiles, 84
Stability, nuclear, and structure of peace, 91
Stability, Third World structures, 93–4
Stalin, J., 53
Standing Consultative Commission (SCC), role, 22
States, proliferation of, 55
Strassman, Fritz, 5
Strategic Arms Limitation Talks, *see* SALT
Strategic deterrence, *see* Deterrence
'Strategic man', 15
Striking, risks of, 24, 25, 26, 27, 28, 29
Suasion, 13
Submarine-launched ballistic missiles, *see* SLBMs
Submarines, missile-carrying, 8, 10, 36; and SALT I, 83–4; vulnerability, 17; *see also* SSBNs
Superiority, strategic: attainment, 9; decline, 20; *see also* Parity
Super-powers: bipolarity, *see* Bipolarity; co-operation, 57–8, 92; decline, 20, 22, 57; deterrence, 67–8; extended deterrence, 19; and lesser nuclear powers, 68, 92, 94; and proliferation, 94; relations, 13, 22, 56, 57–8; responsibility, 22, 57; and Third-world conflicts, 90–5, 100–1, 102

Tactical weapons, 5
Taiwan, nuclear weapons, 20, 43
Targets: accuracy, 6; choice, 2, 60–1; cities, 2, 4, 6, 60–1; military, 2, 6; philosophy of, 6–7, 60–1, 62; retargeting, 64
Technology: change, effects of, 1, 21, 66; and deterrence, 59, 60–70; and flexibility, 64–5, 66; plateau of, 54, 63
Terror, balance of, 8, 13, 14, 17, 54, 62, 94
Thailand, foreign alliances, 57
Theatre weapons: cruise missiles, 5; Europe, 5, 34, 35–6, 46, 51, 77
Third World countries: conflicts, 14, 90–5: and central strategic balance, 90–3, escalation, 93, 94, 101–2, internal, 95, 101–2; domestic needs and nuclear weapons, 98; and extended deterrence, 19; goals, achievement, 98; irrational use of nuclear weapons, 100–1; and medium powers, 92, 93–4; nuclear weapons, 94–5, 96–102; perceptual differences, 99–100; security, and nuclear weapons, 97, 101, 102; Soviet policy, 3, 90, 91, 92, 93, 94; stability, structures of, 93–4; strategic concepts, 100–1, 102; threat, perceptions of, 97; and United States, 90, 91, 92; and vocabulary, strategic, 100
Threat: and deterrence, 11, 13, 29, 35–7; subjective perceptions, 97
Threshold of credibility, 49
'Tirpitz factor', 68
Tlatelolco, Treaty of, 95
Tornado, 51

Triad of weapons, 8, 10; and B-I programme, 73; and MX, 36; and NATO, 10, 11; redistribution, 74; vulnerability, 85
Trident, 36, 45
Triple Alliance, 25
Triple Entente, 25, 26, 29
Tu-2s, 39, 40
Tu-4s, 39, 40
Tu-16s, 39, 40
Tube Alloys, 5
Turkey, foreign policy, 24, 57

United Nations, 7
United States: Allies, 58; arms control policies, 9, 73; B-I programme, 73; and change, 59; and China, 18, 42; decision-making process, 82; defence planning, 11–12, 31, 82, 87, 92; deterrence philosophy, 2, 4, 8–9, 46–7, 48, 53–4, 58, 62, 64, 79, 82, 85–6; diminished nuclear strength, 1, 55, 85; and European nuclear forces, 45–6, 49; Europe, nuclear protection of, 1–2, 10–11, 18–19, 33–4, 35–6, 42, 47, 50, 51, 55; extended deterrence, 19, 31–7, 42; global responsibilities, 56, 61, 91; ICBM vulnerability, 1, 17, 35, 43, 80, 85; and Japan, 34–5, 42; McMahon Act amendments (1958), 46; National Security Study, *NSC 68*, 61, 63; and NATO, 31, 46, 51; political factors in deterrence, 31–2, 86; and SALT, 71–3, 74, 75, 76–7, 84, 85; self-interest, 51; and small independent nuclear forces, 45–6, 49; Soviet relations, 7, 13, 15, 17–18, 40, 42–4, 57, 58, 72, 91, 92; and Soviet strategic doctrine, 78, 86; superiority, early, 8, 9, 54; targeting doctrines, 4, 6, 9; Third World interests, 90, 91, 92; vulnerability, relative, 34, 56, 63

Variety, and arms control, 67
Verification, and SALT, 71, 74
Vertical shelters, 84
Vietnam: and China, 42; 'syndrome', 91; War, effects of, 85, 91
Viner, Jacob, 60
Vulcan, 50, 51
Vulnerability: and central balance, 17, 33, 56; and extended deterrence, 33; ICBMs, 1, 3, 17, 35, 43, 66, 71, 75; increasing, 3, 17, 34, 55; reduction, 2; relative, 33, 56

War: accidental, 15, 17, 93; control of nuclear weapons, 1, 13, 64; feasability of, 8; and risks, alternative, 24–9; weapons suitable for, 14, 66
Weapons: deterrent, 14; nuclear, *see* Nuclear weapons; strategic, definition, 66; for war, 14–15, 66
West Berlin, United States interest in, 33
West Germany: importance, 18; nuclear power, 10, 20, 48, 49, 51
Western countries: Alliance, 31, 32, 47, 58; nuclear philosophy, 2–3, 46–52, 58; perceptions of nuclear weapons, 99–100; and Soviet strategic doctrine, 86–7, 91; and Third World, 55
'Window of opportunity', 1, 29
Wohlstetter, Albert, 8, 17
Wolfe, Thomas W., 85
World War I, events leading to, 24–6
World War II, events leading to, 26–9, 91

Zaïre, French intervention, 92